John Lydgate's

DANCE OF DEATH
AND RELATED WORKS

MIDDLE ENGLISH TEXTS SERIES

The Middle English Texts Series are scholarly texts designed for research and classroom use. Its goal is to make available to teachers, scholars, and students texts that occupy an important place in the literary and cultural canon but have not been readily available in print and online editions. The series does not include those authors, such as Chaucer, Langland, or Malory, whose English works are normally in print. The focus is, instead, upon Middle English literature adjacent to those authors that are needed for doing research or teaching. The editions maintain the linguistic integrity of the original work but within the parameters of modern reading conventions. The texts are printed in the modern alphabet and follow the practices of modern capitalization, word formation, and punctuation. Manuscript abbreviations are silently expanded, and *u/v* and *j/i* spellings are regularized according to modern orthography. Yogh (ȝ) is transcribed as *g*, *gh*, *y*, or *s*, according to the sound in Modern English spelling to which the medieval pronunciation corresponds; thorn (þ) and eth (ð) are transcribed as *th*. Distinction between the second person pronoun and the definite article is made by spelling the one *thee* and the other *the*, and final *-e* that receives full syllabic value is accented (e.g., *charité*). Hard words, difficult phrases, and unusual idioms are glossed either in the right margin or at the foot of the page. Explanatory and textual notes appear at the end of the text, often along with a glossary. The editions include short introductions on the history of the work, its merits and points of topical interest, and brief working bibliographies.

John Lydgate's

DANCE OF DEATH
AND RELATED WORKS

Edited by
Megan L. Cook and Elizaveta Strakhov

Published for TEAMS
(Teaching Association for Medieval Studies)
in Association with the University of Rochester

by

MEDIEVAL INSTITUTE PUBLICATIONS
Kalamazoo, Michigan
2019

Library of Congress Cataloging-in-Publication Data

Names: Cook, Megan L. (Megan Leigh), 1981- editor. | Strakhov, Elizaveta, 1984- editor. | Lydgate, John, 1370?-1451? Dance of death.
Title: John Lydgate's dance of death and related works / edited by Megan Leigh Cook and Elizaveta Strakhov.
Description: Kalamazoo, Michigan : Published for TEAMS (Teaching Association for Medieval Studies) in Association with the University of Rochester by Medieval Institute Publications, 2019. | Series: Middle English texts series | Includes bibliographical references. | Poems in Middle English, one French poem with an English translation. | Summary: "This volume brings together new editions of both texts of John Lydgate's fifteenth-century poem, The Dance of Death, with related Middle English verse from the fourteenth and fifteenth centuries. It also includes a new translation of Lydgate's French source, the Danse macabre. Together, these poems showcase the power and versatility of the danse macabre motif, offering a vivid window into life and death in late medieval Europe. In these poems, we see Death itself help readers remember and process the fundamental paradox of death's universality yet irremediable specificity. In vivid, often grotesque, and darkly humorous terms, these poems ponder life's fundamental paradox: while we know that we all must die, we cannot imagine our own death"-- Provided by publisher.
Identifiers: LCCN 2019034706 | ISBN 9781580443807 (paperback) | ISBN 9781580443814 (hardback) | ISBN 9781580444088 (pdf)
Subjects: LCSH: English poetry--Middle English, 1100-1500. | Death--Poetry.
Classification: LCC PR1203 .J58 2019 | DDC 821/.2--dc23
LC record available at https://lccn.loc.gov/2019034706

ISBN 978-1-58044-380-7 (paperback)
ISBN 978-1-58044-381-4 (hardback)
ISBN 978-1-58044-408-8 (pdf)

Printed and bound by CPI Group (UK) Ltd, Croydon, CR0 4YY

✤ CONTENTS

LIST OF ILLUSTRATIONS

 ## ACKNOWLEDGMENTS

For their financial support of this endeavor, we would like to thank Colby College, Marquette University, and the Mellon Fellowship in Critical Bibliography at Rare Book School. We would also like to express our gratitude to the knowledgeable and helpful staff of the Huntington Library, the British Library, the Bodleian Library, the Coventry County Archives, and the Venerable English College in Rome, especially Professor Maurice Whitehead. For help with research queries both small and large, but in all respects essential, we thank Daniel Davies, Aaron Pratt, R. D. Perry, Sebastian Sobecki, and Daniel Wakelin, with special thanks to C. J. Lambert and Lucas Wood for aid in Latin and French translation quandaries. Finally, we would like to note that the process of compiling and completing this edition has been an uncommonly pleasant and smooth one; for this, we express our deep appreciation to the staff at METS, especially Russell Peck and Pamela Yee, as well as staff editors Katherine Briant and Ashley Conklin. We would also like to thank the National Endowment for the Humanities (NEH) for its longstanding funding of METS.

INTRODUCTION

This volume offers a new edition of both versions of John Lydgate's *Dance of Death* set within their broader cultural and literary contexts. The *Dance* was edited twice in the twentieth century: in the earlier of its two versions, known as the A version, by Eleanor Prescott Hammond in her *English Verse Between Chaucer and Surrey* in 1927 and in both versions by Florence Warren and Beatrice White for the Early English Text Society in 1931.[1] Our edition presents the two versions of Lydgate's *Dance* sequentially, rather than in a parallel-text format as in the EETS edition. We further highlight the origins and context of Lydgate's text by presenting it alongside five other contemporary Middle English poems treating similar themes, two more poems that demonstrate its literary afterlife in England, and a new translation of Lydgate's original French source, the anonymous *Danse macabre*. To introduce this collection, we begin by mapping out the larger contours of the death poetry tradition in late medieval England before moving into discussing the origins of the *danse macabre* tradition in France and tracing its major developments in the literary and visual culture of Europe more broadly. Thereafter we turn to Lydgate's *Dance*, placing it in the wider context of Lydgate's literary activity and tracking its later circulation among its medieval and early modern readers.

LATE MEDIEVAL POETRY ABOUT DEATH: A GENERAL OVERVIEW

Late medieval England, marked by recurrent outbreaks of plague and the Hundred Years War, saw a surge in literature treating death as a dominant theme. Much of it, following the period's predilection for didactic advice literature, took the form of moralizing counsel known as the *ars moriendi*, or "art of dying": how to set one's spiritual affairs in order before death's inevitable advent. Thus, for example, a poem rubricated "Sex observanda omni cristiano in extremis" (The Six Things to be Observed by Each Christian at the End) (DIMEV 1226) walks the reader through six considerations to take when preparing to die: restore property to its rightful owner, settle one's debts, confess, receive penance, receive Communion, and pray. Similarly, in the poem "In Four Points My Will Is Ere I Hence Depart" (DIMEV 2503) the speaker, on his or her deathbed, ruminates on rejoining the earth whence he or she came, contemplates the sins of his or her life, the transitory vanity of the world, and the state of the soul in the afterlife. The programmatic nature of this

---

[1] *English Verse between Chaucer and Surrey*, ed. Hammond, pp. 131–42 (portions of this edition of the text are reprinted in *The Oxford Book of Late Medieval Verse and Prose*, ed. Gray, pp. 69–70) and Lydgate, *The Dance of Death, Edited from MSS. Ellesmere*, ed. Warren and White. Compare also appendix to Lydgate, *Fall of Princes*, ed. Bergen, pp. 1025–44, which offers an edition largely based on the text found in Tottel's 1554 printing of the *Fall of Princes*, on which see below, p. 18.

poetry is reflected in the phrase often appearing within it, "lerne to die," which also serves as the title of Thomas Hoccleve's Middle English verse translation of Henry Suso's *Ars moriendi* (or Book 2, chapter 2 of his larger *Horologium sapientiae*).

Side by side with such poetry, however, emerged a different strain of death poetry that sought to come to terms with dying by staging imaginative encounters with death as a material experience.[2] The following short poem (DIMEV 6459) belongs to what is called the Signs of Death tradition. Originating in commentaries on Hippocrates and transmitted in medieval medical manuscripts, by the twelfth century it developed into its own robust literary strain and wound its way into the immensely popular fourteenth-century preaching handbook *Fasciculus morum*.[3] In this version of the Signs of Death, found in MS Harley 7322, dated to the end of the fourteenth century, the approach of death is rendered in the following terms:

Wonne þin eren dinet: and þi nese scharpet.	*When your ears fill with din; nose; sharpens*
And þin hew dunnet: and þi sennewess starket.	*hue darkens; sinews stiffen*
And þin eyen synket: and þi tunge foldet.	*eyes; speech fails*
And þin honde stinket: and þin fet coldetʒ.	
And þin lippes blaket: and þin teth ratilet.	*blacken; teeth chatter*
And þin hond quaket: and þi þrote ruteletʒ.	*rattles (in death)*
— Al to late. al to late. þen is te wayn atte yate.	*hearse at the gate*
For may þor no man þenne penaunce make.[4]	*there; then*

Organized as a kind of anti-blazon, this poem deploys anaphora (the repetition of words for rhetorical effect) and polysyndeton (the use of numerous conjunctions — in this case, "and" — for rhetorical effect) to prompt its reader to imagine the degradation of his body as a set of grisly images in rapid succession: sharpened nose, darkened skin, sunken eyes, collapsed tongue, etc. A poem found in the thirteenth-century manuscript, Trinity College MS B.14.39 (DIMEV 6595), meanwhile, is even more explicit in the function served by its serialization of images:

> Wose warit wid prute abeit amadde;
> Of heore brein wl waccen a cadde.
> A worim of herre tunke. þat maden her lesunge . . .
> Of herre vombe wacchet ongiltuaches
> Þat glutit & liuit bilacches
> Þe woriste neddre in þe rug bon
> Of þe letchore wacces on
> Asse þis bitit in dede liche; bitit þe soule in helle piche . . . .
>   (Lines 4–6, 9–13)

---

[2] On medieval cultures of death, especially in England, see Ariès, *The Hour of Our Death*, trans. Weaver; Daniell, *Death and Burial in Medieval England*; *Death and Dying in the Middle Ages*, ed. DuBruck and Gusick; Kinch, *Imago Mortis*; and Appleford, *Learning to Die in London*.

[3] Woolf, *The English Religious Lyric in the Middle Ages*, pp. 78–82.

[4] Text from *Political, Religious, and Love Poems*, ed. Furnivall, p. 221, glosses our own. For other examples of the Signs of Death, see DIMEV 6460, 6383, 6437, 6439, 6447, 6459, and 6462. Unless otherwise noted, all glosses and translations given in this introduction are our own.

Whoso fares with pride they are driven mad,
From their brain will wax a caddis;
A worm from their tongue who here told lies . . .
From their belly wax (or wake) maw-worms
(Those) that glut themselves and live by laziness.
The worst adder in the back-bone
Of the lecher waxes alone.
As this happens in the dead body it happens to the soul in the pitch of hell ....[5]

Similar to the lists of tasks to be undertaken by the soul as it prepares itself for death in *ars moriendi* poetry, this serialization serves as a mnemonic device (a pattern constructed to help the reader retain something in her memory). It fixes different sins (pride, lying, gluttony, lechery) onto specific body parts (brain, tongue, belly, spine) and associates those in turn with vermin that reify aspects of decomposition (caddisfly, maggot, worm, adder). The catalogue of body parts, and the particular manner of future decomposition with which those are associated, prompt the reader to make an organized list of mental images, anchoring the image of death in the mind. Vivid — and especially violent or gruesome — serialized images, organized around a central category, are, of course, a fixture of the so-called memorial arts from antiquity through the late Middle Ages, as Mary Carruthers has amply shown.[6]

These death poems, in other words, although they are texts, are designed to function like a mental "image-text," compelling the reader to imagine a set of visualizations organized around a single, central idea.[7] In the case of the poems above, this category is the decomposing human body, but other poems ponder the transience of human attachment to possessions, rules and regulations, and social rank, or consider embodied encounters with death by personifying death into a real figure, capable of dialogue that describes and justifies its actions. This interest in death's material presence produces a vivid poetry eager for new ways to express death's physical and psychological processes on the human body. Furthermore, like their "learn to die" counterparts, these poems also engage in a serializing aesthetic, suggesting that a central impetus of late medieval death poetry is the attempted taxonomization and ordering of the ineffable experience of dying.

THE *DANSE MACABRE* TRADITION

Danse macabre poetry participates in this serializing aesthetic by also prompting the reader to imagine death by means of a serialized catalogue that cues vivid visualizations. Here, however, instead of decomposition, the catalogue consists of successive conversations between Death, embodied as an emaciated humanoid figure, and various representatives of society. Each pair of stanzas in *danse macabre* poems represent a conversation between Death and a member of a different social demographic. These conversations are arranged in descending hierarchical order, beginning with the pope and emperor, moving through representatives of lesser clerical and secular authority (cardinal, king), progressing to more

---

[5] Text and translation, which its editor delightfully entitles "Poem on the Creepy-Crawlies that Grow Out of the Dead Body," from Laing, "Confusion 'Wrs' Confounded," p. 270.

[6] Carruthers, *The Book of Memory*. Compare similar points made by Kinch, *Imago Mortis*, pp. 6–7.

[7] The term "image-text" is introduced by Mitchell in *Iconology*, pp. 154–55 and subsequently elaborated in his *Picture Theory*, especially p. 89n9.

minor ecclesiastical orders (friar, parish priest) down to urban dwellers (lawyer, merchant, etc.), and often ending with the peasant laborer and the infant child. The inexplicable cradle-death of the latter often serves as the apogee of the tradition's ruminations on death's implacability.

In its cross-section of all strata of late medieval European society, the *danse macabre* tradition bears obvious affinities with estates satire. The characters are portrayed as flat types defined by physical characteristics (the cardinal wears his distinctive red hat, the physician has a urine flask, the abbot is corpulent, etc.), stereotypical behavior, and personality traits (the usurer is greedy, the laborer is weary, etc.), which are elaborated without deviation from narrative expectation.[8] Like the catalogues of decomposition in the visually vivid death poetry mentioned above, the flat types of *danse macabre* estates satire similarly help readers remember and thus process the fundamental paradox of death's universality yet specificity: while we know that we must die like everyone else, we cannot imagine our own personal death. Taxonomy, these poems suggest, helps fill that imaginative void.

In this way, the *danse macabre* poems partake of the "image-text" quality of the broader genre of death poetry, like the Signs of Death. Furthermore, two of its earliest instantiations, the anonymous French *Danse macabre* and John Lydgate's near contemporary translation of it into Middle English, were themselves actual image-texts, painted as murals on which stanzas of text were linked to visual images of the dead communicating with the living. The *danse macabre* tradition went on to spawn a rich pan-European iconographic and literary tradition of murals, Books of Hours miniatures, sculptures, blockbooks, incunabula, and broadsides that continued to visually showcase a serializing aesthetic by presenting alternating figures of dead and living, interlinked in the final dance of death.

THE ORIGINS AND POTENTIAL MEANINGS OF "MACABRE"

The earliest mention of a "danse macabre" comes from Jean Le Fèvre's *Le respit de la mort* (1376). In this work, the protagonist (represented as the author himself) is seized by a sudden illness and argues before a tribunal for a *lettre de répit* (letter of continuance) in order to die at a later date. In a passage discussing the illness and death's inevitability, Le Fèvre writes:

> Je fis de Macabré la dance
> qui toutes gens maine a sa tresche
> et a la fosse les adresche,
> qui est leur derraine maison.
>   (lines 3078–81)

> (I did the dance of Macabré
> who leads all men to his dance
> and directs them to the grave,
> which is their final abode.)[9]

In this passage, "Macabré" clearly refers to a person who is in charge of and organizing a dance that eventually wends its way towards one's final resting place.

---

[8] On estates satire, see, in particular, Mann's seminal *Chaucer and Medieval Estates Satire*.

[9] Le Fèvre, *Le respit de la mort*, ed. Hasenohr-Esnos, p. 113.

The phrase *danse macabre* goes on to become the title of a well-known French poem consisting of octosyllabic eight-line stanzas rhyming *ababbcbc*, framed by two brief Latin texts, totaling 556 lines. It was also, according to the *Journal d'un bourgeois de Paris* (1405–49), painted as a mural at L'Église aux Saints Innocents (the Church of the Holy Innocents), started in August 1424 and completed during Lent in 1425.[10] Guillebert de Mets notes more specifically in his *Description de la ville de Paris* (1434) that the *Danse macabre* mural was located in the arcades under the charnel houses of the adjacent cemetery.[11] This detail is noteworthy because, some lines after invoking "de Macabré la dance," Jean le Fèvre's speaker goes on to express dread before the prospect of dying and ending up among the piles of bones at the charnel house of the Innocents (lines 3122–23). This suggests a possible connection between that location and the idea of "Macabré"'s dance as early as 1376, although the Innocents was also the main charnel house in Paris and thus a natural choice for a mural of this theme. The cemetery was one of the oldest in Paris, with historical records going back to 1186; in the fourteenth and fifteenth centuries, it was a bustling area located by Les Halles, the main market, and full of merchants, produce sellers, scribes, and sex workers.[12]

Given the presence of the Saint Innocents reference in Le Fèvre, it is all the more noteworthy that both the *Danse macabre* and its Middle English translation, Lydgate's *Dance of Death*, feature a character named "Machabre," who, like in Le Fèvre, seems to be in charge. In a manuscript made just a year or two after the painting of the mural, Paris, Bibliothèque nationale de France, fr. 14989, the speaker of the work's opening and closing stanzas is named "Machabre docteur"; we observe the same character in Lydgate's translation.[13] That "Macabre" was perceived to be a person overseeing death's dance further resurfaces in a more literal fashion in Guyot Marchant's 1490 printing of a Latin translation of the *Danse*. Here the title page names the text as "*Chorea ab eximio Macabro versibus alemanicis edita et a Petro Desrey . . . nuper emendata . . .*" (The Dance elevated from German verses by the excellent Macabrus and . . . in recent years corrected . . . by Pierre Desrey).[14]

The actual origins of the word "macabre," however, remain obscure. The term has been suggested to be a borrowing from Arabic ("maqābir" meaning "graveyards") or Hebrew ("m'kaber" meaning "undertaker"), though in both cases scholars have found it difficult to offer any clear line of transmission between Arabic and Hebrew burial rites and customs and the Western European *dance macabre* tradition.[15] Gaston Paris suggested that "Macabre" could be a surname derived from "Maccabeus" and cites two *chansons de geste*, *Élie de Saint Giles* and *Anseïs de Cartage*, which give "Macabre" as Saracen names.[16] Florence White notes,

---

[10] *Journal d'un bourgeois de Paris*, ed. Beaune, p. 220.

[11] Guillebert de Mets, *Description de la ville de Paris 1434*, ed. and trans. Mullally, p. 95. Of additional interest is de Mets' detail that the church contains a relic of a young Christian boy allegedly murdered by Jews in 1179 (see p. 142n299).

[12] Dujakovic, "The Dance of Death, the Dance of Life," pp. 210–11.

[13] For more on this manuscript, see the Explanatory Notes to the *Danse macabre*, p. 142.

[14] On the rubric's claim that the French *Danse* is actually translated from German, see further Clark, *Dance of Death in the Middle Ages and the Renaissance*, p. 28.

[15] For an overview of these theories and the arguments against them, see DuBruck, "Another Look at 'Macabre,'" pp. 539–43.

[16] Paris, "Le Danse Macabré de Jean Le Fèvre," p. 132.

in support of this theory, that a Dutch translation of the *Danse macabre* by Anthonis de Roovere is called *Makkabeusdans* (1482) and that "Macabré" is attested as a French surname in the late fourteenth century.[17] Upholding this theory, Joël Saugnieux traces the connection between Judas Maccabeus and death to 2 Maccabees 38:45, in which Judas Maccabeus insists on burying the bodies of soldiers who have sinned through false worship.[18] A final line of thought holds that "Macabre" is instead a variation on the name Macarius, owing to two influential episodes in the *Vita* of Macarius the Great, in which the saint raises a man from the dead and, elsewhere, makes a dead body speak to name its killer, thus demonstrating his power over death. This theory is supported by the widespread folk association of St. Macarius with funeral rites in Central and Eastern Europe.[19]

LITERARY, VISUAL, AND CULTURAL PRECURSORS TO THE FRENCH *DANSE MACABRE*

While it remains unclear what "Macabre" is or who originally wrote the work, the *Danse macabre* seems to have emerged organically from contemporary cultural traditions and beliefs surrounding death and the status of the cadaver. For plague-ravaged late medieval Europe, death was "in the air," so to speak, though recent scholarship has questioned earlier assumptions as to direct correlations between the appearance and spread of *danse macabre* imagery and the epidemiology of the plague.[20] Meanwhile, Jane H. M. Taylor notes the frequent representation of devils in hell as dancing in contemporary French mystery plays.[21] Nancy Caciola finds mentions in Walter Map (1140–c. 1210) and Thomas of Cantimpré (1201–72) of the living witnessing dead bodies dancing in a circle in cemeteries, a detail that she connects with real-life ecclesiastical injunctions prohibiting dancing to commemorate the dead in cemeteries. These reports suggest that dancing in the cemetery was an actual medieval practice, which may have contributed to the poetic and visual *danse macabre* tradition.[22] Caciola further suggests a connection to the widespread Northern European belief in corporeal revenants, or decaying bodies of the newly dead that did not remain in their graves, found in the folklore of Iceland, modern-day Germany and the Netherlands, England, and Northern France and widely reported by figures such as Walter Map, William of Newburgh (c. 1136–c. 1198) and Thomas of Cantimpré. These revenants were understood

---

[17] White, "Introduction," in Lydgate, *Dance of Death*, ed. Warren and White, p. xvii.

[18] Saugnieux, *Les danses macabres de France et d'Espagne*, pp. 15–16. Compare Kurtz, *Dance of Death and the Macabre Spirit*, p. 22. While an allusion to Judas Maccabeus may seem obscure to modern-day audiences, Judas Maccabeus was one of the Nine Worthies alongside Hector, Alexander the Great, Julius Caesar, Joshua, David, Arthur, Charlemagne, and Godfrey of Bouillon, or nine noted great figures of the past listed in numerous late medieval literary works. See further Sperber, "Etymology of Macabre," pp. 394–95.

[19] Strakhov, "Russkie slova," pp. 271–80. Compare Kurtz, *Dance of Death and the Macabre Spirit*, p. 125, on the representation of St. Macarius in a Dance of Death mural in Pisa, Italy.

[20] See Gertsman's overview of this issue in *Dance of Death in the Middle Ages*, pp. 42–44.

[21] Taylor, "Que signifiait 'danse,'" pp. 267–70; see further Gertsman, *Dance of Death in the Middle Ages*, p. 64. Compare Oosterwijk, "Dance, Dialogue and Duality," pp. 17–20; and Eustace with King, "Dances of the Living and the Dead."

[22] Caciola, "Wraiths, Revenants and Ritual," pp. 38–43. See also Taylor, "Que signifiait 'danse,'" pp. 265–67, who points out that medieval popular dance featured leaping of the kind represented in Guyot Marchant's woodcuts accompanying his edition and also notes the ecclesiastical condemnation of dancing at cemeteries.

to be the newly deceased, who lived sinfully and were taken suddenly or inopportunely. Not yet fully decayed and with unfinished business on earth, their connection with the world of the living is not fully severed, allowing them to roam the earth.[23] The belief in revenants' partially decayed state tracks with all known visual representations of the *danse macabre* theme, in which the dead are represented as emaciated, decomposing bodies.

The *Danse* also has important literary precursors. Its dialogic structure resonates with the ubiquitous genre of medieval debate poetry and reminds us, in particular, of the extremely popular genre of the Debate of the Body and the Soul, first emerging in the twelfth-century *Visio Philiberti*, in which allegorizations of the body and the soul, at the point or immediately upon the act of dying, debate worldly vanity, death's inexorability, and the importance of salvation.[24] Beyond this broad literary context are several works with particular formal and thematic features that bear a strong relationship with *danse macabre* poetry. Hélinand of Froidmont's *Les vers de la mort*, written in the 1190s, treats a speaker who addresses himself to Death, repenting of his profligate life and expressing dread before Death's inexorability.[25] Another important source is the so-called *Vado mori*, a late thirteenth or early fourteenth-century work, in which characters from a descending range of social strata (king, pope, bishop, knight, physician, poor man, etc.) lament the inexorability of death and the earthly possessions they must abandon, as they — notably — *move* towards death, beginning and ending their speeches with "Vado mori" (I go to die).[26] However, Death does not appear in any of these works as its own character.

A significant related motif that, like the *Danse*, originates in literature and becomes extremely popular in visual iconography is the legend of the Three Living and the Three Dead. Found all over Europe in over 60 versions, some of its earliest instantiations originate in thirteenth-century France, including one attributed to Baudoin de Condé and the other by Nicole de Margival in manuscript. An alliterative Middle English version of it, entitled *Three Dead Kings*, is found in John Audelay's compilation of his collected works, Oxford, Bodleian Library, MS Douce 302 (c. 1426–31), although scholars do not agree as to his authorship of the poem.[27] In this *memento mori* encounter, three noblemen (in some versions, kings) encounter three dead men in the forest, who warn them to flee life's vanities, though at this point the textual similarities end.[28] By c. 1300, the work became an extremely popular iconographic subject on walls (with records of over 200 murals), in sculpture, and in Books of Hours and psalters across Europe; interestingly, the earliest known murals of

---

[23] Caciola, "Wraiths, Revenants and Ritual" pp. 28–33.

[24] On this genre, see Batiouchkof, "Le débat de l'âme et du corps," Parts 1 and 2; Vogel, "Some Aspects of the Horse and Rider Analogy"; Ackerman, "Parochial Christianity"; and, most recently, Raskolnikov, *Body Against Soul*.

[25] Kurtz, *Dance of Death and the Macabre Spirit*, pp. 12–14. For an edition, see *Les vers de la mort par Hélinant*, ed. Wulff and Walberg.

[26] Kurtz, *Dance of Death and the Macabre Spirit*, pp. 16–17; Clark, *Dance of Death in the Middle Ages and the Renaissance*, pp. 101–02; Oosterwijk, "Dance, Dialogue and Duality," pp. 20–21. For an edition, see "Die Vado-Mori-Elegie," ed. Rosenfeld.

[27] See Audelay, "Three Dead Kings" and the Headnote to its Explanatory Notes, ed. S. Fein, pp. 218–22 and pp. 321–34.

[28] Kurtz, *Dance of Death and the Macabre Spirit*, pp. 17–20; Clark, *Dance of Death in the Middle Ages and the Renaissance*, pp. 95–99; Gertsman, *Dance of Death in the Middle Ages*, pp. 26–29. For an edition, see *Les cinq poèmes des trois morts*, ed. Glixelli.

this text, dating from the fourteenth century, seem to be English, while the French ones all date from the fifteenth century.[29] In its visual instantiations, the legend resonates strongly with the visual quality of *danse macabre* murals in depicting the living in communion with the dead, with the stark contrast between their states vividly underscored by the similarity in their physical stances. The Innocents cemetery featured a carving, dated 1408, of the Three Living and the Three Dead above its doorway that had been commissioned by John of Berry; the later addition of the *Danse macabre* mural to the same spot suggests that the two works were perceived to have a cultural connection.[30] This connection was further strengthened by Marchant's inclusion of a French version of the legend into later editions of the *Danse*.

Additionally, late medieval funeral sculpture, both in England and on the Continent, saw the emergence of the "cadaver effigy," also known as the *memento mori*, or *transi* tomb (*transi* in the sense of "crossed over, transitioned"). This was a Northern European sculptural vogue running from the late fourteenth to the seventeenth century, particularly prominent in England and Northern France. It represented a person's desiccated or decomposing likeness on the lid, sometimes with additional verses describing the occupant's death. In the fifteenth century, these developed into elaborate "double-decker" affairs with an effigy of the deceased represented as newly dead on the first level, followed by an image of a putrefying skeletal body beneath it. The tomb of Henry Chichele, Archbishop of Canterbury, is a noteworthy example of the phenomenon and was constructed in 1424–26, well before his death in 1443, suggesting that it may have served as a literal *memento mori* to its future occupant.[31]

Elina Gertsman further connects the *danse macabre*'s instantiation into mural format with late medieval drama. She notes that individual characters, and the dead bodies interacting with them, are positioned on extant murals across Europe with distinctive visual features and gestures. Facing the viewer in a manner evocative of medieval theater, they are specifically reminiscent, she argues, of *dramatis personae* (cast of characters) illustrations in

---

[29] Two English murals remain extant at the Chapel of Saint Nicolas at Haddon Hall in Derbyshire and at Longthorpe Tower in Cambridgeshire. For more on this iconographic motif, see Binski, *Medieval Death: Ritual and Representation*, pp. 134–38, Kralik, "Dialogue and Violence," and, on the legend's consumption, as both text and image, by the very courtly audiences it seeks most to critique, Kinch, *Imago Mortis*, pp. 109–44.

[30] Kinch, *Imago Mortis*, pp. 136–38. The same collocation is seen at Kermaria in Brittany and Bergamo in Italy (Kurtz, *Dance of Death and the Macabre Spirit*, pp. 78–80 and 121–22). It is further interesting to note that, in his *Vite de' piu eccellenti pittori*, 2:218–21, Giorgio Vasari describes in detail a famous painting, known as *Il Trionfo della Morte* (*The Triumph of Death*), painted at Campo Santo in Pisa in the early-mid fourteenth century; Vasari attributes it to Andrea Orcagna (c. 1308–68), but it has since been attributed to Buonamico Buffalmacco (fl. c. 1315–36). This painting of sinners being driven to hell by demons as Death reigns triumphant also features a small scene derived from the motif of the Three Living and the Three Dead, in which the three noblemen are enjoined to look upon three corpses in open graves by an old man, whom Vasari identifies as Saint Macarius, one of the figures from whom the term "macabre" has been thought to derive; see Sperber, "Etymology of Macabre," p. 399 and Strakhov, "Russkie slova," pp. 278–79.

[31] See, in general, Cohen, *Metamorphosis of a Death Symbol* and, in relation to the *danse macabre*, Binski, *Medieval Death: Ritual and Representation*, pp. 139–52 and Gertsman, *Dance of Death in the Middle Ages*, pp. 29–32.

late medieval manuscripts of mystery plays.[32] Gertsman also points out the parallels between *danse macabre* scenes as rendered on murals and in other visual formats and records of fifteenth-century court masques and mystery plays featuring Death trying to attack other characters.[33] In at least two cases, a *danse macabre* was itself actually performed as some kind of masque: for Philippe Le Bon at court in 1449 (described in the expense account of the duke as a "jeu" [game]), while Jean de Calais performed a "Chorea Maccabeorum" (Dance of Maccabees) at a church in Besançon in 1453.[34]

LATER DEVELOPMENTS IN THE *DANSE MACABRE* TRADITION

Death poetry's stark imagery and vivid portrayals of embodied death both drew inspiration from and inspired new visual cultural forms. As Jane H. M. Taylor argues, the *Danse macabre* mural seems clearly to have been intended to be consumed as an "image-text," not unlike a modern graphic novel.[35] The particular arrangement of the *Danse* as horizontal bands of sequential images and text vertically aligned between speaker and speech, Taylor suggests, produces a tension on the part of the typical medieval reader. The reader would have perceived the sense of the images far more rapidly and immediately than she would have likely read the mural's text but, nevertheless, the full import of the *Danse* could not be gained from the images alone. The *Danse* thus necessitated an active reader asked to process and synthesize two conceptually separate but importantly overlapping narrative systems at once.[36] Seeta Chaganti has further shown the importance of the spatialized dual media format of the *danse macabre*. Placed in large-scale formats in churches, the murals would have invited the viewer to physically displace his body, thus adding a kinetic element to his experience of the mural. Additionally, Marchant's woodcuts, as well as later *danse macabre* images, depict the dead and the living as dancing within architectural spaces, thus creating a doubling effect for a viewer observing the mural within its architectural space. The *danse macabre* thus becomes, she argues, a "multimedia artistic installation."[37]

---

[32] Gertsman, "Pleyinge and Peyntynge," pp. 2–5 and 11–20; this argument is expanded in her *Dance of Death in the Middle Ages*, pp. 79–99.

[33] Gertsman, "Pleyinge and Peyntynge," pp. 7–8.

[34] Gertsman, "Pleyinge and Peyntynge," pp. 8–10. Clark suggests that the common general source accounting for the thematic similarities yet clear independence of the three *danse macabres* texts of Paris, Castille, and Lübeck may be a now lost mystery play (*Dance of Death in the Middle Ages and the Renaissance*, pp. 91–92).

[35] While the original *Danse macabre* mural in Paris is no longer extant, scholars have largely accepted Guyot Marchant's first edition of the *Danse* with accompanying woodcuts in 1485 as a faithful representation of the original, even though it features figures in contemporary dress (Kurtz, *Dance of Death and the Macabre Spirit*, pp. 76–77); Clark, *Dance of Death in the Middle Ages and the Renaissance*, pp. 24–25.

[36] Taylor, "*Danse Macabré* and Bande Dessinée." See further Gertsman, *Dance of Death in the Middle Ages*, pp. 103–24, who offers similar readings of later *danse macabre* murals in other parts of Europe.

[37] Chaganti, "*Danse Macabre* and the Virtual Churchyard," p. 20. This argument is developed at much greater length in *Strange Footing*, pp. 99–185, especially 121–28.

Figure 1. fol. ¶¶ 1v; *A treatise excellent and compendious, shewing and declaring, in maner of tragedye, the falles of sondry most notable princes and princesses with other nobles* (London: Richard Tottell, 1554; STC 3177). "The daunce of Machabree." (Photo: Harry Ransom Center at the University of Texas)

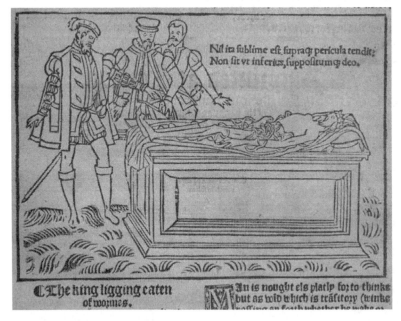

Figure 2. fol. ¶¶ 6; *A treatise excellent and compendious, shewing and declaring, in maner of tragedye, the falles of sondry most notable princes and princesses with other nobles* (London: Richard Tottell, 1554; STC 3177). "The king ligging eaten of wormes." The Latin lines from Ovid's *Tristia* (4.8.47–48) translate as "nothing is so high and above danger, that it is not below and subject to God." (Photo: Harry Ransom Center at the University of Texas)

From 1430 on, *danse macabre* visual motifs appeared on a vast array of surfaces. Two nearly contemporaneous Books of Hours, the first dated c. 1430–35 (now New York, Morgan Library, MS M. 359), the second Book of Hours, dated c. 1430–40 (now Paris, Bibliothèque nationale de France, MS Rothschild 2535), as well as the famous early sixteenth-century *Hours of Charles V*, all illustrate the *danse macabre* in their margins. This suggests that the idea of death as a dance was rapidly adopted as a major visual motif within this devotional genre.[38] Interest in the *danse* was soon not limited to manuscripts: scenes teemed on church murals, wall hangings, stone and wood sculptures, even misericords and bells, in places as far-flung as St. Omer, Kermaria in Brittany (which has the oldest extant mural, dating from c. 1450), Rouen in Normandy, Auvergne, Stratford-upon-Avon, Windsor, Coventry, Roslyn in Scotland, Berlin, Lübeck, Ulm, Basel, Bergamo and Trento in Italy, Javier in Spain, Brussels, Hrastovlje in Slovenia, and Talinn. Unfortunately, many church murals have succumbed to the Protestant Reformation, the French Revolution, and the Second World War, but for centuries the *danse macabre* adorned a dizzying number of surfaces all across Europe.[39]

Inasmuch as the *Danse*'s afterlife was most immediately felt in its powerful influence on iconographic traditions stretching all across Europe, it also importantly extended into the realm of the literary. Aside from Lydgate's *Dance of Death*, discussed below, the mid-late fifteenth century saw, in France, the *Danse macabre des femmes*, attributed to Martial d'Auvergne (c. 1430–1508) and composed between 1466 and 1482, judging from internal textual and manuscript evidence. Clearly directly modeled on the original *Danse* in structure, it features 34 women speaking to "la morte," a dead woman, who counsels them to resign themselves to Death. Like the *Danse*, the women represent all ranks of society, from the queen to the shepherdess, though this text also includes some interesting representation of women in male-dominated professions such as "la theologienne" (the female theologian), as well as a witch and a sex worker. It also presents multiple women at different points of the female life cycle (the maiden, the pregnant woman, several different kinds of wives, the old woman, etc.). Like the *Danse*, the work culminates with a rotting dead queen as a female parallel to the rotting dead king of the *Danse*.[40] The *Danse macabre des femmes* is found in six late fifteenth- and sixteenth-century manuscripts, four of which it shares with the original *Danse macabre*, and was added to later editions of Marchant's *Danse*.[41] Its appearance and collocation with the *Danse* is especially interesting, given that

---

[38] Oosterwijk, "Of Dead Kings," pp. 140–45 and, for a reading of the Morgan Library Book of Hours alongside Lydgate's *Dance*, see Kinch, *Imago Mortis*, pp. 185–226. *The Book of Hours of Charles V*, or Madrid, Biblioteca nacional de España, Cod. Vitr. 24–3, is available fully digitized at http://bdh.bne.es/bnesearch/detalle/bdh0000051953.

[39] See Kurtz, *Dance of Death and the Macabre Spirit*; Clark, *Dance of Death in the Middle Ages and the Renaissance*; Oosterwijk, "Of Corpses, Constables and Kings," pp. 67–76; Gertsman, *Dance of Death in the Middle Ages*; and Oosterwijk, "Money, Morality, Mortality."

[40] See Harrison, "La Grant Danse Macabre des Femmes," and Becker, "La danse macabre au féminin." For an edition, see *The Danse Macabre of Women*, ed. Harrison, pp. 46–133.

[41] The *Danse macabre des femmes* is found with the *Danse* in: Paris, Bibliothèque nationale fonds français 995, fols. 23v–43r; Paris, Bibliothèque nationale fonds français 1186, fols. 98v–108r; Paris, Bibliothèque nationale fonds français 25434, fols. 61r–79v, and Paris, Bibliothèque nationale nouvelles acquisitions françaises 10032, fols. 224r–38r; as well as separately in Paris, Bibliothèque de l'Arsenal MS 3637, fols. 26r–30v and The Hague, Koninklijke Bibliotheek, MS 71 E 49, fols. 285r–93v. Marchant included it in his editions of 1486, 1491, and 1492.

Lydgate's *Dance of Death* departs from its original source precisely in its addition of several female characters.

Castille in the Iberian Peninsula offers us its own unique take on the *danse macabre* theme with the *Dança general de la muerte* that may in fact predate the French mural and text. Extant only in Madrid, Biblioteca de l'Escorial MS B.IV.21, a mid-fifteenth-century manuscript, the text's linguistic features suggest it may have been composed as early as the late fourteenth century.[42] The *Dança* features 33 characters, 22 of whom it shares with the *Danse* (and Lydgate's *Dance*), like the pope, emperor, cardinal, king, knight, squire, archbishop, bishop, merchant, usurer, etc. Speakers engage in the now familiar dialogue with Death, except that here each speaker's words are enclosed by opening and concluding addresses from Death. Other than some of its characters, however, and its dialogic structure, the *Dança* is a completely independent work that demonstrates some thematic overlap, but no textual parallels with the French text or Lydgate's translation. It further reveals its adherence to its own specific sociocultural context by including a rabbi and an *alfaqui* (an Islamic cleric expert in Islamic law).[43] The French *Danse* was separately translated into Catalàn by Pedro Miguel de Carbonell (1437–1517) in 1497, with the addition of several new female characters.[44] (The French *Danse* also seems to have served as the basis for an Italian version, titled *Il ballo della morte*, dated to the late fifteenth or early sixteenth century: here, as in other versions, Death speaks in dialogue form to a variety of characters from different social stations.[45])

In what are now Germany, Switzerland, Denmark, Sweden, and the Netherlands, the tradition reached perhaps its most extensive development, with numerous murals, blockbooks, and incunabula dating from the late fifteenth, sixteenth, and seventeenth centuries. Like France and Castille, the Free City of Lübeck, capital of the Hanseatic League from c. 1200 until the League's demise in 1669, had its own independent *danse macabre*, though it bears some textual similarities to the French *Danse*. This dance was also painted on a mural with both text and image in 1463 before appearing in a 1489 edition with woodcuts. Unsurprisingly, given the city's economic role in the Hansa, the Lübeck dance illustrates middle-class urban dwellers as the largest cross-section of its representation of contemporary society. Other versions, related to this one and separate from the French and Castillian traditions, also circulated in mid-fifteenth-century blockbooks.[46]

Most famous within the Germanic side of the tradition, however, and perhaps best known to modern audiences, are Hans Holbein the Younger's exceptional woodcuts. Holbein began by creating the *Alphabet of Death* in c. 1523, a series of woodcuts of the Latin alphabet

---

[42] Kurtz (*Dance of Death and the Macabre Spirit*, pp. 147–49) and Clark (*Dance of Death in the Middle Ages and Renaissance*, pp. 41–42) suggest it is contemporary to its manuscript, thus postdating the *Danse macabre*, while Gertsman (*Dance of Death in the Middle Ages*, p. 3) suggests it predates it, being c. 1400. Víctor Infantes argues that the poem, partially collocated with works from the 1360s–80s, may be equally as early (*Las danzas de la muerte*, pp. 226–39). See further Saugnieux, *Les danses macabres de France et d'Espagne*, pp. 45–49 for an overview of the complexities of the dating question.

[43] For an edition, see "*Danza general*," ed. Saugnieux, pp. 165–82.

[44] Kurtz, *Dance of Death and the Macabre Spirit*, pp. 149–52; Clark, *Dance of Death in the Middle Ages and the Renaissance*, pp. 45–48.

[45] Kurtz, *Dance of Death and the Macabre Spirit*, pp. 126–27.

[46] Kurtz, *Dance of Death and the Macabre Spirit*, pp. 93–120; Clark, *Dance of Death in the Middle Ages and the Renaissance*, pp. 78–83.

with *danse macabre* imagery.[47] Not long after, he designed the *Images of Death*, forty-one complex and imaginative woodcuts, carved by Hans Lützelburger, in which gruesome cadavers relentlessly tease and torment their harried victims. First published in 1538 in Lyons by Melchior and Caspar Trechsel in a volume entitled *Les simulachres & historiees faces de la mort*, the work went through numerous editions over the next 30 years. In the same period, Holbein also designed a Swiss dagger sheath featuring *danse macabre* elements.[48]

In this way, the theme of death as a material force upon the body diffused widely both into late medieval literature and late medieval iconography, especially iconography in public settings. The *danse macabre* tradition thus reminds us that texts, especially popular texts in the Middle Ages, were also visual, auditory, and performed for a wide audience. In its spread across multiple kinds of media, late medieval death poetry suggests that the most private experience of human life — death — is also its most public.

JOHN LYDGATE'S *DANCE OF DEATH*: ORIGINS AND CONTEXT

Like the French *Danse macabre*, John Lydgate's *Dance of Death* stages a series of dialogues between Death and a variety of figures from across the social stratum, from the highest ecclesiastical and secular authorities (the Pope, the Emperor) to the humblest members of society (the newborn child). In each set of paired stanzas, Death reminds his interlocutor of his or her impending fate, and the character responds with a meditation on the transience of his or her existence, repenting of any ill-advised or misguided behavior. Taking *memento mori* and *ars moriendi* as its themes, the poem enjoins its readers that none shall be spared: all must be prepared to join Death's dance. Shifting between stern admonition, dark humor, and sudden consolation, Lydgate's *Dance of Death* is a vivid and moving example of fifteenth-century didactic poetry, with a message for all.

John Lydgate's *Dance of Death* exists in two versions, which together survive in a total of fifteen manuscripts and two early printed editions, a relatively large number which testifies to the significance and popularity of the poem in a vernacular English context. Fifteenth-century scribes placed the *Dance of Death* alongside other works by Lydgate, as well as by Chaucer and Hoccleve, but almost always in the context of other Middle English writing, suggesting its primary audience was readers who were required or preferred to read works in English rather than Latin or French. Remarkably, given the prevalence of visual iconography of the *Danse macabre* in other contexts, it is never illustrated.

The earliest version of the poem is called the "A" version by Eleanor Prescott Hammond (who uses Oxford, Bodleian Library MS Selden Supra 53 as her base text) and the "Ellesmere version" by White and Warren (who base their edition on San Marino, Huntington Library, MS EL 26.A.13). This version of the poem, consisting of 672 decasyllabic lines in eight-line stanzas rhyming *ababbcbc*, is Lydgate's initial translation of his French source, begun while he was in Paris in 1426 as part of the entourage of the Earl of Warwick. Amy Appleford argues that the A version, like Lydgate's other French to English translations made around this time, was prepared for a specific, likely courtly, audience shortly after his return from Paris.[49] Lydgate testifies to the connection between

---

[47] On the *Alphabet*, see Schwab, "Letters without Words."

[48] Kurtz, *Dance of Death and the Macabre Spirit*, pp. 190–208; Gertsman, *Dance of Death in the Middle Ages*, pp. 169–80.

[49] Appleford, *Learning to Die in London*, p. 88.

his text and the French *Danse macabre* in a five-stanza prologue, identified as the *verba translatoris* (words of the translator), as well as a two-stanza envoy that names Lydgate as the translator. In this *verba translatoris*, Lydgate takes pains to explain that his text is "[l]ike the exawmple wiche that at Parys / I fonde depict oones in a wal" (lines 19–20), positioning himself as an eyewitness to the Parisian paintings. He also notes that his English translation was made with the encouragement of French clerics in Paris:

> Ther, of Frensshe clerkis takyng aqueintaunce,   *French clerics making*
> I toke on me to translatyn al,
> Oute of the Frensshe, Machabres Daunce.
>
> By whos avys and counceil atte the leste,   *advice and counsel at last*
> Thorugh her steryng and her mocioun,   *guidance; suggestion*
> I obeide unto her requeste,   *their*
> Therof to make a playn translacioun   *complete translation*
> In Englissh tonge . . .   *Into the English language*
> (lines 22–29)

Lydgate's journey to Paris in 1426 and decision to translate a French work into English came at a particularly fraught period for late medieval Anglo-French relations, rendering his insistence on the French clerics' request interesting. The decade before had seen Henry V's triumphant and disastrous invasion of Northern France culminating in the Treaty of Troyes in 1420, in which the French government made him next in line for the French throne in exchange for peace. Henry's sudden death in 1422 left England and France with the nine-month-old king Henry VI under the co-regency of his two uncles, Humphrey of Gloucester in England and John of Bedford in France. As he held Paris under military occupation, Bedford was also a patron of the arts, commissioning decorated manuscripts, on the one hand, and appropriating French manuscripts from the royal library for shipment to England, on the other.[50] As Sophie Oosterwijk and R. D. Perry have suggested, many of the *Danse macabre*'s prominent characters representing the ruling and martial classes, like the king and constable, and especially its final figure of the rotting dead king, would have held particularly powerful political resonance for both French and English audiences in the mid-1420s.[51]

In its stated inspiration from the Holy Innocents mural, Lydgate's *Dance of Death* highlights its engagement with the "image-text" quality of late medieval death poetry by adducing an actual painted surface as its textual source. In so doing, Lydgate also gestures to his personal broader interest in manipulating the material form of the text. Lydgate composed verses for public display in guild halls and at Westminster as well as for masques to be performed at court. In this, Lydgate joined a much larger fifteenth-century trend of placing the text beyond the codex on wall hangings, murals, rolls, tombs, wood paneling,

---

[50] On Bedford's patronage and export of Northern French art and literature to England, see Reynolds, "'Les angloys, de leur droicte nature'" and Stratford, "The Manuscripts of John, Duke of Bedford."

[51] Oosterwijk, "Of Dead Kings" and Perry, "Lydgate's *Danse Macabre* and the Trauma."

even clothing, or what Heather Blatt has called the "extracodexical text".[52] Lydgate's *verba translatoris* insist on the crucial importance of the extracodexical and "image-text" quality of both the French *Danse* and his English translation:

> Considerith this [i.e. Death], ye folkes that ben wys,   *are wise*
> And it enprentith in youre memorial,   *imprint; memory*
> Like the exawmple wiche that at Parys   *Paris*
> I fonde depict oones in a wal . . .   *once*
> [. . . .]
> That proude folkes, wiche that ben stout and bold,   *valiant*
> As in a mirrour toforn in her resoun   *before*
> Her ougly fine may cleerly ther bihold . . .   *Their ugly end*
>   (lines 17–20, 30–32)

Both the extracodexical text of the Parisian mural, Lydgate claims, and this textual English translation will produce a powerful mental image of death for their readers, on which the latter are meant to meditate. Immediately after this moment, Lydgate reiterates that the "Daunce at Seint Innocentis / Portreied is . . . To shewe this world is but a pilgrimage . . ." (lines 35–37), drawing our attention again to the centrality of the extracodexical Parisian mural to his project. Thus, even as he is himself producing a written text, Lydgate demonstrates an acute awareness of the relationship between text and image in the late medieval death poetry tradition.

In this way, the A version of the *Dance of Death* testifies to Lydgate's evident close knowledge of the French *Danse macabre* in its urban setting as well as to his engagement with other cultural trends in the late medieval death poetry and extracodexical traditions. That said, Lydgate's text is also, importantly, an independent contribution to the *danse macabre* tradition. The A version features some marked departures from its French source: in addition to the *verba translatoris* at the beginning of the poem and envoy at the end, this version includes six speakers who are not found in the French *Danse*. Of these — the empress, lady of great estate, abbess, juror, tregetour (court magician) and an "amorous lady" — four are women (all of the speakers in the French *Danse* are men). Lydgate thus notably depicts some of the earliest female figures in the *danse macabre* tradition, anticipating the later French *Danse macabre des femmes* by several decades. Apart from these insertions, the A version of the poem follows exactly the order of speakers found in most manuscripts of the French text.

The A version of the *Dance of Death* survives today in nine manuscripts, the earliest of which, Bodleian Library MS Selden Supra 53, dates from the second quarter of the fifteenth century. The remaining eight were copied in the mid- to late-fifteenth century. The poem was also printed as a supplement to Lydgate's *Fall of Princes* in Richard Tottel's 1554 edition, where it was illustrated with two woodcuts apparently specially produced for it, indicating continued interest into the sixteenth century (see Figures 1 and 2 above). Among the A manuscripts, there is a strong association between the *Dance of Death* and the work of Lydgate's fellow Chaucerian Thomas Hoccleve. In particular, Hoccleve's *Series*, which

---

[52] Blatt coined this term as the title of a panel co-organized by her and Elizaveta Strakhov at the Sewanee Medieval Colloquium on 10–11 March, 2017; see further *Participatory Reading*, especially pp. 142–56. On this trend see, in particular, Sponsler, "Text and Textile," "Lydgate and London's Public Culture," and *The Queen's Dumbshows*; Floyd, "St. George and the 'Steyned Halle,'" and Gayk, *Image, Text, and Religious Reform*, pp. 84–122.

includes his translation of Henry Suso's *Ars moriendi*, mentioned above, appears in five of the manuscripts containing the A version, while Hoccleve's *Regiment of Princes* appears in seven. As a translation, the *Dance of Death* fits nicely alongside these other works, which are also translations, but there are thematic connections as well: a taste for didactic examples, inducements to meditate on one's own death, and attention to practical concerns grounded in the urban world of fifteenth-century London.

Of the A manuscripts, New Haven, Bodley, Coventry, Laud, and Selden are particularly closely related. The contents of New Haven, Selden, Laud, and Bodley overlap completely, containing the *Dance of Death*, Hoccleve's *Series*, and the *Regiment of Princes*. Coventry — probably a slightly later manuscript — incorporates this same cluster of texts into a larger collection. Barbara Shailor argues that the Beinecke, Laud, and Bodley manuscripts were copied at about the same time, and perhaps in the same scriptorium (although by different scribes).[53] The Selden manuscript is slightly older than this trio of manuscripts, suggesting that the group of texts contained in both it and its descendants were in fact brought together quite early, perhaps within a decade or two of Lydgate's initial translation of the *Dance of Death*.

The second, later version of the *Dance of Death*, which we, following Hammond, refer to as the "B" version, uses the same stanza form, meter, and rhyme scheme as the A version. In 1530, at the commission of London city official John Carpenter, Lydgate undertook a revision of the poem, which was then painted on the interior walls of the Pardon Churchyard at St. Paul's Cathedral, this time with accompanying images.[54] Some reworking and reorganization of the text occurred at this stage: the *verba translatoris* was removed from the beginning of the poem, and the envoy was omitted at the end, although the stanza attributing the translation to Lydgate was retained. New speakers were added, several of which emphasize the poem's urban context, notably the mayor, the canon, and the artisan. Altogether, the B version contains 584 lines, as opposed to the A version's 672 lines. Although the material is reorganized, because the B version contains the figures added in the A version but not present in the French *Danse*, it is clear that this version constitutes a revision of the earlier version rather than a fresh reworking of the French source.

The B version of the poem exists today in full in six manuscripts. Chaganti suggests that the B manuscript tradition ultimately derives from transcriptions of the text that accompanied *Dance of Death* murals at St. Paul's; while this cannot be conclusively proven, both versions of the poem appear to have been circulating in manuscript by the middle decades of the fifteenth century.[55] The majority of the *Dance of Death* manuscripts date from the second half of the fifteenth century, aside from Cotton Vespasian A.xxv, a fragmentary copy of the Lansdowne manuscript dating to c. 1600. Unlike other Middle English texts that circulated in multiple versions, such as *Piers Plowman*, there are no hybrid copies but, notably, in the Selden manuscript, a later fifteenth-century hand has added two stanzas to its text — Death's address to the Empress and her reply — from the B version, indicating awareness of multiple versions of the text. The contents of manuscripts containing the Lansdowne and Selden versions of the poem generally do not overlap, although both frequently include other works by Lydgate as well as pieces by Chaucer. They also include saints' lives, secular didactic pieces, and proverbs. Taken as a group, the manuscripts of the

---

[53] Shailor, *Catalogue of the Medieval and Renaissance Manuscripts in the Beinecke*, 2:475.

[54] Appleford, *Learning to Die in London*, pp. 89–97 and "The Dance of Death in London."

[55] See Chaganti, *Strange Footing*, pp. 160–63.

poem testify to the *Dance of Death*'s ability to signify in a wide variety of literary and devotional contexts in fifteenth-century England.

Ultimately, it was the Lansdowne version of the poem that reached the widest and most expansive audience, through its installation at St. Paul's. While there are other Middle English poems that evoke the *danse macabre* motif in whole or in part, the version of the *Dance of Death* found with the murals in the Pardon Churchyard of St. Paul's appears to have been the iconic iteration of Lydgate's *Dance* in late medieval and early modern England. Two manuscripts of the B version (Bodley and Corpus Christi) describe it specifically as the "St. Paul's Dance," a note by John Stow in the Trinity College Cambridge manuscript of the Selden version describes the poem's connection to St. Paul's, and texts ranging from the popular fifteenth-century Middle English poem "Erthe upon Erthe" to Thomas More's *Four Last Things* reference or allude to it.[56]

In contrast to the un-illustrated manuscripts of Lydgate's poem, the St. Paul's Dance reasserts the *Dance* as an image-text, combining visual and verbal elements into a unified whole as they would have appeared in the version of the *danse* Lydgate encountered in Paris. Anchored, as Appleford has shown, to a number of important civic and religious institutions, the Dance of St. Paul's achieved wide renown.[57] Although the Pardon Churchyard was not a burial ground like the Holy Innocents in Paris, it was a public space, religious yet proximate to secular commercial activities — in this case, the center of the London book trade in St. Paul's Churchyard. In his *Survey of London*, John Stow describes the Pardon Courtyard as it appeared in the second quarter of the sixteenth century:

> About this Cloyster, was artificially & richly painted, the dance of Machabray, or dance of death, commonly called the dance of Pauls: the like wherof, was painted about S. Innocents closter at Paris, in France: the metres or Poesie of this dance, were translated out of French into English by Iohn Lidgate, Monke of Bery & with the picture of Death leading all estates, paynted about the Cloyster.[58]

This mural must have been one of the great attractions at the medieval St. Paul's. The St. Paul's Dance survived the fifteenth century and the first wave of Protestant iconoclasm, but it was destroyed with the rest of the Pardon Churchyard in 1549 by the orders of Lord Protector Somerset, whose principal target appears to have been the shrine of Thomas Becket that stood at the center of the churchyard.[59] The popularity of the visual tradition surrounding Lydgate's *danse macabre* is confirmed by its spread beyond the St Paul's churchyard. Lydgate's *Dance* also seems to have been separately copied onto wall hangings placed at the Clopton Chapel of the Church of the Holy Trinity at Long Melford, as per a 1529 inventory of the chapel where they are described as "[t]hree long cloths hanging before the rood loft, stained, or painted, with the Dawnce of Powlis."[60] These *Dance of Death* cloths, interestingly, joined wooden panels featuring stanzas from Lydgate's *Testament* and

---

[56] For other fifteenth- and sixteenth-century allusions and references to the *Dance of Death*, see Gray, "Two Songs of Death," pp. 53–64.

[57] Amy Appleford, *Learning to Die in London*, pp. 89–97 and "The Dance of Death in London."

[58] Stow, *A Survey of London*, ed. Thoms, p. 122.

[59] *St. Paul's: The Cathedral Church*, ed. Keene, Burns, and Saint, p. 122.

[60] Dymond and Paine, *The Spoil of Melford Church*, p. 23; see also Floyd, "Writing on the Wall," 34n9,10.

other Marian verse for a multimedia Lydgatian experience.[61] A "Daunce of Poulys" was also painted at the Guild Chapel of the Holy Cross in Stratford-upon-Avon, and John Stow's description of it suggests that it also derives from Lydgate's *Dance of Death*.[62] Additionally, Cotton Vespasian A.XXV, containing the B version, begins with the rubric, "An history and daunce of deathe of all estate and degres writen in the cappell of Wortley of Wortley Hall," suggesting yet another physical location for Lydgate's *Dance*.[63]

Unfortunately, very little archaeological evidence of the St. Paul's Dance remains. Therefore, to understand the poem's reception in the years following its immediate publication and subsequent installation in the Pardon Churchyard, we turn to printed books. Even here, there are some gaps: neither the *Dance of Death* itself nor the poems it appears with most often in manuscript — Hoccleve's *Regiment of Princes* and the *Series* — are printed during the first half-century of print. Our earliest print witness to Lydgate's text is a partial copy of the B version that appears in a Book of Hours printed in Paris for the London bookseller Richard Fakes around 1521 (STC 15932). Although the *Dance* does appear alongside some devotional texts in manuscript, the liturgical function and continental origins of this book differentiate it significantly from the manuscripts. No title or attribution to Lydgate is given. The layout resembles printed versions of the *danse macabre* from France and Germany, with the textual exchange between Death and the living in the lower half of the page, and a woodcut depicting their encounter in the upper half. There is every reason to suspect these cuts were originally produced for use in books for the French market, and patterns of wear suggest that they had been used prior to the 1521 printing. The only surviving copy of this book, at the Bodleian Library, is incomplete. (The full B text includes 24 more speakers; this would constitute exactly one additional signature of this duodecimo book.)

This Book of Hours reflects Lydgate's *Dance of Death*'s continued utility as a devotional text beyond the fifteenth century and into the sixteenth. Richard Tottel's 1554 edition of Lydgate's *Fall of Princes*, which includes the *Dance of Death* as an epilogue, demonstrates its lasting literary import. Tottel printed the *Dance* just five years after the destruction of the Pardon Churchyard, and it is reasonable to assume that both he and his customers would have been able to recall the *Dance of Death* as it appeared there. Tottel does not include a full program of illustrations, which would have been expensive for a work included as a supplement rather than printed as a title in its own right, but he does include a woodcut depicting a procession of notables — the Pope, an emperor, a king, a cardinal, and a bishop — each escorted by a skeleton, with a large crowd (including a child visible on the far right) following behind, and another showing "the king lying eaten by wormes," which corresponds to the final image offered in both the A and B recensions of the poem. The

---

[61] See Trapp, "Verses by Lydgate"; Griffith, "A Newly Identified Verse Item"; Floyd, "Writing on the Wall," pp. 29–127; and Davis, "Lydgate at Long Melford."

[62] Floyd, "Writing on the Wall," p. 117 and n143.

[63] On the manuscript, see Lydgate, *Dance of Death, Edited from MSS, Ellesmere*, ed. Warren and White, pp. xxviii-ix.

courtiers gathered around the deceased monarch are in recognizably Tudor dress, updating the visual context of the poem for a new audience.[64]

Although they do not include Lydgate's text, sixteenth-century broadside ballads offer a different kind of glimpse of the *danse macabre*'s evolution in early modern England. In her EETS edition, White calls this phase the "degeneration of the *Danse Macabre*"; a more generous reading might consider how Lydgate's *Dance of Death*'s presence for more than 120 years in a public place gave it an enduring cultural life in London, and how it may have inspired later printed materials that — though ephemeral — also frequently circulated in public spaces and combined text and image to dramatic effect.[65] The *Dance and Song of Death*, for example, was printed by John Awdeley in 1569. Figures familiar from the medieval *danse macabre* tradition — the beggar and the king, the wise man and the fool — join hands with skeletons in a circular roundel around an open grave, upon which sits a grotesque figure beating a drum and playing a pipe, identified as "Sickness, Deaths minstrel."[66] In the four corners of the print, Death accosts a merchant, judge, prisoner, and pair of lovers as they go about their business, his outstretched hands indicating that they, too, must join in the dance. The text — four quatrains and a six-line stanza — is not related to Lydgate's, but it carries forward the idea of a verbal dialogue between Death and the living that is a consistent feature of the *danse macabre* tradition. The print's overall effect is of dynamic movement organized around the strongly delineated central point of the grave.

While the Book of Hours and *Fall of Princes* edition of Lydgate's *Dance of Death* can be understood as extending the functions of the fifteenth-century manuscripts of the poem into the era of print culture, the Awdeley broadside and others like it might be thought of as a synthesis of the two earlier vectors for the circulation of Lydgate's text, the bibliographic and the spatial or architectural. The ballads, of course, are printed material and contain text, but they are also inherently visual and, thanks to the low price point and frequent public dissemination of broadsides, retained some of the accessibility of the St. Paul's Dance.

THE RELATED WORKS

To contextualize Lydgate's poem, we have additionally selected five late medieval poems that similarly dramatize encounters between the dead and the living and ask their readers in some way to confront their own eventual demise. Each of these poems evokes one or more of the features that Florence Warren identifies as defining the *danse macabre* tradition: social satire, the idea that before death all are equal, and a confrontation between the living and the dead.[67] These are as follows:

---

[64] We see this same kind of sartorial visual updating in Marchant's 1485 edition of the *Danse*. Tottel's association of the *Fall of Princes* with Lydgate's poetry on death also resonates with another of Lydgate's own poems on death, included in this edition, "Death's Warning to the World" (DIMEV 4905), which is actually an independently circulating five-stanza extract of the *Fall of Princes* with additional stanzas appended to it. For more information, see the Explanatory Notes, pp. 129–31.

[65] Lydgate, *Dance of Death, Edited from MSS, Ellesmere*, ed. Warren and White, p. 100. For a discussion of the broadsides, see pp. 100–07.

[66] Compare "The Three Messengers of Death" (DIMEV 5387) in this edition, in which Sickness is one of Death's messengers (line 13).

[67] See Lydgate, *Dance of Death, Edited from MSS, Ellesmere*, ed. Warren and White, p. xii.

• John Lydgate, "Death's Warning to the World" (DIMEV 4905)

Composed by John Lydgate and drawn partly from the *Fall of Princes*, this poem consists of eight stanzas of seven decasyllabic lines rhyming *ababbcc* (otherwise known as rhyme royal). It asks readers to imagine a personified Death (in two of its manuscripts it is accompanied by large-scale illustrations of Death) and exhorts them to "lerne for to dye." It thus connects the emphasis on death as a material force with the didacticism common in late medieval death poetry and so demonstrates Lydgate's interest in poetry about death elsewhere in his œuvre.

• "Three Messengers of Death" (DIMEV 5387)

This anonymous poem is included in two monumental anthologies of devotional literature: Vernon (Oxford, Bodleian Library, MS Eng. poet. a.1) and Simeon (London, British Library, MS Additional 22283). Consisting of 56 octosyllabic quatrains rhyming *abab*, this metrical homily describes the effects of Death's "three messengers," namely Chance, Sickness, and Old Age, emphasizing the universality and inevitability of death as an equalizing force. Like Lydgate's *Dance* and "Death's Warning" above, it relies on vivid allegory to achieve its representation of death.

• "A Warning Spoken by the Soul of a Dead Person" (DIMEV 3624)

This anonymous early fifteenth-century poem in the Signs of Death genre consists of eight quatrains with lines of eight or nine syllables rhyming *abab*. It offers a poetic analogue to the gruesome detail that often marks late medieval visual representations of the dead and the dying, and it does so in the form of an address from the dead to the living. An anti-blazon of sorts, it dwells on the putrefaction of individual parts of the human body, exemplifying the late medieval fascination with death's material presence.

• "A Mirror for Young Ladies at their Toilet" (DIMEV 3454)

"A Mirror for Young Ladies at their Toilet" is an anonymous late medieval poem in three stanzas of five decasyllabic lines (on its variable rhyme scheme, see Headnote to this work in Explanatory Notes, p. 136). It precedes Lydgate's *Dance of Death* in London, British Library, MS Harley 116 and warns readers that death may strike down even those in the flower of their youth and beauty. Like Lydgate's poem, it brings female figures into the death poetry tradition, and its French rubric gestures to the cross-Channel quality of the *danse macabre* tradition. It also constitutes an early English example of an acrostic, spelling out the Latin motto MORS SOLVIT OMNIA ("Death loosens all").

• "The Ressoning betuix Deth and Man" (DIMEV 4000), ascribed to Robert Henryson

This poem, ascribed to the Middle Scots poet Robert Henryson, consists of six stanzas of eight decasyllabic lines rhyming *ababbcbc*. It clearly evokes the *danse macabre* in staging a debate between Death and the living and in its focus on varied social strata. The poem is found in the Bannatyne manuscript (Edinburgh, National Library of Scotland, MS

Advocates 1.1.6), where it appears ascribed to Robert Henryson (c. 1430–1500); see Headnote to this work in Explanatory Notes, p. 137. It represents an important continuation of the poetic tradition established by Lydgate's *Dance of Death*, given the prominence of its attributed author and the manuscript in which it is found.

We also include editions of two sixteenth-century poems in the *danse macabre* tradition, which demonstrate its continued vitality up to and beyond the Henrician reforms and the destruction of the *danse macabre* mural at St Paul's.

- "The Dawnce of Makabre" (DIMEV 4104)

In this sixteenth-century poem of twelve seven-line stanzas of irregular lines rhyming *ababbcc* (or rhyme royal), Death addresses the reader and, by extension, the world. While offering a narrower social scope than Lydgate's poem, it maintains the structure of a dialogue between death and a worldly speaker. Its later date emphasizes the extent and influence of the English *danse macabre* tradition.

- "Can Ye Dance the Shaking of the Sheets" (DIMEV 956)

A similar work, "Can Ye Dance the Shaking of the Sheets," consists of eleven stanzas of seven lines with lines of eight or nine syllables and an *ababccc* rhyme scheme. It is preserved in a seventeenth-century recusant collection, now London, British Library, MS Additional 15225, though the poem itself dates to an earlier period. Like "The Dawnce of Makabre," the poem has Death as its speaker and exhorts an unspecified addressee toward penance. In this, it echoes other written texts and, perhaps, visual work in the *danse macabre* tradition through emphasizing dancing with one's winding sheet and the inevitability of death for representatives of all social strata.

EDITORIAL PRINCIPLES

In accordance with METS editorial guidelines, we have used modern English spelling conventions for words with *v/u* and *i/j*, and have provided modern equivalents for thorns, yoghs, and eths. We have silently expanded scribal abbreviations and have also brought into conformity with modern English spelling *the/thee* and *of/off*. Where they occur at the beginning of a word and signal a capital letter, double *ff*s become *F*, and when *e* at the end of a word receives syllabic value it is marked with an accent (e.g., *cité*). Punctuation is also editorial; especially in the poems by Lydgate, we have tried to refrain from intervention except when it enhances clarity, to better reflect the poems' loose, paratactic syntax. The names of allegorical figures (e.g. Death) and proper nouns have been capitalized. Word division has also been regularized; for example, *i feer* becomes *ifeere* (*Dance of Death* [Lansdowne] line 55). In our modern English translation of the *Danse macabre*, we have similarly striven for clarity and simplicity. We have not sought to replicate the original's rhyme or meter but, instead, simply to remain as literal as possible while offering a smooth reading experience. In particular, given the text's heavy use of proverbs, we have either looked for English parallels or for equivalent expressions that render the original into a fluid contemporary idiom: we note particular deviations from literal sense in our Explanatory Notes.

Our edition of Lydgate's poem is based on fresh transcriptions of the base manuscripts of each of the two versions of the *Dance of Death*. Following Hammond, we take Oxford, Bodleian Library, MS Selden Supra 53 as our base text for the A version. In our Textual Notes, we have marked instances where our readings differ from those found in Florence Warren and Beatrice White's EETS edition, which uses Huntington Library MS EL 26.A.13 as its base. We also add variants from three more manuscripts (Coventry, New Haven, and Rome) to Warren and White's textual apparatus. Our base text for the B version of the *Dance of Death* is London, British Library, MS Lansdowne 699. This is also the manuscript used by Warren and White, and our textual notes indicate moments where we depart from their edited version of the poem. We also refer readers to Warren's notes for variant readings from the Cotton manuscript of the poem, an incomplete and very late copy, perhaps dating to the early seventeenth century, which differs in significant ways from other manuscripts of the B recension.

JOHN LYDGATE, DANCE OF DEATH: A VERSION (SELDEN)

fol. 148r	¶ Verba Translatoris	*Words of the Translator*
	O yee folkes harde-hertid as a stone,	
	Wich to the worlde have al your advertence,	*attention*
	Liche as it shulde laste evere in oone —	*Like; always the same*
	Where is your witt, wher is your providence	*wit; preparation for the future*
5	To se aforn the sodeine violence	*in advance; sudden*
	Of cruel Dethe, that ben so wis and sage,	*prudent*
	Wiche sleeth, allas, by stroke of pestilence	
	Bothe yong and olde, of lowe and hy parage?	*parentage*
	Deeth sparith not lowe ne hy degré.	*status*
10	Popes, kynges, ne worthy emperours —	
	Whan thei shyne most in felicité,	*prosperity*
	He can abate the fresshnes of her flours,	*their flowers*
	The bright sonne clipsen with his shours,	*eclipse; its showers*
	Make hem plunge from her sees lowe.	*fall low from their high positions*
15	Magré the myght of alle these conquerours,	*In spite of*
	Fortune hath hem from her whele ythrowe.	*them; thrown*
	Considerith this, ye folkes that ben wys,	*are wise*
	And it enprentith in youre memorial,	*imprint; memory*
	Like the exawmple wiche that at Parys	*Paris; (see note)*
20	I fonde depict oones in a wal	*once*
	Ful notably, as I reherce shal:	*as I will tell*
	Ther, of Frensshe clerkis takyng aqueintaunce,	*French clerics making*
	I toke on me to translatyn al,	
	Oute of the Frensshe, Machabres Daunce.	
fol. 148v	By whos avys and counceil atte the leste,	*advice and counsel at last*
26	Thorugh her steryng and her mocioun,	*guidance; suggestion*
	I obeide unto her requeste,	*their*
	Therof to make a playn translacioun	*complete translation*
	In Englissh tonge, of entencioun[1]	
30	That proude folkes, wiche that ben stout and bold,	*valiant*

---

[1] *Into the English language, intending*

As in a mirrour toforn in her resoun   *before*
Her ougly fine may cleerly ther bihold,   *Their ugly end*

By exaumple that thei in her ententis   *their intentions*
Amende her lif in every maner age.   *every stage of their life*
35   The wiche Daunce at Seint Innocentis
Portreied is with al the surplusage   *with all the rest*
To shewe this worlde is but a pilgrimage
Yeven unto us our lyves to correcte.   *Given*
And to declare the fyne of oure passage   *relate; outcome; journey*
40   Right anoon my stile I wille directe.   *stylus*

¶ Verba Auctoris   *Words of the Author*
O creatures ye that ben resonable   *who are reasonable*
The liif desiring wiche is eternal,
Ye may se here doctrine ful notable,   *see*
Youre lif to lede wich that is mortal,
45   Therby to lerne in especial   *in particular*
Howe ye shul trace the Daunce of Machabre,   *follow*
To man and womman yliche natural,   *alike*
For deth ne spareth hy ne lowe degré.   *does not spare*

In this mirrour every wight may finde   *person*
50   That him bihoveth to goo upon this daunce.   *That he must go*
Who goth toforn or who shal goo behinde,   *goes first*
Al dependith in Goddis ordinaunce.   *God's plan*
Wherfore eche man lowly take his chaunce;   *humbly*
Deeth spareth not pore ne blood royal.
55   Eche man therfore have in remembraunce:
Of o mater God hath forged al.[1]

fol. 149r   ¶ Deeth to the Pope
O yee that ben set most hie in dignité
Of alle estatis in erthe spiritual,   *Out of all religious positions on earth*
And like as Petir had the soverenité
60   Overe the chirche and statis temporal: *Over both the Church and worldly affairs*
Upon this daunce ye firste bigyn shal,
As moste worthy lorde and governour,
For al the worship of youre astate papal   *high esteem; papal estate*
And of lordship to God is the honour.   *dominion*

¶ The Pope aunswerith
65   First me bihoveth this daunce for to lede   *it is proper for me*
Wich sat in erthe hiest in my see —   *Who; seat of authority*

---

[1] *God has made everyone from the same matter*

The state ful perillous ho so takith hede
To occupie Petris dignité —[1]
But al for that Deth I may not fle,
70 On his daunce with other for to trace,   *to follow*
For wich al honour, who prudently can se,
Is litel worth that dothe so sone pace.   *so soon pass [away]*

¶ Deeth to the Emperour
Sir Emperour, lorde of al the ground,   *earth*
Soverein prince and hiest of noblesse: *preeminent; nobility*
75 Ye must forsake of golde your appil round,
Septre and swerd and al youre hy prowesse.   *Scepter; sword; martial deeds*
Behinde leve your tresour and ricchesse,
And with othir to my daunce obeie.   *obey*
Agein my myght is worth noon hardinesse;   *Against; no valor*
80 Adamis children alle thei mosten deie.   *Adam's children (i.e., humanity); must*

¶ The Emperour answerith
I not to whom that I may apele   *know not; appeal*
Touching Deth wiche doth me so constreine.   *Concerning; compel*
Ther is no gein to helpe my querele,   *aid; complaint*
But spade and pikois my grave to ateyne,   *pickaxe; reach*
85 A simple shete — ther is no more to seyne —   *to say*
To wrappe in my body and visage,   *face*
Therupon sore I may compleine   *fervently*
That lordis grete have litel avauntage.   *advantage*

fol. 149v ¶ Deeth to the Cardinal
Ye ben abaisshid, it semeth, and in drede   *upset; full of dread*
90 Sir Cardinal — it shewith by youre chere —   *expression*
But yit forthy ye folowe shulle in dede   *you shall follow forth in death*
With othir folke my daunce for to lere.   *to learn*
Youre grete aray al shal bileven here,   *fine clothing; shall be left*
Youre hatte of reed, youre vesture of grete cost.   *red hat; [ecclesiastical] garment*
95 Alle these thingis rekenyd wele yfere:[2]
In greet honour good avis is lost.   *judgment*

¶ The Cardinal answerith
I have grete cause — certis this is no faille —   *certainly; mistake*
To ben abaisshid and greetly drede me,   *upset; to have great dread*
Sithen Deeth is come me sodeinly to assaille,   *Because; to attack me suddenly*
100 That I shal nevere heraftir clothed be
In grys ne ermyn like to my degré,   *gray fur (possibly squirrel); ermine*

---

[1] Lines 67–68: *The very dangerous position, whoso takes heed / To occupy St. Peter's rank*

[2] *Each and every one of these valuable things adjudicated together*

My hatte of reed leve eke in distresse,   *leave also*
By wiche I have lerned wel and see
Howe that al joie endith in hevynesse.   *sorrow*

¶ Deeth to the Kyng
105   O noble kyng, moste worthi of renoun,   *renown*
       Come forthe anone for al youre worthinesse,   *at once; nobility*
       That somtyme had aboute yow enviroun   *on all sides*
       Greet rialté and passing hy noblesse.   *royalty; very high nobility*
       But right anoone al youre grete hynes   *immediately; great status*
110   Sool fro youre men in hast ye shul it lete.[1]
       Who moste aboundith here in greet ricches   *abounds*
       Shal bere with hym but a sengle shete.

¶ The Kynge answerith
       I have not lernyd here aforn to daunce   *heretofore*
       No daunce in sooth of footyng so savage,   *in truth; frenzied*
115   Wherfore I see by clere demonstraunce: *by clear proof*
       What pride is worth force or hy lynage?   *power; noble birth*
       Deeth al fordothe — this is his usage —   *destroys; practice*
       Greet and smale that in this worlde sojourne.
       Who is most meke I hold he is most sage,   *meek; wise*
120   For we shal al to dede asshes tourne.

fol. 150r   ¶ Deeth to the Patriarke
       Sir Patriarke, alle youre humble chere   *attitude*
       Ne quite yow not, ne youre humilité.   *Do not acquit you*
       Youre double crosse of gold and stones clere,   *double cross*
       Youre power hoole, and al youre dignité   *whole; rank*
125   Some othir shal of verrey equité   *in accordance with divine law*
       Possede anoone, as I reherce can.   *as I can say*
       Trustith nevere that ye shal pope be,   *(see note)*
       For foly hope deceiveth many a man.   *foolish*

¶ The Patriarke aunswereth
       Worldly honour, greet tresour, and richesse
130   Have me deceivid sothfastly in dede.   *truly in death*
       Myn olde joies ben turned to tristesse.   *sadness*
       What vailith it suche tresour to possede?   *What use is it; possess*
       Hy clymbyng up a falle hath for his mede;   *for its reward*
       Grete estates folke wasten oute of noumbre.[2]
135   Who mountith hy — it is sure and no drede —   *rises high*
       Greet berthen dothe hym ofte encoumbre.   *burden*

---

[1] *Alone from your men in haste you will [it] surrender*

[2] *Folk waste more great estates than can be numbered*

¶ Deeth to the Constable

It is my right to reste and yow constreine   *arrest; detain*
With us to daunce, my maister Sir Constable,
For more strong than evere was Charlemayne   *Charlemagne*
140 Deeth hath aforced and more worshipable,   *forced; worthy of respect*
For hardines, ne knyghthood — this is no fable —
Ne stronge armure of plates ne of mayle.   *plate armor; chainmail*
What geyneth armes of folkes moste notable   *What gain is*
Whan cruel Deeth luste hem to assaile?   *desires them*

¶ The Constable answerith

145 My purpos was and hool entencioun   *entire intent*
To assaille castelles and mighty forteresses,
And bringe folke unto subjeccioun,
To seke honour, fame, and grete richesses.
But I se wel that al worldly prowesses   *see clearly; earthly valor*
150 Deeth can abate, wich is a grete dispite.   *demolish; vengeance*
To him aloone sorwe and eke swetnesses,   *alone; also*
For agein Deeth is founded no respite.   *against; is found; reprieve*

fol. 150v   ¶ Deeth to the Archebisshop

Sir Archebisshoppe, whi do ye yow withdrawe   *retreat*
So frowardly as it were by disdeyn?   *insolently; with contempt*
155 Ye muste aproche to my mortel lawe: *draw near to*
It to contrarie it were not but in veyn.   *to oppose*
For day by day, ther is noon othir geyn,
Deeth at hande pursueth every coost.   *course of action*
Prest and dette mote be yolde agein,[1]
160 And at o day men counten with her oost.   *the last day; reckon; host*

¶The Archibisshoppe answereth

Allas, I woote not what partie for to flee,   *don't know where to flee*
For drede of Dethe I have so grete distresse,
To ascape his myght I can no refute se.[2]
That who so knewe his constreint and duresse,   *whoever; oppression; cruelty*
165 He wolde take resoun to maistresse.   *mistress*
Adewe, my tresour, my pompe, and pride also,   *Goodbye*
My peintid chaumbres, my port, and my fresshnesse,
For thing that bihoveth nedes must be do.[3]

---

[1] *Loans and debt must be paid again*

[2] *I see no refuge in which to escape his power*

[3] Lines 167–68: *My painted rooms, my demeanor, and my cheerfulness, / For the thing that is required to do must be done*

¶Deth to the Baroun
Ye that amonge lordis and barouns
170   Hav had so longe worship and renoun,
Forgete youre trumpetis and youre clariouns.
This is no dreme ne simulacioun.   *deception*
Somtime youre custome and entencioun   *desire*
Was with ladies to daunce in the shade,
175   But ofte it happith, in conclusioun,
That o man brekith that anothir made.   *one; breaks*

¶ The Baroun or the Knyht answerith
Ful ofte sithe I have bene auctorised   *times; authorized*
To hie emprises and thinges of greet fame.   *enterprises*
Of hie and lowe my thanke also devised,   *gratitude; contrived*
180   Cherisshed with ladies and wymmen hie of name.
Ne nevere on me was put no defame   *No slander was ever put on me*
In lordis court, wiche that was notable.
But Deethis strook hath made me so lame —   *stroke; helpless*
Undre hevene in erthe is nothing stable.

fol. 151r   ¶ Deeth to the Lady of Grete Astate   *Estate*
185   Come forthe anone, my lady and princesse,
Ye muste also goo upon this daunce.
Nowt may availle youre grete straungenesse,   *No help will be; haughtiness*
Nouther youre beauté, ne youre greet plesaunce,   *Neither; charm*
Youre riche aray, ne youre daliaunce,   *fancy clothes; flirting*
190   That sumtyme cowde so many holde on honde   *could; hold in your sway*
In love for al youre double variaunce.   *duplicity*
Ye mote as nowe this footing undirstonde.

¶ The Lady answerith
Allas, I see ther is none othir boote.   *remedy*
Deeth hath in erthe no lady ne maistresse,   *mistress*
195   And on his daunce yit muste I nedis foote.   *yet; step*
For ther nys qwene, contesse, ne duchesse
Flouringe in beauté ne in fairnesse   *Flourishing; fair appearance*
That she of Deeth mote Dethes trace sewe.   *dance behold*
For to youre bewté and countirfeet fresshnesse   *false youthfulness*
200   Owre rympled age seith farewele, adewe.   *Our wrinkled age; goodbye*

¶ Deeth to the Bisshoppe
My lorde sir Bisshoppe, with youre mytre and croos,   *miter and cross*
For al youre ricchesse, sothly I ensure,   *truly I assure you*
For al youre tresour so longe kept in cloos,   *privately owned*

	Youre worldly goodes and goodes of nature,[1]	
205	And of youre sheep the gostli dredeful cure,	*flock; spiritual pastoral duty*
	With charge committid to youre prelacie,	*prelacy (i.e., office of bishop)*
	For to acounte ye shulle be broughte to lure.	*brought under control*
	No wight is sure that clymbeth overe hie.	*person; secure*

¶ The Bisshoppe answerith

	My herte truly is nouther glad ne myrie	*neither; happy*
210	Of sodein tidinges wiche that ye bring.	*Because of the unexpected news*
	My festis turned into simple ferye	*food (fare)*
	That for discomfort me list nothing syng;	*desire*
	The worlde contrarie nowe to me in workyng	
	That alle folkes can so disherite.	*disinherit*
215	He that al withhalt, allas, at oure parting,	*withholds*
	And al shal passe save only oure merite.[2]	

fol. 151v   ¶ Deeth to the Squier

	Come forth Sir Squier, right fresshe of youre aray,	*youthful; attire*
	That can of daunces al the newe gise:	*knows; new fashion*
	Though ye bare armes fressh horsed yisterday,	
220	With spere and shelde at youre unkouthe devise,[3]	
	And toke on yow so many hy emprise,	*undertaking*
	Daunceth with us, it wil no bettir be;	
	Ther is no socour in no manere wise,	*assistance of any kind*
	For no man may fro Dethes stroke fle.	

¶ The Squier aunswerith

225	Sithen that Dethe me holdith in his lace,	*Because; snare*
	Yet shal Y speke o worde or Y pace:	*I; one; before; go*
	Adieu, al myrthe, adieu nowe, al solace;	
	Adieu, my ladies, somtime so fressh of face;	*youthful*
	Adieu, beuté, plesaunce, and solace!	*charm*
230	Of Dethes chaunge every day is prime;	*a new beginning*
	Thinketh on youre soules or that Deth manace,	*before Death threatens*
	For al shal rote, and no man wote what tyme.	*decay; knows*

¶ Deeth to the Abbot

	Come forth, Sir Abbot, with youre brood hatte,	*broad*
	Beeth not abaisshed (though ye have right).	*upset; good reason*
235	Greet is your hede, youre bely large and fatte;	*belly*
	Ye mote come daunce though ye be nothing light.	*must*

---

[1] *Your earthly goods and natural goods (e.g., crops)*

[2] *Everything will pass away except our good deeds*

[3] Lines 219–20: *Though you carried arms and rode a new horse yesterday / With spear and shield according to your outlandish fancy*

Leveth youre abbey to some othir wight,   *person*
Youre eir is of age youre state to occupie.   *heir; position*
Who that is fattest, I have hym behight,   *designated*
240   In his grave shal sonnest putrefie.   *soonest decay*

¶ The Abbot answerith
Of thi thretis have I noon envie   *threats; grudge*
That I shal nowe leve al governaunce.
But that I shal as a cloistrer dye —   *cloistered monk*
This doth to me passinge grete grevaunce.   *causes me exceedingly great offense*
245   Mi liberté nor my greet habondaunce[1]
What may availe in any manere wise?   *help in any kind of way*
Yit axe I mercy with hertly repentaunce,   *ask; heartfelt*
Though in diynge too late men hem avise.   *examine themselves*

fol. 152r   ¶ Deeth to the Abbesse
And ye, my lady gentil Dame Abbesse,   *of noble rank or birth*
250   With youre mantels furred large and wide,   *sleeveless overgarment*
Youre veile, youre wymple passinge of greet richesse,[2]
And beddis softe ye mote nowe leie aside,   *bedding; turn*
For to this daunce I shal be youre guyde.
Though ye be tendre and born of gentil blood,   *delicate; noble*
255   While that ye lyve for youresilfe provide,   *prepare yourself*
For aftir Deeth no man hath no good.   *possessions*

¶ The Abbesse answerith
Allas, that Deeth hath thus for me ordeined
That in no wise I may it not declyne,   *way; avoid*
Though it so be ful ofte I have constreyned   *very often; compelled*
260   Brest and throte my notes out to twyne,   *to sing*
My chekes round vernysshed for to shyne,   *coated (i.e., as with a cosmetic)*
Ungirt ful ofte to walke atte large —   *Ungirdled; out and about*
Thus cruel Dethe dothe al estates fyne.   *bring to an end*
Who hath no ship mote rowe yn bote or barge.   *must; boat*

¶ Deeth to the Bally
265   Come forthe, Sir Bailly, that knowen al the gise,   *ways*
By youre office, of trouthe and rightwisnes.
Ye must come to a newe assise   *session of civil court*
Extorciouns and wronges to redres.
Ye ben somonyd as lawe bit expres,   *summoned; as required by law*
270   To yelde acountes, the Juge wole yow charge,   *give accounts*

---

[1] *My legal privileges nor my great wealth*

[2] *Your veil, your headdress of exceedingly great richness*

Wiche hath ordeyned, to exclude al falsnes,

That every man shal bere his owne charge.   *accept responsibility for*

¶ The Bayly answerith

O thou, Lorde God, this is an hard journé,

To whiche aforne I tooke but litel hede.   *before; paid little attention*

275   Mi chaunge is turned and that forthinkith me.   *fortune; unsettles me*

Sumtyme with juges what me list to spede   *liked to accomplish*

Lay in my myght by favour or for mede.   *power through favors or bribes*

But sithen ther is no rescuse by bataille,   *Because; deliverance by battle*

I holde hym wys that cowde see indede

280   Agein Deeth that none apele may vaille.   *no appeal will prevail*

fol. 152v   ¶ Deeth to the Astronomere

Come forthė, maister, that loken up so ferre

With instrumentis of astronomy

To take the grees and heighte of every sterre.   *degrees and height*

What may availe al youre astrologie,   *help*

285   Sethen of Adam alle the genolagie,   *Since; descendants*

Made ferst of God to walke uppon the grounde,

Deeth dooth areste? Thus seith theologie,

And al shal die for an appil round.

¶ The Astronomere answerith

For al my craft, kunnynge, or science   *knowledge*

290   I cannot finde no provisioun,   *provision (i.e., against Death)*

Ne in the sterris serche oute no defence,

By domefiynge ne calculacioun,   *By locating the position of the stars*

Safe finally — in conclusioun —   *Except*

For to discrive oure kunnyng every dele,   *explain; in every aspect*

295   Ther is no more by sentence of resoun: *by doctrine*

Who lyveth aright mote nedis dye wele.   *must necessarily die well*

¶ Deeth to the Burgeys

Sir Burgeis, what do ye lenger tarie   *longer delay*

For al youre aver and youre greet ricchesse?   *possessions*

Though ye be straunge, deynous, and contrarie,   *haughty, scornful; cross*

300   To this daunce ye mote yow nedis dresse,   *you must necessarily prepare yourself*

For youre tresour, plenté, and largesse   *plenty; abundance*

From othere it cam and shal unto straungers.

He is a fool that in suche bysynes   *business*

Woot not for whom he stuffith his garners.   *Knows; storerooms*

¶ The Burgeis aunswerith

305   Certis to me it is greet displesaunce   *Certainly; displeasure*

To leve al this and may it not assure.   *I may not secure it*

Houses, rentes, tresour, and substaunce: *material goods*

	Deeth al fordothe, suche is his nature.	*destroys*
	Therfore wys is no creature	
310	That set his herte on good that moot dissevere.	*must fall away*
	The worlde it lente, and he wille it recovere,[1]	
	And who most hath lothest dieth evere.	*loathes to die always*

fol. 153r   ¶ Deeth to the Chanoun

	And ye, Sir Chanoun, with many grete prebende,	
	Ye may no lenger have distribucioun	*a share [of alms]*
315	Of golde and silver largely to dispende,	*extravagantly to squander*
	For ther is nowe no consolacioun,	
	But daunce with us for al youre hie renoun,	*lofty reputation*
	For ye of deeth stonde uppon the brink.	
	Ye may therof have no dilacioun,	*postponement*
320	Deeth comyth ay whan men lest on him think.	*always; least*

¶ The Chanoun answerith

	My benefices with many a personage,	*parsonage*
	God wote, ful lite may me nowe comforte.	*knows, very little*
	Deeth hath of me so grete avauntage;	
	Al my ricches may me not disporte.	*cheer me up*
325	Amys of grys, thei wille agein resorte	*Garments of gray; again; return*
	Unto the worlde, surplys and prebende;	*surplice*
	Al is veinglorie, truly to reporte,	
	To die wel eche man shulde entende.	

¶ Deeth to the Marchaunt

	Ye riche marchaunt, ye mote loke hiderwarde,	*must; over here*
330	That passid have ful many divers londe,	*various*
	On hors, on foot, havynge moste reward	*esteem*
	To lucre and wynnyng, as I undirstond:	*To profit and wealth*
	But nowe to daunce ye mote yeve me youre honde,	*must; give*
	For al youre laboure ful litel availeth now.	*helps*
335	Adieu, veinglorie, bothe of free and bonde!	*master and servant*
	No more coveite than thei that have ynow.	*covet; enough*

¶ The Marchaunt answerith

	By manie an hil and many a straunge vale	*foreign valley*
	I have traveilid with my marchandise,	
	Overe the see do carie many a bale	*sea; measurement of goods*
340	To sundry iles, mo than I can devise.	*tell*
	My herte inwarde ay fret with covetise,	*always loaded*
	But al for nought — nowe Deeth doth me constreine —	*detain*

---

[1] *The World loaned it and will retrieve it*

By wiche I seie, by recorde of the wise,
Who al enbraceth litel shal restreine.   *embraces; restrain*

fol. 153v   ¶ Deeth to the Chartereux   *Carthusian*
345   Yeve me youre hond with chekis dede and pale,   *Give*
        Causid of wacche and longe abstinence,   *wakefulness (i.e., for a vigil)*
        Sir Chartereux, and youresilfe avale   *help yourself*
        Unto this daunce with humble pacience.
        To stryve agein may be no resistence;   *against*
350   Lenger to lyve set not youre memorie.   *direct not your attention*
        Thow I be lothsom as in apparence,   *loathsome*
        Above alle men Deth hath the victorie.

        ¶ The Chartereux aunswerith
        Unto the worlde I was dede longe agone   *ago*
        By my ordre and my professioun.   *[Carthusian] order*
355   Though every man, be he nevere so stronge,
        Dredith to die by kindly mocioun   *natural instinct*
        Aftir his flesshly inclinacioun,
        But plese it to God my soule for to borowe
        From fendis myght and from dampnacioun;   *the Devil's power; damnation*
360   Some bene today that shulle not be tomorwe.   *are*

        ¶ Deeth to the Sergaunt
        Come forthe, Sir Sergant with youre statly mace;
        Make no defence ne no rebellioun.
        Not may availe to grucche in this cace,   *aid; complain; case*
        Though ye be deynous of condicioun,   *arrogant by nature*
365   For nouther pele ne proteccioun   *appeal*
        May yow fraunchise to do nature wrong.   *empower*
        For ther is noone so sturdy champioun;
        Though he be myghty, another is as stronge.

        ¶ The Sergeant answereth
        Howe dare this Dethe sette on me areste,   *take me into custody*
370   That am the kinges chosen officere,   *Who*
        Wiche yisterday bothe west and este
        Min office dide ful surquidous of chere?   *haughty; attitude*
        But nowe this day I am arestid here   *detained*
        And may not flee, though I hadde it sworn.
375   Eche man is lothe to die, ferre and nere,   *unwilling*
        That hath not lerned for to die aforn.   *before*

fol. 154r   ¶ Deeth to the Monke
        Sir Monke also, with youre blak habite,   *black habit*
        Ye may no lenger holde here sojour.   *sojourn*
        Ther is nothing that may yow here respite,   *reprieve*

380	Agein my myght yow for to do socour.	*Against; to render assistance*
	Ye mote acounte touching youre labour,	*must; concerning*
	Howe ye have spent it in dede, worde, and thought.	
	To erthe and asshes turneth every flour;	
	The life of man is but a thing of nought.	

¶ The Monke answerith

385	I hadde levere in the cloistre be	*would rather; cloister*
	At my book and studie my service,	*the Mass*
	Wiche is a place contemplatif to se,	
	But I have spent my life in many vice,	
	Liche as a fool dissolut and nyce.	*Like; fool; frivolous*
390	God of his mercy graunt me repentaunce,	
	By chere outwarde harde to devise.	*appearance*
	Alle be not mery wich that men se daunce.	*see*

¶ Deeth to the Usurere

	Thou Usurer, loke up and biholde:	
	Unto wynnynge you settist al thi peine,	*profit; effort*
395	Whos covetise wexith nevere colde.	*grows*
	Thy gredy thrust so sore thee doth constreine,	*thirst; powerfully*
	But you shalt nevere thi desire ateyne.	
	Such an etik thin herte frete shal	*consuming passion; devour*
	That, but of pité God his hande refreine,	*unless; stay*
400	O perillous strook shal make thee lese al.	*One dreadful; lose*

¶ The Usurere answerith

	Nowe me bihoveth sodeinly to dey[1]	
	Wiche is to me grete peine and greet grevaunce.	
	Socour to finde I see no maner wey,	*Assistance*
	Of golde ne silver by no chevesaunce.	*relief*
405	Deeth thorugh his haste abit no parveaunce	*makes no provisions*
	Of folkes blinde, that cannot look wel.	
	Ful ofte happith by kinde or fatal chaunce	*nature; accident*
	Some have faire eyghen that see nevere adele.	*good eyes; a bit*

fol. 154v	¶ The Pore Man to the Usurere	
	Usuré to God is ful grete offence	
410	And in his sight a grete abusioun.	*abuse*
	The pore borwith par cas for indigence,	*borrow because of*
	The riche lent by fals collucioun	*lend; conspiracy*
	Only for lucre in his entencioun.	*profit*
	Deeth shal hem bothe to acountes sette,	*take to account*

---

[1] *Now it is appropriate for me to die suddenly*

415	To make rekenynge by computacioun;	*settle accounts; counting*
	No man is quit that is bihinde of dette.	*discharged [from debt]; behind*

¶ Deeth to the Fisician — *Physician*
Maister of phisik, wiche on youre uryne — *medicine; who; urine; (see note)*
So loke and gase and stare agein the sonne, — *gaze; against*
For al youre craft and studie of medicine,
420   Al the practyk and sience that ye konne, — *practical and theoretical knowledge*
Your lyves cours so ferforthe is ironne. — *to a great extent; run*
Agein my myght youre craft may not endure
For al the golde that ye therby have wonne.
Good leche is he that can himsilfe recure. — *doctor; cure*

¶ The Fisician answerith
425   Ful longe agon that I unto phisik — *ago; medicine*
Sette my witt and my dilligence,
In speculatif and also in practik, — *theorizing; practice*
To gete a name thorugh myn excellence,
To finde oute agens pestilence
430   Preservatives to staunche it and to fine, — *Protections; stop; end (it)*
But I dar seie, shortly in sentence, — *concisely*
Agens Deeth is worth no medicine.

¶ Deeth to the Amerous Squier
Ye that be gentil, so fresshe and amerous, — *noble; youthful; amorous*
Of yeres yonge, flouringe in youre grene age,
435   Lusty, free of herte, and eke desirous, — *Vigorous; also filled with desire*
Ful of devises and chaunge in youre corage, — *intrigues; inconstancy; heart*
Plesaunt of port, of look, and of visage — — *deportment; appearance*
But al shal turne into asshes dede,
For al bewté is but a feint ymage, — *beauty; unreliable image*
440   Wiche stelith aweye or folkes can take hede. — *steals away before; take notice*

fol. 155r   ¶ The Squier answerith
Allas, allas I can nowe no socour — *know; assistance*
Agens Dethe for mysilfe provide.
Adieu, of youthe the lusty fresshe flour, — *lively youthful*
Adieu, veinglorie of bewté and of pride, — *beauty*
445   Adieu, al service of the god Cupide,
Adieu, my ladies, so fressh, so wel besein, — *youthful; good looking*
For agein Dethe nothing may abide,
And windes grete gon doun with litil reyn.[1]

---

[1] *And great winds die down with a little rain*

¶ Deeth to the Gentilwomman Amerous

Come forthe, maistresse, of yeris yonge and grene   *mistress; fresh*

450   Wiche holde youresilfe of bewté sovereyne.   *preeminent*

As faire as yee was somtyme Polycene,   *fair; once Polyxena*

Penolope, and the quene Eleyne,   *Helen*

Yit on this daunce thei wente bothe tweine,   *Yet; both of them*

And so shulle ye for al youre straungenesse.   *despite; haughtiness*

455   Though daunger longe in love hath lad youre reine,   *resistance; reign*

Arestid is youre chaunge of doubilnesse.   *Halted; faithlessness*

¶ The Gentilwomman answerith

O cruel Deeth that sparest none estate,

To old and yonge thou art indifferent.

To my bewté thou hast yseide chekmate,

460   So hasty is thi mortal jugement.   *swift*

For in my youthe this was myn entent,

To my service many a man to have lured.

But she is a fool, shortly in sentement,   *concisely*

That in hir bewté is too moche assurid.

¶ Deeth to the Man of Lawe

465   Sir Advocate, short processe for to make,   *legal argument*

Ye mote come plete afore the highe Juge.   *plead your case; before*

Many a quarel ye have undirtake   *complaint*

And for lucre to do folke refuge,   *profit; legal redress*

But my fraunchise is so large and huge   *body of legal rights*

470   That counceile none availe may but trouthe.

He skapith wisly of Deeth the greet deluge   *escapes; flood*

Tofore the doom who is not teint with slouthe.   *Before; judgment; tainted*

fol. 155v   ¶ The Man of Lawe answerith

Of right and resoun by Naturis lawe,

I cannot putte agein Deeth no defence,

475   Ne by no sleighte me kepe ne withdrawe   *cunning; protect nor excuse myself*

For al my wit and my greet prudence

To make apele from his dredful sentence.   *appeal*

Nothing in erthe may a man preserve

Ageins His myght to make resistence;

480   God quite al men like as thei deserve.   *repays*

¶ Deeth to the Jourrour

Maister Jurrour, wiche that at assise   *Juror; sessions of civil court*

And atte shires questes doste embrace,   *shire's inquests; illegally influence*

Departist londe like to thi devise,   *Divided; scheme*

And who most yaf moste stode in thi grace: *gave (i.e., bribed)*

485   The pore man lost londe and place;   *position*

For golde thou cowdest folkes disherite.   *disinherit*

But nowe lete se, with thi teint face,   *see; guilty*
Tofore the Juge howe thou canst thee quite.   *Before; acquit yourself*

¶ The Jourour answerith
Somtyme I was clepid in my cuntré   *called; country*
490   The bellewedir, and that was not a lite.   *bellwether; small thing*
Nought loved but drad of lowe and hie degré,   *feared by*
For whom me list by crafte I coude endite,   *I pleased; cunning; convict*
And hange the trewe and the theef respite;   *reprieve*
Al the cuntré by my worde was lad.   *led*
495   But I dar sey, shortly for to write   *quickly*
Of my dethe many a man is glad.

¶ Deeth to the Minstral
O thou mynstral, that canst so note and pipe   *sing*
Unto folkes for to do plesaunce,   *delight*
By the right honde I shal anoone thee gripe
500   With these other to goo upon my daunce.
Ther is no scape neither avoidaunce   *escape*
On no side to contrarie my sentence,   *resist; judgment*
For in musik, by craft and acordaunce,   *harmony*
Who maister is shewe his science.   *knowledge*

fol. 156r   ¶ The Minstral answerith
505   This newe daunce is to me so straunge,
Wondir diverse and passingly contrarie.   *Extraordinarily unusual; very inconsistent*
The dredful fotyng doth so ofte chaunge,   *hazardous steps*
And the mesures so ofte sithes varie,   *patterns; continually vary*
Wiche nowe to me is nothing necessarie,   *Which is to me not at all profitable*
510   If it were so that I myght asterte,   *escape*
But many a man (if I shal not tarie)   *delay*
Ofte daunceth but nothing of herte.   *although his heart's not in it*

¶ Deeth to the Tregetour   *Court magician*
Maister John Rikele, sometyme Tregetour   *(see note)*
Of noble Harry, Kyng of Engelond   *England*
515   And of Fraunce the mighty conquerour:
For alle the sleightes and turnyng of thin hond   *hand*
Thou must come ner this daunce to undirstond.   *near*
Nought may availe al thi conclusions,   *help; intentions*
For Deeth shortly, nouther on see ne lond,   *in brief; sea*
520   Is nought deceivid by none illusions.   *any*

¶ The Tregetour answerith
What may availe magik natural,   *sorcery*
Or any craft shewid by apparence,   *conjuring*
Or cours of sterres above celestial,

	Or of the hevene al the influence,	
525	Ageins Deeth to stonde at defence?	
	Legerdemeyn nowe helpith me right nought.	*Sleight of hand*
	Farewel, my craft and al suche sapience,	*wisdom*
	For Deth moo maistries yit than I hath wrought.[1]	

¶ Deeth to the Parsoun

	O Sir Curat that bene nowe here present,	
530	That had youre wordly inclinacioun,	
	Youre herte entire, youre studie, and entent	
	Moste on youre tithes and oblacioun,	*offerings*
	Wiche shulde have bene of conversacioun,	*manner of living*
	Mirrour unto othir, light and exaumplarie:	*example*
535	Like youre desert shal be youre guerdoun,	*worth; reward*
	And to eche labour dewe is the salarie.	*due*

fol. 156v ¶ The Persoun answerith

	Maugré my wille I must condiscende,	*Despite; acquiesce*
	For Deeth assailith every lifly thing.	*living*
	Here in this worlde who can comprehende	
540	His sodein stroke and his unware comyng?	*sudden; unforeseen*
	Farewele, tithis, and farewel, myn offryng,	*tithes*
	I mote goo counte in ordre by and by,	*go to judgment*
	And for my shepe make a just rekenyng;	
	Whom He aquyteth I holde he is happy.	*believe*

¶ Deeth to the Laborer

545	Thou, laborer, wiche in sorwe and peine	
	Hast lad thi life in ful greet travaile,	*toil*
	Thou moste eke daunce and therfore not disdeyne,	*also; do not be angry*
	For if thou do, it may thee not availe.	*help*
	And cause why that I thee assaile	*attack*
550	Is oonly this: from thee to dissevere	*to separate*
	The fals worlde that can so folke faile.	
	He is a fool that weneth to lyve evere.	*desires*

¶ The Laborer answerith

	I have wisshed aftir Deeth ful ofte,	
	Al be that I wolde have fled hym now —	*Although*
555	I had levere to have leyn unsofte	*rather; uncomfortable*
	In winde and reyn and have gone at plow,	
	With spade and pikoys and labourid for my prow,	*pickaxe; fortune*
	Dolve and diched and at the carte goone.	*Worked hard at manual labor*

---

[1] *And Death has wrought yet more stratagems than me*

560   For I may seie and telle pleinly howe
     In this worlde here ther is reste none.

     ¶ Deeth to the Frere Minour
     Sir Cordeler, to yow myn hand is raught   *extended*
     To this daunce yow to conveie and lede,
     Wiche in youre preching have ful ofte itaught: *taught*
     Howe that I am moste gastful forto drede   *terrifying*
565   (Al be that folke take therof noon hede).   *Although*
     Yit is ther noon so stronge ne so hardy,   *no one; fearless*
     But Deth dare reste and let for no mede,   *capture; free; compensation*
     For Deeth eche hour is present and redy.

fol. 157r   ¶ The Frere answerith
     What may this be that in this world no man
570   Here to abide may have no sureté?   *certainty*
     Strengthe, ricchesse, ne what so that he can,   *nor anything else he can do*
     Worldly wisdom: al is but vanité.   *vanity*
     In grete astate ne in poverté   *estate*
     Is nothing found that may fro Dethe defende.
575   For wiche I seie, to hie and lowe degré,
     Wys is that synner that dooth his life amende.

     ¶ Deeth to the Childe
     Litel enfaunte that were but late borne,   *infant; recently*
     Shape in this worlde to have no plesaunce,   *Created; delight*
     Thou must with other that goone here toforn   *before*
580   Be lad in haste by fatal ordinaunce.   *led; predetermined judgment*
     Lerne of newe to goo on my daunce,   *again*
     Ther may noon age escape in soth therfroo.   *escape; in truth there from*
     Lete every wight have this in remembraunce: *person*
     Who lengest lyveth moost shal suffre woo.

     ¶ The Childe answerith
585   A, A, A — o worde I cannot speke.   *one*
     I am so yonge, I was bore yisterday.
     Deeth is so hasty on me to be wreke   *eager to do me harm*
     And list no lenger to make no delay.   *desires*
     I cam but nowe and nowe I goo my way,
590   Of me no more no tale shal be told.
     The wil of God no man withstonde may,
     As sone dieth a yonge man as an old.   *soon*

     ¶ Deeth to the Clerke
     O ye Sir Clerke, suppose ye to be free
     Fro my daunce or youreselfe defende,
595   That wende have rysen unto hie degré   *thought to; position*

	Of benefices or some greet prebende?	
	Who clymbeth hiest sometyme shal dissende.	*descend*
	Lat no man grucche agens his fortune,	*complain against*
	But take in gree whatevere God hym sende,	*good will*
600	Wich ponissheth al whan tyme is oportune.	*Who punishes*

fol. 157v   ¶ The Clerke answerith

Shal I that am so yonge a clerke nowe deye
Fro my service and have no bettir guerdoun?   *reward*
Is ther no geyn ne no bettir weye,   *scheme*
No sure fraunchise ne proteccioun?   *privilege*
605   Deeth makith alweie a short conclusioun.   *always a quick end*
Too late ware whan men bene on the brinke;   *aware*
The worlde shal faile and al possessioun,[1]
For moche faileth of thing that foles thinke.   *fools*

¶ Deeth to the Hermyte
Ye that have lived longe in wildernesse
610   And ther contynued longe in abstinence;
Atte laste yet ye mote yow dresse   *must; prepare*
Of my daunce to have experience,
For ther agein is no recistence.
Take nowe leve of thin ermytage.   *hermitage*
615   Wherfore eche man adverte this sentence: *take note of; wisdom*
That this life here is no sure heritage.   *inheritance*

¶ The Hermite answerith
Life in desert callid solitarie   *solitary*
May agein Dethe have no respite ne space.   *reprieve*
At unset our his comyng doth not tarie,   *unspecified hour; delay*
620   And for my part welcome be Goddes grace,
Thonkyng hym with humble chere and face   *Thanking; attitude*
Of al his yiftes and greet haboundaunce,   *gifts; abundance*
Fynally affermynge in this place,
No man is riche that lackith suffisaunce.   *contentment*

¶ Deeth ayein to the Hermite
625   That is wel seide, and thus shulde every wight   *person*
Thanke his God and alle his wittis dresse   *direct*
To love and drede Hym with al his herte and myght,
Seth Deeth to ascape may be no sikernesse.   *Since; certainty*
As men deserve God quit of rightwisnesse   *repays*
630   To riche and pore uppon every side.

----

[1] *The world and possessions shall all fail*

A bettir lessoun ther can no clerke expresse,
Than til tomorwe is no man sure to abide.

fol. 158r   ¶ The Kyng ligging dead and eten of wormes
          Ye folke that lokyn upon this portrature,
          Biholdyng here alle the estates daunce,
635   Seeth what ye bene and what is youre nature: *See; are*
          Mete unto wormes, not ellis in substaunce.   *Meat; nothing else*
          And have this mirrour evere in remembraunce,
          Howe I lie here somtyme crownyd kyng,   *once*
          To alle estates a trewe resemblaunce
640   That wormes food is fyne of oure lyvyng.   *final end*

          ¶ Machabre the Doctour
          Man is not ellis, platly forto thinke,   *nothing else; plainly*
          But as a winde wiche is transitorie,
          Passinge ay forthe, whether he wake or winke,   *always; sleep*
          Towarde this Daunce. Have this in memorie,
645   Remembringe ay ther is no bet victorie   *always; better*
          In this life here than fle synne at the leste.   *fleeing; at least*
          Than shul ye regne in Paradys with glorie;   *shall*
          Happy is he that maketh in hevene his feste.   *feast*

          Yit ther be folke mo than six or sevene,   *Yet; more*
650   Reckles of liif in many maner wise,   *many different ways*
          Like as ther were helle none ne hevene.   *neither hell nor heaven*
          Suche false errour lete every man dispice.   *despise*
          For hooly seintis and oolde clerkis wise
          Writen contrarie her falsnes to deface.   *their falseness; refute*
655   To lyve wel — take this for best emprice —   *undertaking*
          Is moche worth whan men shul hens pace.   *much; hence*

          ¶ Lenvoye de Translator   *The envoy of the Translator*
          O ye, my lordis and maistres alle in fere   *altogether*
          Of aventure that shal this Daunce rede,   *By chance*
          Lowly I preie with al myn herte entere   *Humbly; entire*
660   To correcte whereas ye see nede.
          For nought ellis I aske for my mede,   *reward*
          But goodly support of this translacioun
          And with favour to sowpouaile drede,   *encourage reverence*
          Benignely in youre correccioun.   *With good will*

665   Out of the Frensshe I drewe it of entente,   *with purpose*
          Not worde by worde but folwyng the substaunce.
          And fro Paris to Engelonde it sente
          Oonly of purpos yow to do plesaunce.   *delight*
          Rude of langage (I was not born in Fraunce),

670   Have me excusid; my name is John Lidgate.
             Of her tunge I have no suffisaunce   *their language; fluency*
             Her corious metris in Englisshe to translate.   *Their unfamiliar meters*

             Here endith the Daunce of Deeth.

John Lydgate, Dance of Death: B Version (Lansdowne)

fol. 41r	¶ Incipit Macrobius	*(see note)*
fol. 41v	O creatures ye that been resonable,	*have reason*
	The liff desiryng which is eternall,	
	Ye may seen heer doctrine ful notable,	*see*
	Your liff to leede which that is mortall,	*life*
5	Therby to lerne in especiall	*in particular*
	How ye shal trace the daunce which that ye see	*follow*
	To man and wooman yliche naturall,	*alike*
	For Deth ne sparith hih nor lowe degre.	*does not spare*

	¶ Angelus	*Angel (see note)*
	In this myrrour every man may fynde	
10	That hym behovyth to goon upon this daunce.	*That he must go*
	Whoo goth before or who goth behynde,	*goes*
	All dependith in Goddis ordynaunce.	*God's plan*
	Wherfore eche mann lowly take his chaunce;	*humbly*
	Deth spareth nothir poore nor blood roiall.	*royal*
15	Eche man therfore have this in remembraunce:	
	Of oon mateer God hath forgid all.[1]	

	¶ Papa	*Pope*
	Ye that be sett hih in dignyté	
	Of all estatis in erthe spirituall,	*Out of all religious positions on earth*
	And lik to Petir have the sovereynté	
20	Ovir the chirche most in especiall:	*in particular*
	Upon this daunce ye first begynne shall,	
	As most worthi lord and governour,	
	For al the worshippe of your estat papall	*high esteem; papal estate*
	And of all lordshippe to God is the honour.	*dominion*

	¶ Responsum	*Response*
25	First me bihovyth this daunce with Deth to leede,	*It is proper for me*
	Wich sat in erthe hihest in my see —	*Who; seat of authority*
	Thestat ful perilous whoso takith heede	

---

[1] *God has made everyone from the same matter*

43

To occupie Seynt Petris dignyté —[1]
But for al that fro Deth I may nat flee,   *from*
30   Upon this daunce with othir for to trace,   *with others; to follow*
For sich honour, who prudently can see,   *such*
Is litel worthe that doth so soone passe.   *pass [away]*

fol. 42r   ¶ Imperator   *Emperor*
Sir Emperour, lord of all the ground,   *earth*
Most sovereyn prynce surmountyng of noblesse: *preeminent; nobility*
35   Ye must forsake of gold your appill round,
Septre and swerd and all your hih prowesse.   *scepter; sword; martial deeds*
Behynde yow lat tresour and richesse,   *leave*
And with othir to my daunce obeye.
Ageyn my myth vaileth non hardynesse;   *Against; might; prevails; valor*
40   Adamis children all thei must deye.   *Adam's children (i.e., humanity)*

¶ Responsum
I not to whom I may appele,   *know not; appeal*
Whan Deth me sailith that doth me constreyn.   *assails; compel*
Ther is no gynne to socour my quarele,   *aid; assist; complaint*
But spade and picois my grave to atteyne,   *pickaxe; reach*
45   A symple shete — ther is no more to seyn —   *to say*
To wrappen in my body and visage,   *face*
Wherupon sore I me compleyn   *fervently*
That lordis grete have litel avauntage.   *advantage*

¶ Cardinalis   *Cardinal*
Ye be abaissht, it seemeth, and in drede,   *upset; full of dread*
50   Sir Cardynall — it seemeth bi your cheer —   *expression*
But for al that ye folwe shal in deede   *you shall follow; indeed*
With othir estates this daunce for to leer.   *to learn*
Your gret array al shal levyn heer,   *fine clothing; shall be left*
Your hatt of red, your vesture of gret cost.   *garment*
55   Al these thynges rekenyd weel ifeere:[2]
In gret worship good avys is lost.   *judgment*

¶ Responsum
I have gret cause — trewly it is no faile —   *certainly; mistake*
To been abaissht and gretely to dreede me,   *upset; to have great dread*
Sith Deth is come me sodeynly tassaile,   *Because; to attack me suddenly*
60   That I shall nevir hereaftir clothid be
In grise nor ermyn lik to my degré;   *gray fur (possibly squirrel); ermine*
Myn hat of red levyn heer in distresse,   *leave*

---

[1] Lines 27–28: *The very dangerous position, whoso takes heed / To occupy St. Peter's rank*

[2] *Each and every one of these valuable things adjudicated together*

Bi which I have lernyd weel and see
How that al joie eendith in hevynesse.   *sorrow*

fol. 42v ¶ Imperatrix   *Empress*
65 Lat se your hand, my lady dame Empresse,   *Let [me] see*
Have no disdeyn with me for to daunce.   *scorn*
Ye may aside leyn al your richesse,   *leave aside*
Your fresh attyres, devises of plesaunce,   *fancy clothes; stratagems of flattery*
Your soleyn cheeris, your strange countenaunce,   *distant expression; haughty attitude*
70 Your clothis of gold most uncouthly wrouht,   *outlandishly made*
Havyng of Deth ful litel remembrance.
But now ye se weel al is come to nouht.   *nothing*

¶ Responsum
What availeth gold, richesse, or perre,   *What use is; wealth; precious stones*
Or what availeth hih blood or jentylnesse,   *high birth or nobility*
75 Or what availeth freshnesse or beaute,   *radiance*
Or what is worth hih porte or straungenesse?   *haughty attitude; aloofness*
Deth seith chekmat to al sich veyn noblesse.   *checkmate; vain*
All worldly power now may me nat availe:
Raunsoun, kynrede, frenshippe, nor worthynesse,   *Ransom; kindred; friendship*
80 Syn Deth is come myn hih estate tassaile.   *Because; to attack*

¶ Patriarcha   *Patriarch*
Sir Patriarch, ful sad and humble of cheere,   *attitude*
Ye mote with othir gon on this daunce with me.   *must*
Your dowble cros of gold and stonys cleer,   *double cross*
Your power hool, and al your dygnyté   *whole; rank*
85 Som othir shal of trouth and equité   *truth and fairness*
Be possessid in hast, as I rehers can.   *as I can say*
Trust nevyr that ye shal pope be,
For foly hope disseiveth many a man.   *foolish*

¶ Responsum
Worldly honour, grete tresour, and richesse
90 Have me disseyved sothfastly in deede.   *deceived; truly indeed*
My joies old be turned to distresse.
What availeth it sich honour to possede?   *What use is it; such; possess*
Hih clymbyng up a fal hath to his meede;   *for its reward*
Gret estat folk waste out of noumbre.[1]
95 Whoso mountith hihest stondith most in drede,[2]
Such hevy berden doth hem ofte encoumbre.

---

[1] *Folk waste more great estates than can be numbered*

[2] *Whoever rises highest stands most in dread*

fol. 43r ¶ Rex   *King*

Right noble kyng, most worthi of renoun,   *renown*

Cum forth anon for al your worthynesse,   *Come; at once; nobility*

That somtyme had so gret possession,   *possession of lands*

100   Rewmys obeyng unto your hih noblesse.   *Realms; high nobility*

Ye most of nature to this daunce yow dresse   *must; naturally; prepare yourself*

And fynally your crowne and sceptre leete.   *leave*

For whoso most haboundith in gret rychesse   *abounds*

Shal bere with hym but a sengle sheete.   *single [winding] sheet*

¶ Responsum

105   I have nat lernyd heer afforn to daunce   *heretofore*

No daunce in soth of fotyng so savage,   *in truth; frenzied*

Wherbi I see ful cleerly in substaunce: *in essence*

What pride is worth force or hih parage?[1]

Deth all fordoth — this is his usage —   *destroys; practice*

110   Gret and smal that in this world sojourne.

Who that is most meek hath most avauntage,

For we shul all to dede asshis torne.

¶ Archiepiscopos   *Archbishop*

Sir Archebisshop, whi do ye so withdrawe   *retreat*

Your look, your face as it wer bi disdeyn?   *with contempt*

115   Yee must obey to my mortal lawe:

It to constreyne it were but in veyn.   *to control*

For day bi day, be right wele certeyn,

Deth at hond pursewith every coste.   *course of action*

Preestes and Deth may nat be holden ageyn,   *Loans; delayed*

120   For at oon our men contith wit ther oste.   *the [last] hour; reckon; host*

¶ Responsum

Allas, I wot nat what partye for to flee,   *don't know where to flee*

For dreede of Deth I stonde in sich distresse,   *such*

Tescape his power I can no refute see.[2]

But who that knewe his constreynt and duresse,   *oppression; cruelty*

125   He wolde take reson to maistresse   *mistress*

And seyn adieu pompe, and pride also,   *say goodbye*

My peynted paleys, my tresour, and richesse.   *painted palace*

Thyng that behovyth nedis must be do.[3]

fol. 43v ¶ Princeps   *Prince*

Riht myhty prynce, be rith weell certeyn   *be completely certain*

---

[1] *What kind of power or high birth is worth taking pride in?*

[2] *I see no refuge in which to escape his power*

[3] *The thing that is proper to do must be done*

130	This daunce to yow is not eschewable.	*not avoidable*
	For more myhty than ever was Carlemayn,	*Charlemagne*
	Or worthy Arthour of prowes ful notable	*military deeds*
	With al his knyhtes of the Rounde Table —	
	What did ther platis, ther armour, or ther maile,	*plate armor; chainmail*
135	Ther strong corage, ther sheeldes defensable,	*spirit; defensive shields*
	Ageyns Deth availe whan he hem dide assaile?	*them*

¶ Responsum

	My purpos was and myn entencion	*intent*
	To assege castellis and myhti forteresses,	*besiege; castles; mighty*
	Rebellis to bryng unto subjeccion,	
140	To seeke worship, fame, and grete rychesses.	
	But I se weel that al wordly prowesses	*earthly valor*
	Deth can abate, wherof I have despite.	*demolish; contempt*
	To hym allon sorwe eke swetnesses,	*alone; also*
	For ageyns Deth is founde no respite.	*against; reprieve*

¶ Episcopos   *Bishop*

145	Com ner, Sir Bisshoppe, with your myteer and croos,	*miter and cross*
	For al your richesse, soth I yow ensure,	*truly I assure you*
	For al your tresour so longe kepte in cloos,	*privately owned*
	Your wordly goodis and goodis of nature,	*earthly goods; natural goods (e.g., crops)*
	And of your sheep the gostly dreedful cure,	*spiritual serious duty*
150	With charge commytted to your prelacie,	*prelacy (office of the bishop)*
	For to acounte ye shal be brouht to lure.	*brought under control*
	No wiht is sewr that clymbith on hih.	*person; secure*

¶ Responsum

	Of these tidynges I am nothyng glaad,	*not at all*
	Which Deth to me so sodeynly doth bryng.	*suddenly*
155	It makith my face and countenaunce ful saad	
	That for discomfort me lyst nothyng to syng;	*desire*
	The world contrary to me in werkyng	
	Which al estatis can so disherite.	*disinherit*
	And needis we must onto our departyng,	
160	And al shal passe save oonly our merite.[1]	

fol. 44r	¶ Comes et Baro	*Earl and Baron*
	Erl or Baron, which that thourh regiouns	*through*
	Have sore laboured for worship and renoun,	*earnestly*
	Forget your trompetis and your clariouns.	
	This is no dreem nor symulacioun.	*deception*
165	Somtyme your custom and your entencoun	*desire*

---

[1] *Everything will pass away except our good deeds*

Was in estat and wordly wurshippe to glade,   *to take joy*
But often tyme it happith, in conclusion,
Oo man brekyth that anothir made.   *One; breaks*

¶ Responsum
Ful often tyme I have ben auttorised   *authorized*
170   To hih empryse and thyng of gret fame.   *martial deeds*
Of gret estatis my thank also devised,   *gratitude; contrived*
Cherishid with princes and lordis hih of name,
Nor nevyr on me was put no diffame   *No slander was ever put on me*
In roial courtes, which that weer notable.
175   But Deth unwarly al power makith lame,   *unexpectedly; helpless*
And undir hevene in erthe is nothyng stable.

¶ Abbas et prior   *Abbot and prior*
Sir Abbot and Priour with your brood hatt,   *broad*
To been abassht ye have a maner riht.   *upset; good reason*
Gret is your hed, your bely rounde and fatt;   *belly*
180   Ye must come daunce thouh ye be nat liht.
Leven your lordshippe to som othir wiht,   *Leave; person*
Your eyer is of age your state to ocupye.   *heir; position*
Whoso is fattest to hym I have behiht,   *him I have designated*
In his grave sonnest shal putrefie.   *soonest; decay*

¶Responsum
185   Of thy manace I have no gret envye   *threat; grudge*
That I shal leve al maner governaunce.
But that I shal as a cloistrer die —   *cloistered monk*
This doth to me somwhat the lesse grevaunce.   *somewhat lesser offence*
My libertes nor my gret aboundaunce,[1]
190   What may thei availe in any maner wise?   *help; any kind of way*
Yit aske I mercy with devoute repentaunce,
Thouh toforn Deth too late men them avise.   *examine themselves*

fol. 44v ¶ Abbatissa   *Abbess*
And ye, my lady gentyl dame Abbesse,   *of noble rank or birth*
With your mantyl furryd large and wide,   *sleeveless overgarment*
195   Your veile, your wympil, your ryng of gret richesse,   *headdress*
And beddis softe ye must now leyne aside,   *bedding; turn (put)*
For to this daunce I must be your gyde.
Thouh ye be tendre, born of gentil blood,   *delicate; noble*
Whil that ye live yoursilf provide,   *prepare yourself*
200   For aftir Deth no man hath no good.   *possessions*

---

[1] *My legal privileges nor my great wealth*

¶ Responsum

Allas, that Deth hath for me so ordeyned

That in no wise I may nat hym eschewe;   *way; escape*

Unto this daunce of riht I am constreyned   *rightly; compelled*

That heer with othir I must his trace sewe.   *follow his steps*

205   This pilgrymage to every man is dewe,   *due*

An ernest mateer, a mateer of no jape.   *matter; joke*

Who that is alwey redy shal nevir rewe   *regret*

The hour abydyng that God hath for hym shape.   *awaiting; created*

¶ Iudex   *Judge*

That hand of youres, my Lord Justice,

210   That have rewlid so long the lawe,   *ruled*

Weel may men holde yow war and wise,   *Well; knowledgeable*

So that this drauht be weel drawe;   *drawn*

Escape shal ye nat, wold ye never so fawe,   *desirous*

Sich dome to have as ye have yoven in soth.[1]

215   Wherfore men seyn of an old sawe: *adage*

Weel is hym that alwey weel doth.   *well*

¶ Responsum

Allas, ne were that myn entent

Was weele dressid, thouh I othirwhile erryd.   *intended well; otherwise*

Now shuld I uttrely be shamyd and shent   *harmed*

220   For many causes that I have oftyn deferrid,   *referred to a higher court*

Sauff mercy oonly now were I marrid.[2]

Blissid therfore is every wiht,   *Blessed; person*

As bi Holy Scriptur may ben averrid,   *demonstrated*

That in all tyme doth lawe and kepith riht.

fol. 45r ¶ Doctor utrisque Iuris   *Doctor of both laws*

225   Com forth, Doctour of Canon and Cyvile.

In bothe these lawis of long contynuaunce,

Your tyme hath spent — bewar ye did no gile —   *deceit*

In your mateers for to han fortheraunce.   *matters; personal benefit*

Now must ye lerne with me for to daunce;

230   All your lawe may yow nat availe.   *assist*

Giff me your hand and make no perturbaunce:

Your hour is come — this is withouten faile.

¶ Responsum

A mercy, Jhesu, whow mankynde is freele   *frail*

And litel tyme in this worlde abydyng;

---

[1] *Such judgment to have as you have given in truth*

[2] *Except for mercy, I would now be destroyed*

235	No man of his liff hath charter nor seele.	*life; seal*
	Therfore it may be likned in all thyng	
	Unto a flour so amorously floorsshyng,	*ardently flourishing*
	Which with a froste bigynneth riht sone to fade.	*immediately*
	Whan cruell Deth his massage list to bryng,	*message; chooses*
240	Al liffly thyng he bryngeth in the shade.	*living*

	¶ Miles et armiger	*Knight or squire*
	Knyht or Scwyer, riht fressh of your aray	*attire*
	That can of daunses al the newe gise:	*knows; dances; fashion*
	Thouh ye bare armes wele-horsid yisterday,[1]	
	With speere and sheeld at your uncouth devise,	*of outlandish design*
245	And took upon yow many strange emprise,	*remarkable deeds*
	Dansith with us, it wole no bettir be;	
	Ther is no socour in no maner wise,	*assistance of any kind*
	For no man may from Dethis power flee.	

	¶ Responsum	
	Sith that Deth me holdith in his lace,	*Because; snare*
250	Yit shal I speke a woord or I pace:	*Yet; before; go*
	Adieu, al myrthe, adieu now al solace;	
	Adieu, my ladies somtyme so fressh of face;	*youthful*
	Adieu, beauté that lastith but short space!	*time*
	Of Dethis chaunge every day is pryme;	*a new beginning*
255	Thynk on your sowlis or that Deth manace,	*before Death threatens*
	For al shal rote, and no mann wot what tyme.	*decay; knows*

fol. 45v	¶ Maior	*Mayor*
	Com forth, Sir Mayr, which had governaunce	
	Bi pollicie to rewle this cité:	*policy; rule*
	Thouh your power were notable in substaunce,	*great*
260	To flee my daunce ye have no liberté.	*freedom*
	Estate is noon nor wordly dygnyté	*There is no status or worldly rank*
	That may escape on of my daungeris.	*any; powers*
	To fynde rescew exaumple ye may se	
	Nouthir bi richesse nor force of officeres.[2]	

	¶ Responsum	
265	What helpith now thestat in which I stood,	*the estate*
	To rewle cites or comouns to governe,	*rule; populaces*
	Plente of richesse, or increce of good,	*increase*
	Or olde wynnyng that cometh to me so yerne?	*wealth; quickly*

---

[1] *Though you bore arms well on horseback yesterday*

[2] Lines 263–64: *You cannot find examples in which someone escaped / Because of their riches or the power of their office*

Deth al defaceth, whoso list to lerne;   *desires*
270   Me for tareste he comyth on so faste.   *to arrest*
Eche man therfore shold afore discerne   *in advance*
Prudently to thynk upon his laste.

¶ Canonicus Regularis   *Canon Regular*
Lat see your hand, Sir Chanon Reguler,
Somtyme ysworn to religion,   *vowed*
275   As humble soget and obedienceer,   *subject; subordinate*
Chastly to live lik your profession.   *according to*
But ther may be no consolacion
Ageyn my sawes sodeyn and cruell,   *decrees*
Except oonly — for short conclusion —
280   Who liveth in vertu mot nedis dey weel.   *virtuously must*

¶ Responsum
Whi shulde I grutche or disobeye   *complain*
The thyng to which, of verrey kyndly riht,   *by truly natural right*
Was I ordeyned and born for to deye,
As in this world is ordeyned every wiht?   *person*
285   Which to remembre is nothyng liht;   *no small thing*
Prayng the Lord that was sprad on the Roode   *Praying; spread; Cross*
To medle mercy with His eternal myht   *mix; power*
And save the sowles that he bouht with his blood.

fol. 46r   ¶ Decanus   *Dean*
Sir Dean or Chanon, with many gret prebend,
290   Ye may no lenger ha distribuciouns   *have; a share [of alms]*
In gret array your tresour to dispende,   *fine clothing; to squander*
With all your richesse and your possessiouns,
For Kynde hath sett hir revoluciouns,   *Nature*
Eche man som day to daunce on Dethis brynk.
295   Therof ye may have no dilaciouns,   *delays*
For Deth cometh evir whan men lest on hym thynke.   *always; least*

¶ Responsum
My divers cures, my riche personages —
Allas ful litel thei may me now comforte.   *very little*
Deth upon me hath geten his avantages;   *got the better of me*
300   All my richesse can make me now no sporte.   *no consolation*
Amys of grey, thei must ageyn resorte   *Fine garments of grey; return*
Unto the world with many a gret prebende;
For which trewly, as clerkis can reporte,
To deye weel eche man sholde entende.

¶Monialis   *Monk*
305   Thouh ye be barbid and claad in clothis blaake,   *tonsured; wearing*

Chastly receyved the mantil and the ryng,   *mantle; ring*
Ye may nat the cours of nature forsake,
To daunce with othir now at my comyng.
In this world is non abidyng,   *no one living*
310   Nouthir of maide, widewe, nor wiff,   *Neither*
As ye may seen heer cleerly bi wrytyng,
That ageyns Deth is founde no preservatiff.   *protection*

¶ Responsum
It helpith nat to stryve ageyn Nature,
Namely whan Deth bigynneth tassaile,   *begins to attack*
315   Wherfore I counseil every creature
To been redy ageyn this fel batayle.   *fierce battle*
Vertu is sewrer than othir plate or maile,   *Virtue; more secure; either armor; chainmail*
Also nothyng may helpe more at sich a nede
Than to provide a sur acquytaile
320   With the hand of almesse to love God and drede.[1]   *alms*

fol. 46v   ¶ Chartreux   *Carthusian*
Yeve me your hand with chekis ded and pale,   *Give*
Causid of watche and long abstynence,   *wakefulness (i.e., for a vigil)*
Sir Chartreux, and doth your chyne vale   *lower your chin*
Unto this daunce with humble pacience.
325   To stryve ageyn may be no resistence;   *against*
Lenger to live set nat your memorie.   *direct not your attention*
Thouh I be lothsom outward in apparence,   *loathsome*
Above all men Deth hath the victorie.

¶ Responsum
Unto this world I was ded ago ful longe
330   Bi myn ordre and my profession.   *[Carthusian] order*
Thowgh every man, be he nevyr so strong,
Dredith to deye bi naturall mocion   *natural instinct*
Afftyr his flesshly inclynacion,
Plese it the Lord my sowle for to borwe   *borrow*
335   Fro feendis myht and fro dampnacion;   *the Devil's might; damnation*
Som arn today that shal nat be tomorwe.   *are*

¶ Sergeant in lawe
Come neer, Sir Sergeant, short processe for to make,   *legal argument*
Ye must cum pleete afore the Juge on hihe,   *plead your case before*
Many a quarell thouh ye have undirtake   *complaint*
340   And for lucre doon folk gret remedie.   *profit; legal redress*

---

[1] Lines 318–20: *Nothing does more to help / And provide an acquittal in such a difficult situation / Than demonstrating one's love and dread of God through the giving of alms*

Ther shal your sotil wittis be deemyd foly,   *crafty*
Yif sleathe and covetise be nat exiled.   *sloth; covetousness*
Bewar bitymes and labour for mercy,   *promptly*
For thei that trust most themsilf ar sonnest bigiled.   *themselves; deceived*

¶ Responsum
345   Of riht and reson bi Natures lawe,
       I can alleggen nor make no diffence,   *make a formal legal claim; defense*
       Nor bi sleihte nor statute me withdrawe   *cunning; myself excuse*
       Tescape awey from this dreedful sentence,   *To escape*
       For al my witt nor gret prudence.
350   No thyng in erthe may no man preserve
       Ageyns His myht to make resistence;
       God qwyteth al men lyke as they deserve.   *repays*

fol. 47r ¶ Generosa   *Rich Gentlewoman*
       Com forth maistresse, of yeeres yong and grene   *mistress; fresh*
       Which hold yoursilff of beauté sovereyn.   *preeminent*
355   As fair as ye was whilom Polliceene,   *once; Polyxena*
       Penolope and the queen Eleyn,   *Helen*
       Yit on this daunce thei went bothe tweyn,   *Yet; both of them*
       And so shal ye for al your strangenesse.   *despite; haughtiness*
       Thouh deynous daungeer longe hath lad your reyn,   *scornful resistance; reign*
360   Unto this daunce ye mote your fotyng dresse.   *must; footing; turn*

¶ Responsum
       O cruel Deth that sparist non estat,
       To old and yong thou art indifferent.
       To my beauté thou hast seyd chekmat,   *checkmate*
       So hasty is thi mortall jugement.   *swift*
365   For in my youthe this was myn entent,
       To my servise many a man to have lurid.   *lured*
       But she is a fool, shortly in sentement,   *concisely*
       That in hir beauté is too myche assurid.

¶ Magister in Astronomia   *Master of astronomy*
       Com forth, mayster, that loken up so ferre
370   With instrumentis of astronomye
       To take the grees and hithe of every sterre.   *degrees and height*
       What may availe al your astrologye,   *help*
       Sith of Adam al the genealogie,   *Since; descendants*
       Maade first of God to walke upon the gronde,
375   Deth doth arrest? Thus seith theologie,
       And alle shul deie for an appyll rounde.

¶ Responsum
       For al my craft, connyng, or science   *knowledge*

	I can fynde no provision,	*provision (i.e., against death)*
	Nor in the sterris serche out no difference,	
380	Bi domofyeng nor calculacion,	*By locating the position of the stars*
	Sauff fynaly — in conclusion —	*Except*
	For to descrive our connyng every deel,	*explain; in every aspect*
	Ther is no more bi sentence of reson,	*by doctrine*
	Who livith aryght most nedis deye weel.	*must necessarily die well*

fol. 47v ¶ Frater   *Friar*

385	Com forth, thou frere, to thee myn hand is rauht	*extended*
	Upon this daunce thee to conveie and lede,	
	Which in thi prechyng hast ful ofte tauht,	*taught*
	How that I am gastfull for to dreede	*terrifying*
	(Althouh that folk take ther of non heede).	
390	Yit is ther non so strong nor so hardy,	*no one; fearless*
	But I dar arrest hym and lett for no meede,	*confine; free; compensation*
	For Deth eche hour is present and redy.	

¶ Responsum

	What may this be that in this world no man	
	Heer for tabide may have no sureté?	*to abide; certainty*
395	Strengthe, richesse, nor what so that he can:	*nor anything else he can do*
	Of wordly wisdam is al but vanité.	*vanity*
	In gret estate nor in poverté	
	Is no thyng founde that may fro Deth deffende,	
	For which I sei to hih and lowe degré,	
400	Wis is the synner that doth his liff amende.	

¶ Sergaunt

	Com forth, thou Sergeant with thi stately maas;	
	Make no deffence nor no rebellion.	
	Nouht may availe to grotchen in this caas,	*aid; complain; case*
	Thouh thou be deynous of condicioun,	*arrogant by nature*
405	For nouthir appele nor protectioun	*appeal*
	May thee franchise to do nature wrong.	*empower*
	For ther is non so sturdi a champioun;	
	Thouh he be myhty, Deth is yit mor strong.	

¶ Responsum

	How darst thou, Deth, set on me arrest,	*take me into custody*
410	Which am the kyngis chosen officeer	*Who*
	And yistirday walkyng est and west	
	Myn office did with ful dispitous cheere?	*scornful attitude*
	But now this day I am arrested heere	*detained*
	And may nat flee, thouh I hadde it sworn.	
415	Eche man is loth to deie, ferr or neer,	*unwilling to die*
	That hath nat lernyd for to deie afforn.	*before*

fol. 48r ¶ Iurour   *Juror*
    Maister Jurour, which that at assises   *sessions of civil court*
    And at shiris questis didist enbrace,   *shire's inquests; illegally influence*
    Departist lond aftir thi devises,   *Divided; schemes*
420   And who most gaff most stood in thi grace: *gave (i.e., bribed)*
    The poore man lost bothe lond and place;   *position*
    For gold thou coudist folk disherite.   *disinherit*
    But lat se now, that withynne so short a space,   *see; time*
    Before the Juge how thow canst thee acquyte.   *acquit yourself*

    ¶ Responsum
425   Somtyme I was callid in my contré   *country*
    The bellewedir, and that was nat a lite.   *bellwether; not a small thing*
    Nat lovid but drad of hih and lowe degré,   *feared by*
    For whom me list bi craft I coude endite,   *I pleased; cunning; convict*
    Hang the trewe and the theef acquyte;
430   Al the contre bi my woord was lad.   *led*
    But I dar say, shortly for to write,   *quickly*
    Of my deth many oon wole be ful glad.   *multiple ones (i.e., many) will*

    ¶ Mimus   *Minstrel*
    Gentil menstral, shewe me now thi witt,   *skill*
    How thou canst pleye or foote ariht this daunce.   *step correctly*
435   I dar weel sei that an harder fitt   *tune*
    Than this fil nevyr unto thi chaunce.   *befell; luck*
    Look therfore what may best avaunce   *assist*
    Thi sowle as now and use that I reede: *advise*
    Refuse nyce play and veyn plesaunce;   *foolish merriment and vain delight*
440   Bettir late than nevyr to do good deede.

    ¶ Responsum
    Ey, benedicité, this world is freele.   *Oh, bless; changeable*
    Now glad, now sory, what shal men use?
    Harpe, lute, phidil, pipe — farwell! —   *fiddle*
    Sautry, sithol, and shalmuse,   *psaltery; stringed instrument (cithole); reed flute*
445   Al wordly myrthe I here refuse.   *reject*
    God graunte me grace of sich penaunce,   *such*
    As may myn old synnes excuse,
    For alle be nat mery that othirwhyle daunce.   *otherwise*

fol. 48v ¶ Famulus   *Attendant*
    Servant or officer in thyn office,
450   Yif thou hast ben as God wold and riht,   *If; desires; righteous*
    To pore and riche doon pleyn justice,   *complete*
    Fled extorcioun with al thi myht,
    Than maist thou in this daunce go liht,   *easily*
    Or elles ful hevy shalt thou be thanne.   *then*

| 455 | Whan alle domys shal fynaly be diht, | *judgments; made* |
| | Go we hens, the tyde abidith no man. | *time waits for* |

¶ Responsum
	Shal I so sone to Dethis daunce,	*soon*
	That wend to have lyved yeeris many mo	*Who; supposed; more*
	And sodeynly forsake al my plesaunce	*delight*
460	Of offices and profites that long therto?	*belong*
	Yit oon thyng I consel or I go —	*before*
	In office lat no man doon outrage,	*injury*
	For dreede of God and peyn also;	
	Also service is noon heritage.	*inheritance*

¶ Phisicus   *Physician*
465	Ye phisiciens for mony, that loken so fast	*money; intently*
	In othir mennys watris what thei eyle,	*urine; ails them*
	Look weel to yoursilf or att last	*Attend to yourself*
	I not what your medicynes nor crafte may availe,	*know not; help*
	For Deth comyng sodeynly doth assaile	*attack*
470	As weel lechis as othir — that shal ye knowe.	*easily physicians*
	Atte Last Jugement, withouten any faile,	
	Whan al men shal repe as thei have sowe.	

¶ Responsum
	Allas too long and too myche in phisik	*medicine*
	For lucre I plyed al my bisynesse,	*profit; plied; business*
475	Bothe in speclacion and in practik,	*theorizing; practice*
	To knowe and konne al bodily siknesse.	*understand*
	But of gostly helthe I was reklesse,	*spiritual well-being; ignorant*
	Wherfore shal helpe nothir herbe nor roote,	*neither*
	Nor no medicyne, sauff Goddis goodnesse,	*except*
480	For ageyns Deth is fynaly no boote.	*remedy*

fol. 49r   ¶ Mercator   *Merchant*
	Come, riche marchant, and looke hidirward,	*over here*
	Which hast passid thorow many dyvers lond,	*various*
	On hors, on foote, havyng most reward	*esteem*
	To lucre and wynnyng, as I undirstonde:	*To profit and wealth*
485	But now to daunce thou must yeve me thyn hond.	*give*
	Al thyn old labour, wher is it become now?	
	Adieu, veynglorie, bothe of fre and bonde!	*master and servant*
	Non more coveitith than he that hath inow.	*No one; covets; enough*

¶ Responsum
	Bi many an hill and many strong vale	*By; foreign valley*
490	I have travailid with my marchaundise,	
	Bi straunge seeis carried many a bale,	*seas; unit of measurement for goods*

To sondri iles, more than I can devise.   *tell*

Myn hert inward evir frett with covetise   *always loaded*

But al for nouht — Deth doth me constreyne —   *detain*

495 For which I sei, bi record of the wise,

Who al enbracith, he lityl shal restreyn.   *embraces; restrain*

¶ Artifex   *Artisan*

Yeve hidir thyn hand, thou Artificeer,   *Give here; Craftsman*

For ther is founde no subtilité   *cleverness*

Bi witt of man that fro my daungeer   *power*

500 To save hymsilff can have no liberté.   *ability*

My strook is sodeyn, fro which no man may flee,

Bi coriousté nor cunnyng of fressh devise.   *ingenuity; new plans*

Kynde hath ordeyned it will non othir be: *Nature; it will not be otherwise*

Eche man mote passe whan deth settith assise.   *must; session of civil court*

¶ Responsum

505 Ther is no craft serchid out nor souht,

Cast nor compassid, bi old nor newe entaile —   *Reckoned or measured; design*

I se ful weel withynne myn owen thouht —

Ageyns Deth ther may nothyng availe;   *help*

She pershith sheeldis, she pershith plate and maile,   *pierces; (see note)*

510 Ageyns hir strok cunnyg nor science,   *cleverness; knowledge*

Whan that hir list mortally to assaile —   *chooses*

Allas, allas — ther may be no deffence.

fol. 49v ¶ Laborarius   *Laborer*

Thou, Labourer, which in sorwe and peyn

Hast lad thi liff and in gret travaile,   *toil*

515 Thou must here daunce and therfore nat disdeyn,   *do not be angry*

For thouh thou do it, may thee nat availe.   *help*

And cause whi that I thee assaile   *attack*

Is oonly fro thee for to dissevire   *in order to separate*

This fals world that causith folk to faile.

520 For he is a foole that wenyth to liven evir.   *desires*

¶ Responsum

I have wisshid aftir Dethe ful oft,   *very often*

Althouh I wold have fleed hym now —

I had levir to ha leyn unsoft   *rather to have lain uncomfortable*

In wynde and reyn and gon forth at the plouh,

525 With spade and picoys laboured for my prouh,   *pickaxe; fortune*

Dolvyn and dikid and atte cart goon.   *Worked hard at manual labor*

For I may seyn and pleynly avow:

In this world here rest is ther noon.

¶ Infans   *Child*
Litil child that were but late born,   *recently*
530   Shape in this world to have no plesaunce,   *Created; delight*
Thou must with othir that goon her toforn   *go here before*
Be lad with hem with sotyl ordynaunce.   *led; skillful judgment*
Lerne of newe to gon on this daunce,   *again*
Ther may non age in soth skape therfro.   *in truth; escape; from there*
535   Lat every wiht have this in remembraunce: *person*
Whoso lengest levith most shal sofren woo.   *suffer*

¶ Responsum
A, A, A — o worde I cannat speke.   *one*
I am ful yong, I was born yisterday.
Deth is ful hasty on me to been wreke   *eager to do me harm*
540   And of his strok list make no delay.   *desires*
I cam but now and now I go my way,
Of me no more tale shal be tolde.
The will of God no man withstond may,
For as sone deieth a yong sheep as an olde.

fol. 50r   ¶ Heremita   *Hermit*
545   Ye that have lived long in wildirnesse
And contynued long in abstynence:
Tyme is come that ye mote yow dresse   *must prepare*
Of my daunce to have thexperience,
For ther ageyns is no resistence.
550   Take now leve of thyn hermitage.
Wherfore eche man advertise this sentence: *take note of; wisdom*
That this liff heer is but a pylgrymage.   *(see note)*

¶ Responsum
Liff in deserte callid solitarye
May ageyns Deth have no respite nor space.   *reprieve*
555   At unsett howr his comyng doth nat tarye,   *unspecified hour; delay*
And for my part welcom be Goddis grace,
Thankyng my Lord with humble cheer and face   *attitude*
Of his yiftis such as I have assayed,   *gifts; determined*
Fynally affermyng in this place,
560   No man is riche, but he that halt Hym payed.   *he who pleases the Lord*

¶ Conclusio   *Conclusion*
Ye folk that loken upon this scripture,
Conceyveth heer that al estatis daunce,   *Understand*
Seth what ye be and what is your nature: *See*
Mete unto wormys, nat ellis in substaunce.   *Meat; nothing else*
565   And have this myrrour ay in remembraunce   *always*
Before your mynde aboven al thyng:

To all estatis a trew resemblaunce
That wormes foode is ende of your lyvyng.

What is mannys liff but a countenaunce   *outward show*
570   Or as a puff of wynde that is transitorie,
As may be weel perceived bi this Daunce?
Therfore ye that reden this storye,
Keepe thentent in your memorye,   *the intent*
And it shal steer yow into gostly liff,   *spiritual life*
575   Teschewe peyn and come unto glorie,   *To avoid punishment*
And be your socour in al gostly stryff.   *help; spiritual struggle*

fol. 50v Be nat afferd this scriptur in tyme of pley   *afraid; pleasure*
In your mynde to revolve and reede.   *contemplate*
For trust trewly ye shal nevir the sonner deye,   *sooner*
580   But it shal cause yow synne for to dreede;
The which refusid, ye shal have gret meede.   *reward*
Therfore among have mynde on this lettir   *continually*
And use vertu, prayer, and almesse deede,   *charitable deeds*
And than I dar sey ye shal doon the bettir.

Explicit

OTHER LATE MEDIEVAL POEMS ABOUT DEATH

JOHN LYDGATE, "DEATH'S WARNING TO THE WORLD" (DIMEV 4905)

Syth that ye lyste to be my hostesse,	*Since; desire*
And in youre book to set myne image,	*book; my image*
Wake and remembre wyth grete avyses	*much consideration*
Howe my custome and mortall usage	
5 Ys for to spare nether olde ne yonge of age,	*nor*
But that ye nowe in thys world levyng	*living*
Afore be redy, or I my belle rynge.	*Be ready in advance, lest*

My dredefull spere full sharpe ygrounde,	*spear; very; honed*
Doth yow now lo here thys manace:	*you; threaten*
10 Armoure ys noonne that may withstande hys wounde,	*There is no armor*
Ne whomme I merke, ther ys non other grace	*whom I mark; no other*
To fynde respite of day, oure, ne space;	*reprieve; brief while*
Wherfore be redy and have no dysdeyne,	*Therefore; take no offence*
Yef of my commyng, the tyme be uncerteyne.	*Although*

15 Remembre, youre yeres almost past be;	
Of flowryng age lasteth but a seasoun;	*age of flourishing (i.e., youth)*
By procese at ey men may see	*In due course with their own eyes*
Beauté declyneth, hys blossom falleth doune.	*falls down*
And lytyll and lytyll by successioun	*by degrees*
20 Cometh croked elde unwarly crepyng,	*old age; unexpectedly*
With hys patent purely thanne manysshyng.[1]	

The gospell byddeth than wake and pray,	*bids them*
For of my commyng there is no tyme sette;	
Ne no manne knoweth whenne he shall dye,	*knows; die*
25 Ne agayne myne entré no gate may be shutte;	*against my entry*
Twene me and kynde there is a knot unknyt,	*Between; creation; loosened*
That in thys worlde every lyvyng creature	*living*
For Adams synne must dye of nature.	*sin; naturally*

---

[1] *With his patent powerfully threatening them (i.e., people whom old age visits)*

Thyese balades that thus ben wrytenne here be tak owte   *are written; are taken*
of the book of Johnne Lucas and sayde to the peple that
shall see thys lytell tretyse in tyme to come.

	O worldely folke, averteth and take hede	*take notice*
30	What vengeaunce and punicyoun	*punishment*
	God shall take after ye be dede	*you are dead*
	For youre trespas and youre transgressioun,	
	Whiche breke his preceptys ayenst al reasoun;	*against all reason*
	Ye have foryete how with his precious bloode,	*have forgotten; blood*
35	Yow for to save, he dyed onne the Roode.	*In order to save you; the Cross*

	Lerne for to dye and hate for to lye;	*hate to live [in sin]*
	Of olde offens amonge have repentaunce;	*sins constantly*
	And, to eschewe al scorne and mokry	*mockery*
	Ayenst vyces, do almes and penaunce,	*Against; do (perform)*
40	And for to have moste souveranly plesaunce	*highest pleasure*
	To sewe the pathes of oure lorde Jhesu,	*show (reveal)*
	Trewe exampeleré of grace and vertew,	*True exemplar; virtue*

	Whyche for oure sake and oure redempcioun	*Who*
	And for oure love was nayled to a tre,	*tree (i.e., the Cross)*
45	Suffred payne and passioun,	*pain*
	And nothyng asketh of hygh ne lowe degree	
	Recompensed ayenwarde for to be,	
	But that we sette all holy oure ententes	
	For to fulfyll Hys commaundmentys.[1]	

50	Wherby menne may, that prudent be and wyse,	
	The joyes clayme, whiche be eternall,	*claim the joys*
	And entré in to paradyse,	*again*
	From whens Adam had a fall;	*whence*
	To whyche place above celestiall	
55	O Cryste Jhesu, so brynge us to that glory,	
	Whyche by thy dethe had the victory. Amen.	

---

[1] Lines 46–49: *And asked for no kind / Of compensation, whether great or small, / Other than that we fully place our intention / Into fulfilling His commandments*

"THREE MESSENGERS OF DEATH" (DIMEV 5387)

Her biginneth a tretis — *Here; treatise*
Of threo messagers of deth, iwis. — *three; certainly*

The mon that is of wommon ibore, — *man; woman; born*
His lyf nis heere but a throwe. — *is not; little while*
So seith Job us heer bifore — *says*
Al in a bok that I wel knowe.

5   He hedde is muynde al of his deth; — *occupied his mind entirely with*
Wel sore he con grone and grunte, — *can groan (complain)*
And seide his lyf nas bote a breth. — *was not but a breath*
Heer mou we none stounde stunte. — *never tarry briefly*

From Deth may no mon be fre; — *free*
10   For his righte wol he not lete. — *will; surrender*
Now beoth ther messagers thre — *there are; three*
Among monkuynde for to meete: — *With mankind; clash*

Aventures, Seeknesse, and Elde, — *Chance (Accident), Sickness; Old Age*
Theos beoth messagers of Deth. — *These are*
15   To hem we moten us alle yelde — *must; yield*
And louten ther ur maystres geth.[1]

Whon Deth cometh that is so derk, — *dismal (wicked)*
Ther may no mon him withstonde;
I take witnesse on a noble clerk — *appeal for reference to*
20   That wrot theos vers with his honde: — *wrote; hand*

Mors vetat athletas;
Ego mortis nescio metas;
Inter res letas
Caveat sibi quelibet etas.[2]

---

[1] *And bow there where our masters go*

[2] Lines 21–24: *Death is an obstacle to wrestlers; / I do not know the bounds of Death; / In happy times, / Let him beware, regardless of his age*

25	Deth, he sleth this kempes kene,	*slays; stalwart wrestlers*
	And kynges in heore worthly won,	*their splendid abode*
	Riche and pore alle bidene,	*together*
	Yong ne old, spareth he non.	*spares*
	Ther is on of this messagers	*one*
30	That of no mon wol take mede.	*reward*
	He is so hardi and so fers	*brave; fierce*
	That alle men of him have drede.	*fear*
	The messager hette Aventours.	*is named Chance (Accident)*
	Ageynes him may beo no strif;	
35	Whon he cometh to a monnes hous,	*man's*
	He taketh bothe hosebonde and the wyf.	*both husband*
	He taketh the child in his cradel,	
	Theih he beo bot o niht old;	*Though; but one night*
	The kniht and horse in his sadel	*saddle*
40	I-armed, beo he never so bold.	
	Of him beo uche mon iwar	*each; vigilant*
	And mak him clene, ar he beo hent.	*himself guiltless, lest he be snatched*
	For ther nis no geynchar	*is no escape*
	Whon Aventures cometh to tornement.	*challenge*
45	Mony mon lihth in dedly synne	*lies; sin*
	And weneth that he beo not veyghe,	*believes; doomed*
	And Aventures cometh with his ginne	
	And hontuth til he have his preye.	*hunts; has*
	In dedly sunne he is ifounde	*sin; found*
50	Withouten schrift and repentaunce.	*confession*
	He geth in to helle grounde,	*goes; grounds of hell*
	Ther to suffre his penaunce.	
	Seint Poul bit we schulden awake —	*bids; should*
	This clerkes witen as wel as I —	*know*
55	That we schulden us clene make	*make ourselves pure (i.e., confess)*
	And of ur sinnes ben sori.	*our; be repentant*
	And bote we ben, we schulen abugge;[1]	
	Ther schal no pledur plede that.	*advocate plead*

---

[1] *And unless we be repentant, we shall pay the price*

Ther God us fynt, he wol us jugge —   *finds; judge*
60   Nou uche mon be war bi that.   *Now each; mindful of that*

For Aventures wol come as a thef   *will; thief*
Be nihte, whon mon ben aslepe,   *By night*
And taken awey that him is leef.   *that which pleases him*
Nou awaketh, that ye mowe him kepe.   *you may; ward off*

65   Another messager ther is
Of Deth, whon Crist wol him sende —   *wishes to send him*
Seknesse — ic have iherd ar this   *heard before*
The messager is swithe hende.   *exceedingly skilled (crafty)*

Whon Seeknesse cometh to a mon,
70   He may bewar yif he is sleih,   *clever*
And greithen his in, yif that he con,   *make ready his home; can*
And thenken that Deth is swithe neih.   *think; very nigh*

For Seknesse cometh apertely;   *openly (without hesitation)*
He ne dareth not in his den.   *lurk; lair*
75   Hit is ure lordes cortesy   *our*
With Seknesse for to warne men.

Mony men, whon that heo beoth seke,   *they are sick*
To Jhesu Crist a clepen and criye   *call; cry*
And to his mylde mooder eke   *his gentle mother also*
80   And sigge: "Now thou help, Marie!   *say*

Yif that we mowe be sound and save   *may; safe*
And kevere, that we mowen habben ur hele,   *delivered; may have; salvation*
Al the good that we have
For Godes love we wolen hit dele."   *distribute [as alms]*

85   We love wel God in al ur thought
While we beo seeke and sore smerte.   *are sick; in pain*
Whon we beoth hol, we loven him nought,   *are healthy; love*
He nis no lengor in ure herte.   *longer; our*

Cum fero langorem,
90   *Fero religionis amorem;*
Expers langoris
Non sum memor huius amoris.[1]

---

[1] Lines 89–92: *When I endure sickness, / I bear love of religion. / Lacking sickness, / I am not mindful of this love*

Of Crist ne taketh he non hede;
He nath no more with him to donne.   *Nor has; to do*
95   To thonken him for his goode dede;   *thank*
He thenketh no more theruppone.   *thinks*

Suche men ben ofte alone ilet   *are; left*
To pleye as the foul in the lift,   *bird; air*
Til Aventures have with hem met,
100   Bereveth hem bothe hosel and schrift.   *Deprives; Eucharist; confession*

Men oughten holden up bothe heore honden   *their hands*
To God, while heo ben hol and feere,   *they are hale and hearty*
To sende, whon he wol hem fonden,   *wishes; to find*
Seeknesse to ben heore messagere.   *be; their*

105   Seynt Poul seith, ure Lordes kniht,
In a pistel that he wrot,   *epistle*
That he was strengest and most of miht   *strongest; might*
Whon God him with Seknesse smot.

Now ichulle siggen ou of Elde;   *I wish to speak to you*
110   Of messagers he is the thridde.   *third*
Whon monnes hed biginneth to elde,   *When man's attention (head); to grow old*
He may not do but beodes bidde.   *recite prayers*

And he leoneth uppon his crucche,   *leans*
Whon Deth him bekneth, comen he mot.   *beckons; must*
115   Hit helpeth nought thauh he grucche,   *though he grumbles*
He schal withstonde never a fot.   *not even a foot*

Also fareth Elde as doth a sweyn   *behaves; servant*
That stondeth at his lordes yate   *gate*
And mot not wenden in ageyn,   *may not walk*
120   For the porter that is therate.   *Because of; right there*

For no yiftes that he may yiven,   *gifts; give*
Ne feire wordes that he mai speken,   *fair; speak*
He worth out atte yate idriven;   *shall at [the] gate be driven out*
Anon the yate for him is steken.   *shut*

125   Yif a mon may libben heer   *If; live here*
And ben of pouwer for to go   *be; power; to reach*
The elde of fourescore yer,   *old age; eighty years*
That other del is serwe and wo.   *remainder [of his life]; sorrow*

For hose wole his lyf beholde   *he who wishes to*
130   From biginnynge to the ende,

Wel ofte may his herte colde　　　　　　　　　　　*grow cold [with fear]*
That not what wey he schal wende.　　　　　　　　*does not know; way*

Wel we witen we schule be ded;　　　　　　　　　　*know; shall*
Ur dwellyng her nis bote a while.　　　　　　　　*here is not but*
135　Jhesu Crist us wisse and rede,　　　　　　　　*instructs; teaches*
That never the Fend ne do us gyle.　　　　　*[So] that the Devil never can deceive us*

Nou is Deth a wonder thing　　　　　　　　　　　　*Now; strange*
And grislich for to thenken on.　　　　　　　　　*horrible; think*
He ne spareth emperour ne kyng,　　　　　　　　　*spares*
140　Ne pope for al the good that he con.　　　　　　*knows*

Wher ben heo that biforen us weoren,　　　　　*are they who were before us*
That weore so mihti in heore deden?　　　　　　*their deeds*
Houndes ladden and haukes beeren　　　　　　　　*led; hawks bore*
An hontyng heighe uppon heore steeden?　　*hunting loftily; their steeds*

145　Deth hit hath hem al byraft,　　　　　　　　*it; them all snatched away*
With hem ther nis no more pley.　　　　　　　　　*action (activity)*
And al that bereth monnes schaft,　　　　　　　*bear human shape*
Schal go that ilke selve wey.　　　　　　　　　　*very same*

Uche mon may be sore aferd　　　　　　　　　　　　*afraid*
150　That hath a soule for to save,
Whon he geth bi a chirche yerd　　　　　　　　　*goes; yard*
And seoth wher dede men beth igrave.　　　　*sees; dead; are buried*

Riche men habbeth riche stones,　　　　　　*have elaborate gravestones*
That alle men mouwe biholde:　　　　　　　　　　*So that; may*
155　Therunder liggeth foule bones,　　　　　　　　*lie*
Ibeddet al in cloth of colde.[1]

Wel pore halle ther is imaked　　　　　　　　　*Very poor; made*
Withouten eny worldes winne;　　　　　　　　　*any worldly wealth*
Save a clout, men beoth al naked,
160　Whon Deth is comen, icast therinne.[2]

The halle roof is cast ful lowe,
Ther beoth none chaumbres wyde;　　　　　　　　*are no*
Me may reche the helewowe　　　　　　　*Men; touch (reckon); end wall*
And the wal on uche a syde.　　　　　　　　　　*each*

---

[1] *Fully provided with a cold cloth (marked by the chill of death, i.e., a winding sheet)*

[2] Lines 159–60: *When Death has come, men are cast therein / all naked, other than a shroud*

165	Heore bodies that weoren so softe ibathen	*Their; were so gently bathed*
	And ibrought forth with mete and drynk,	*reared*
	Ther hit schal crepe ful of mathen —	*creep; maggots*
	In al this world nis foulore stynk.	*there is no fouler*

	A mon that such a bodi seye,	*sees*
170	Whon wormes hit hath thorwsouht,	*dug through*
	He oughte wepe with his eye	*weep*
	And evere have him in his thouht.	*always; thought*

	Ther nis non so luyte ne so muche,	*is no one so slender or so big*
	That is of flesch, blod, and bon,	
175	That we ne schule ben alle suche,	*all the same*
	Whon we ben huled under a ston.	*are kept*

	Hou may eny mon be proud	*How; any*
	For eny thing that he may gete,	*get*
	Whon he is huled under a schroud,	*kept; shroud*
180	That thing that is wormes mete?	*meat*

	That thing that is ur moste fo —	*our greatest foe*
	Therfore we don a gret folye	*do; folly*
	To love that thing that doth us wo,	*causes us woe*
	And eke ur dedliche enemye.	*also [is] our mortal*

185	Yif a mon may libben heer	*live here*
	As longe as dude Matussalé —	*did Methuselah*
	Nighene hundred and nyne and sixti yer	*Nine*
	So longe on eorthe livede he —	

	That nis not also muche tyme	*is not as much*
190	Ageynes the tyme that cometh afterward	*In comparison with*
	As fro the sonne rysing to prime:	*the time between six and nine a.m.*
	To sunfol men that is ful hard.	*sinful; difficult*

	That, I schal seye, nou taketh kepe,	*So that; take heed*
	I drawe to witnesse seynt Austyn:	*Augustine*
195	That a mon schal more wepe	*weep*
	That damned is to helle pyn	*pains of hell*

	Then is water under the sonne,	*Than [there is]; sun*
	And he wepe uche day a ter.	*each; tear*
	Aviseth ow now, yif that ye cunne,	*Contemplate; if you can*
200	And doth that ye ne come not ther.	*act so that*

| | A mon that dampned is to helle, | |
| | His peyne may not ben forbought, | *punishment; redeemed* |

Ac endeles he schall ther dwelle;   *But rather*
Almes dede helpeth him nouht.   *Alms-giving; not at all*

205   Thei alle men that libbeth nouthe   *Even if; live now*
Weore prestes masses to synge,   *Were to sing priests' Masses*
And duden al that thei ever couthe,   *did; could*
Ne scholden him of pyne bringe.[1]

That ilke soule that is dryven   *same; driven*
210   With fendes in atte helle yate,   *fiends; hell's gate*
And his juggement be him yiven,   *is given to him*
To bidde merci hit is to late.   *it; too*

Hevene hit is ure heritage,   *it (Heaven); our inheritance*
To ure bihove hit is diht.   *sake; prepared*
215   We han do feuté and homage   *have done fealty*
To ure Lord, as hit is riht.   *our; right*

Synful mon, yif that he falleth,   *falls*
Arys up and mak thi pees,   *make your peace*
And cum to Crist, whon that he calleth   *calls*
220   To joye that is endeles.

He that is almihti kyng,   *almighty*
That heighe sitteth in Trinité,   *sits aloft*
Graunt us alle his blessyng.
Amen, Amen, par charité.   *by charity*

---

[1] *[That] would not deliver him from punishment (see note)*

"A Warning Spoken

by the Soul of a Dead Person" (DIMEV 3624)

Here is a good counseil for synful men to take heede to while
thei ben in this liif.   *they are; life*

    Mi leeve liif that lyvest in welthe,   *dear beloved; lives; prosperity*
    In mete, and drinke, and fayr schroud,   *food; garment*
    In richesse, honour, and in bodili helthe,
    Loke therfore thou be nought proud.   *so that*

5   But whanne thou art in thi beste lekinge,   *when; delight*
    Have mynde sum tyme, I thee rede,   *Remember; instruct*
    How foule thou schalt lie and stynke   *shall*
    A litil after that thou art deed.   *dead*

    I was ful fair, now am I foul;   *all*
10   My faire fleisch bigynneth forto stinke;   *flesh*
    Wormis fynden at me greet prow: *in me great benefit*
    I am hire mete; I am hire drinke.   *their food*

    I ligge wounded in a clout;   *lie wound; shroud*
    In boordis narwe I am nailid.   *narrow boards; nailed*
15   Allas, that evere I was proud.
    Now alle mi freendis ben to me failid.   *have failed me*

    In mi riggeboon bredith an addir kene;   *spine grows; cruel adder*
    Min eiyen dasewyn swithe dymme;[1]
    Mi guttis roten; myn heer is grene;   *guts rot; hair; colorless*
20   Mi teeth grennen swithe grymme.[2]

    Mi bodi that sumtyme was so gay   *beautiful*
    Now lieth and rotith in the grounde;   *lies; rots*
    Mi fair hed is al now goon awai,   *head; away*
    And I stynke foulere than an hounde.

---

[1] *My eyes swiftly grow faint and dim*

[2] *My teeth are swiftly bared in a fierce snarl*

25 Mi faire feet, mi fyngris longe, *fingers*
Myn eiyen, myn eeren, and mi lymes alle *eyes; ears; limbs*
Noon wil now with other honge, *Not at all; hold together*
But everech wole from other falle.[1] *fingers*

I rede every man that wiis wil be, *instruct; wise*
30 Take kepe herof that I have seid. *heed of that which*
Thanne may he sikir of heven be *Then; sure (bound) to obtain heaven*
Whanne he schal in erthe be laid. *When*

---

[1] *But thoroughly wish to fall from one another*

"A MIRROR FOR YOUNG LADIES AT THEIR TOILET" (DIMEV 3454)

C'est le myrroure pur lez jofenes dames a regardir
aud maytyne pur lour testes bealment adressere.[1]   *(see note)*

Maist thou now be glade, with all thi fresh aray,   *May; adornment*
One me to loke that wyl dystene thi face.[2]   *To look on me, who will discolor your face*
Rew one thy self and all thi synne uprace.   *Repent of your sins; root out*
Sone shalte thu flytte and seche another place.   *Soon; you flee; seek*
5 **S**horte is thy sesoun here, thogh thou go gay.   *season; although; are fashionably dressed*

O maset wriche, I marke thee with my mace.   *frightened wretch; [ceremonial] club*
Lyfte up thy eye, beholde now, and assay.   *test your strength [in combat]*
Vche loke one me aught to put thee in affray;   *Each look on; frighten you*
I wyll not spare thee, for thou arte my pray.   *are my prey*
10 **T**ake hede, and turne fro synne while thu hast space.   *from sin; time*

O thought, wel thee heele to this, thaught ye say nay;[3]
My tyme muste nedis comme as I manace,   *must come; threaten*
Ne lengthe one lyfe may lepe oute of my lace.[4]   *(see t-note)*
I smyte, I sle, I woll graunte no mane grace.   *smite; slay; will; no man*
15 **A**ryse, awake, amend here while thou may.   *correct yourself*

---

[1] *This is the mirror for young ladies to behold in the morning for arranging their hair beautifully*
[2] *To look on me, who will discolor your face*
[3] *O thought, take proper refuge in this, although you say no*
[4] *Nor can [even] one lifetime leap from my snare (i.e., death is unavoidable)*

"THE RESSONING BETUIX DETH AND MAN,"
ASCRIBED TO ROBERT HENRYSON (DIMEV 4000)

Deth

	O mortall man, behold, tak tent to me,	*pay heed*
	Quhilk sowld thy myrrour be baith day and nicht.	*Which should; both; night*
	All erdly thing that evir tuik lyfe mon die.	*earthly; was alive may die*
	Paip, empeirur, king, barroun, and knycht,	*Pope; baron*
5	Thocht thay be in thair riall stait and hicht,	
	May not ganestaind quhen I pleiss schute the derte.[1]	
	Waltownis, castelis and towris nevir so wicht	*Walled towns; towers; sturdy*
	May nocht risist quhill it be at his herte.	*while; heart*

Man

	Now quhat art thow that biddis me thus tak tent	*what; bids; pay heed*
10	And mak ane mirrour day and nicht of thee,	*a mirror*
	Or with thy dert I sowld richt soir repent?	*Lest; should deeply*
	I trest trewly of that thuw sall sone lie.	*about that you shall readily be lying*
	Quhat freik on fold sa bald dar manniss me	*person on earth so bold dare threaten*
	Or with me fecht outhir on fute or horss?	*fight whether; foot*
15	Is non so wicht or stark, in this cuntré,	*no one; brave; fierce; region*
	But I sall gar him bow to me on forss.	*shall make; by force*

Deth

	My name at me forsuith, sen that thow speiris,	*to me in truth, since; ask*
	Thay call me Deid, suthly I thee declair,	*They; Death, truthfully*
	Calland all man and woman to thair beiris	*Calling; their biers*
20	Quhenevir I pleiss, quhat tyme, quhat place, or quhair.	*please; where*
	Is nane sa stowt, sa fresche, nor yit sa fair,	*no one; so mighty; youthful*
	Sa yung, sa ald, sa riche, nor yit sa peur,	*old; poor*
	Quhairevir I pass, owthir lait or air,	*Wherever; whether late; early*
	Mon put thame haill on forss undir my cure.[2]	

---

[1] Lines 5–6: *Although they may be in their royal and lofty [social] estate, / [They] may not put up a fight when I please to shoot the dart*

[2] *[But he] may put himself wholly by force under my care (see note)*

Man

25	Sen it is so that nature can so wirk	*Since; true; work*
	That yung and awld with riche and peure mon die,	*old; poor; may*
	In my yowtheid allace I wes full irk.	*youth alas; stubborn*
	Cuwld not tak tent to gyd and governe me,	*Could not pay heed; guide*
	Ay gude to do, fra evill deids to fle,	*Always good; from; deeds; flee*
30	Trestand ay yowtheid wold with me abyde,	*Trusting always; would; abide*
	Fulfilland evir my sensualitie	*appetite*
	In deidly syn and specialy in pryd.	*mortal; especially; pride*

Deth

	Thairfoir repent and remord thy conscience.	*fill with remorse*
	Think on thir wordis I now upoun thee cry:	*these words*
35	O wrechit man, O full of ignorance,	*wretched*
	All thi plesance thow sall richt deir aby.	*delight; purchase at a great price*
	Dispone thy self and cum with me in hy	*Make arrangements for; quickly*
	Adderis, askis, wormis meit for to be.	*Adders', lizards', worms' meat*
	Cum quhen I call, thow ma me not denny,	*may; deny*
40	Thocht thow war paip, empriour, and king al thre.	*Though; were pope; all three*

Man

	Sen it is swa fra thee I may nocht chaip,	*Since; so from; escape*
	This wrechit warld for me heir I defy	*wretched world; here I disavow*
	And to thee, Deid, to lurk under thi caip,	*Death; cower; cape*
	I offer me with hairt rycht humly,	*offer myself; heartfelt; humbly*
45	Beseiking God the divill myne ennemy	*Beseeching; [that] the devil*
	No power haif my sawill till assay.	*has my soul to attack*
	Jesus, on thee with peteous voce I cry	*piteous*
	Mercy un me to haif on Domisday.	*on; have; Judgment Day*

Finis quod Hendersone	*The end. By Henryson*

POEMS IN THE
DANCE OF DEATH TRADITION

"THE DAWNCE OF MAKABRE" (DIMEV 4104)

O ye al whilk that by me cummes and gothe,	*who; come and go; (see note)*
Attende and behold this warldes vanyté.	*world's vanity*
To lyke symylitude, be ye lefe or lothe,	*alike appearance; loving or loathing*
Sal ye cum for al your warldly prosperité.	*Shall; come worldly*
5 Thinne abydyng here is in no stabilité:	*Thine; permanence*
Yowthe sal passe and his verteus swage	*shall; diminish*
Deth sal cum and lyfe sal hafe passage.	*have*
Why art thou so sett in prowde elacyon,	*arrogance*
And with the desyres of worldly covetyse?	*covetousness*
10 Why in wrathe has thou syche distrubacoun	*disturbance*
With invyos swellyng of gret malyce?	*envious*
Glotony usyng wher les wald suffyce?	*Gluttonous; less would*
Brynnyng in slomer and slawly in corayge,	*Burning in slumber; slothful in desire*
Or to be lycheros for al syche life has sone pasayge.	*lecherous; soon*
15 Thogh gleteryng thou be as byrnysched gold bright,	*glittering; burnished*
None to thee lyke thee semes in lusty purtrature.	*handsome form*
Ilk men byn stowte in his perfyte right,	*These; bold; their*
Enformed with bewtes by nature,	*Developed; beauties*
And with strenth also to fortefye thi fygure.	*strength; their*
20 The day sal cum thou sal out of this warld wende	*shall come; go*
Thi mortal fayte of thee sal make ane ende.	*an end*
Wher is Salomon now with al his prudence,	*Solomon*
Or myghty Sampson, duk invyncybyll,	*Sampson, duke*
Tullyus the retrysciane with al his eloquence,	*Cicero; rhetorician*
25 Or Arystotil in witt moste sensybyll,	*Aristotle*
Or this emprour Octavy mest pessybyll,	*Octavian; most peaceable*
Or swete Jonathas ful amyabyll.	*Jonathan; amiable*
Wher bene thies clerkes so experte in clergy,	*are; learned doctrine*
Thies kynges and prynce myghty and stronge	
30 Al ar thai gone and close with twynkillyng of ane ee.	*buried; an eye*
Of this warldly joy the feste dures not longe.	*worldly; feast endures*
That joy is endyd as a schadow us emonge.	*shadow; among*

Here is no lastyng ese ne no tranquyllité   *ease*
Bot labour, travell, and myche adversyté.   *travail*

35   Remembyr thi selfe — here is no sykyr abydynge,   *secure dwelling*
     And se how this warld is so transitory.
     Thou must departe, here is no long dwellynge
     As Job says in his funerall obsequye,   *sad funeral rites*
     In whos servyse thou may lerne to dye,[1]
40   Whos tretys is a perfyte evydence   *treatise (book); complete*
     To schew what sal be after thine existence.

     O erthly man, why rejoyces thou thee of gudes erthly,   *earthly possessions*
     Sen erthe sal to erth, what is thi cause?   *Since*
     Remembyr thi selfe on ilk syde verely.   *each; truly*
45   No chartyr may help, byll scrow, ne clawse,[2]
     Thine abydyng here is bot a lytel pawse   *pause*
     It vanysches away and that hastely   *quickly*
     As teches experience dayly.   *experience teaches [us] daily*

     We that wer sum tyme in this wardles passayge   *world's passage*
50   War myghty strong and replete in ryches   *Were*
     Into powdyr we sal fall, be we never so sayge,   *powder; never so wise; (see note)*
     Of wardly joy syche is the progresse.   *such*
     O barayne saule that is so witles,   *barren soul*
     That in the lyfes space cannot remembyr
55   Thi selfe, safe that sal be dust ilk membyr.   *except; every limb*

     Why is thi hert so sett in gladnes?
     For to wormes mete thou art grathed and made,   *worms' food; prepared*
     For erth is gifen to erth in sothfastnes,   *given; in truth*
     The flesche is borne into dethe to be hade.
60   O wretchyd man, whi art thou so glad,
     With syche daliaunce and fals elacoun?   *dalliance; arrogance*
     Why wantes thou reson and discrecoun?   *lack*

     Man, remembyr of the dawnce of makabre,   *Dance of Macabre*
     How lordes spritual and also temperall,   *spiritual and earthly lords*
65   Yowthe nor age ther has none lyberté,   *freedom*
     Bot must passe be Dethes dedes mercyall.   *by Death's merciful deeds*
     Wherfore lat it be oft in thi memoriall,   *let; memory*
     For the tyme sal aproche hence for to wende   *to go*
     And to a lyke semblande be broght to ende.   *semblance*

---

[1] *By whose example you may learn to die well*

[2] *No charter will help, nor receipt, nor (legal) clause*

70   When Deth sal smyte thee with his mercyal darte,   *strike (smite); merciful*
        By paynes strong throghe thi hert rote,   *heart's root*
        Mynysteryng the poyntes of his sore arte,   *Administering; activities; painful*
        No help ne socour than nedes to mote.[1]
        Resembyl this fygure, ther is none other bote   *remedy*
75   And thi reward hafe, owther gode or yll,   *have; either*
        When the tyme cummes *ite venite* to fulfyll.   *come and go*

        Who sum ever it be that by this cummes and gothe,
        Stande and behold this litterall scripture
        And it se and over rede, be thou lefe or lothe,   *willing or unwilling*
80   Thi wepyng teres fast sched in gode ure.   *good fortune*
        Thou art now as I was in warldly fygure;   *worldly form*
        I was as thou art, sum tyme be dayes olde.   *by*
        O pray ye al for me, I pray yow a thowsand-folde.   *ask*

---

[1] *No help or comfort then is needed*

"CAN YE DANCE THE SHAKING OF THE SHEETS" (DIMEV 956)

A dolfull daunce and song of death
Intituled: the shakeing of the sheetes

Canne yea dance the shakinge of the sheetes,   *(see note)*
     A daunce that everie man most dooe?
Can yea trime it up with daintie sweetes,
     And everie thinge that longs there too?   *belongs*
5   Make readie then your winding sheete,
And see how yea canne besturre youre feete,
For Death is the man that all must meete.

Bringe away the beggar and the king,
     And everie man in his degree;
10   Bring away both ould and yongest thinge;
     Come all to Death and follow me —
The courtier with his loftie lookes,
The lawier with his learned bookes,   *lawyer*
And the banker with his beating hookes.   *(see note)*

15   Marchantes that make your mart in France,   *business (market)*
     In Italie, and all about,
Know you not that you and I must daunce,
     With both our heeles wrapt in a clout?   *a [burial] cloth*
What meane you to make your houses gay
20   And I must take the tenant away,
And digge for your sakes the clods of clay?   *(i.e., a grave)*

Thinke on the solempe syses last,   *solemn assizes*
     How sodenlie in Oxfordshire   *suddenly; (see note)*
I came and made the judges agast,
25   And justices that did appear,
And tooke both Bell and Baram away,   *(see note)*
And manie a worthie man that day,
And all their bodies brought to clay.

Thinke you I dare not come in scooles,   *schools*
30   Where all the cunninge clarkes be most?   *clerics*

85

Take not I away both wise and fooles?
      And am not I in everie coast?
Assure youreselves noe creature can
Make Death afraid of any man,
35   Or know my comminge where or when.

And you that are busie-headed fooles   *busy-headed (distracted)*
      To brawle for everie peltinge straw,   *brawl; worthless*
Know yea not that I have readie tooles
      To cut away youre craftie law?
40   And you that foolishly buy and sell,
And thinke you make your market well,
Must daunce with Death wheresoever you dwell.

Where be they that make their leases stronge,
      And joyne about them land to land?
45   Doe yea acount to live soe longe,   *expect*
      To have all the world come to your hand?
Noe, foolish nowell, for all thy pence   *ne'er-do-well; money*
This night thy soule must sure goe hence —
Then whoe shall toile for thy defence?

50   And you that leane on your ladies lappes,
      And lay your heades upon her knee,
Doe you thinke to play with bewties pappes,   *beauties' breasts*
      And not to come and daunce with me?
Noe, faith, fair laddes and ladies all,
55   I'le make you come when I do call,
And find you a pipe to dance withall.

Pryd must have a prittie sheete, I see,   *Pride; pretty*
      For properly he learnes to daunce,
Come away, my wanton wench to me
60   As gallantlie as your eye doth glance;
And all good fellowes that swash and flash   *swagger*
In reds and yellows of revell dash,   *revelry*
I warrant you neede not be soe rash.

For I cane quicklie coole you all,
65   How hot or stout soever you be,
Both high and lowe, both great and small,
       I nought doe feare your highe degree.
The ladie faire, the beldam ould,   *old grandmother*
The champion stout, the souldier bould,
70   Must all with me to erthie mould.   *soil*

Take time therefore while it is lent,
    Prepare youreselves with me to daunce,
Forget mee not, your lives lament —
    I come oft-times by soden chance.   *sudden*
75   Be readie therefore, watch and pray
That when my minstrell pypes his play
Yea may to heaven daunce readie way.

    finis   *end*
    Thomas Hill

Nec pictura decus pompam luxumque relegat,
In que choris nostris ducere festa monet.

¶ Doctor loquitur
Discite vos choream cuncti qui cernitis istam
Quantum prosit honor gaudia divitie;
5   Tales estis enim matina morte futuri
Qualis in effigie mortua turba vocat.

¶ Le docteur
O, creature raisonnable,
Qui desires vie eternelle,
Tu as cy doctrine notable
10   Pour bien finer vie mortelle.
La danse macabre s'appelle
Que chascun a danser apprant.
A homme et femme est mort naturelle;
Mort n'espargne petit ne grant.

¶ Le docteur
15   En ce mirouer chascun puet lire
Qu'il le convient ainsi danser.
Cilz est eureux qui bien s'i mire;
La mort le vif fait avancier.
fol. 1v   Tu vois les plus grans commancier,
20   Car il n'est nul que mort ne fiere.
C'est piteuse chose y penser:
Tout est forgié d'une matiere.

¶ Le mort au pape
Vous qui vives certainement
Quoy qu'il tarde ainsi danserez.
25   Mais quant? Dieu le scet seulement.
Advisies comment vous ferez.
Damp pape, vous commancerez.
Comme le plus digne seigneur,

THE DANSE MACABRE, TRANSLATION BY ELIZAVETA STRAKHOV

The painting does not reject glory, pomp, and indulgence
It begs us to lead into these festivities with our dances.

¶ The Teacher speaks
You, all you who behold that dance,
Learn how great is the profit of honor, joy, riches;
5   For this is how you shall be in the morning with Death,
Like the ones in dead effigy whom the mob summons.

¶ The Doctor
O, creature endowed with reason,
You who long for eternal life,
You have before you an important precept
10   For properly ending your mortal life.
It is called the *Danse macabre*,
Which everyone learns to dance.
Death is natural to men and women;
Death spares neither the lowly nor the lofty.

¶ The Doctor
15   In this mirror everyone can read
That he must dance like this.
Happy is the man who can see himself in it well;
Death makes the living come forward.
You see the loftiest take the first step,
20   For there is no one whom Death does not strike.
It is a pitiable thing to consider here:
Everyone is fashioned from the same material.

¶ Death to the Pope
You who are alive assuredly
Sooner or later will dance like this.
25   But when? Only God knows.
Consider what you will do.
Lord Pope, you will begin.
As the most venerable suzerain,

En ce point honnoré serez:
30   Aux grans maistres est deu l'onneur.

        ¶ Le pape
        Hee, fault il que la danse maine
        Le premier, qui suis dieu en terre?
        J'ay eu dignité souveraine
        En l'esglise comme Saint Pierre,
35   Et, comme aultre, mort me vient querre.
        Encor point morir ne cuidasse,
        Mais la mort a tous maine guerre.
        Peu vault honnour qui si tost passe.

        ¶ Le mort
        Et vous, le nompareil du monde,
40   Prince et seigneur, grant emperierre,
fol. 2r Laissier fault la pomme d'or ronde,
        Armes, ceptre, timbre, baniere.
        Je ne vous laire pas d'arriere.
        Vous ne povez plus seignorir;
45   J'enmaine tout — c'est ma maniere.
        Les filz Adam fault tous morir.

        ¶ L'empereur
        Je ne scay devant qui j'appelle
        De la mort, qu'ainsi me demaine.
        Armer me fault de pic, de pelle,
50   Et d'un linseul; ce m'est grant paine.
        Sus tous ay eu honneur mondaine,
        Et morir me fault pour tout gaige.
        Et qu'est ce de mortel demaine?
        Les grans ne l'ont pas davantaige.

        ¶ Le mort
55   Vos faites l'esbay, ce semble,
        Cardinal — sus legierement,
        Suyvons les autres tous ensemble.
        Riens n'y vault esbayssement.
        Vous avez vescu haultement
60   Et eu honneurs a grans devis:
        Prenez en gré l'esbatement.
        Es grans honneurs se pert l'advis.

fol. 2v ¶ Le cardinal
        J'ay bien cause de m'esbahir
        Quant je me voy de si pres prins.
65   La mort m'est venue envair:

<blockquote>
You will be honored in this regard:
</blockquote>

30   Honor is owed to great lords.

¶ The Pope

Ah, must I, who am God on earth,
Lead the dance first?
I had sovereign power
In the church like Saint Peter,
35   And, like any other, Death comes to seek me out.
I was not at all expecting to die,
But Death wages war on everyone.
Such fleeting honor is worth little.

¶ Death

And you, peerless on earth,
40   Prince and lord, great emperor,
You must give up the golden orb,
The arms, the scepter, the crest, and the banner.
You I will not leave behind.
You cannot rule any longer;
45   I carry off everything — that's my style.
All Adam's sons must die.

¶ The Emperor

I do not know before whom to appeal
Against Death, who leads me away like this.
I must arm myself with a pick-axe, a shovel,
50   And a shroud; this is extremely hard for me.
I possessed glory on earth above all others,
And dying is all I have to show for it.
And what about mortal dominion?
The lofty do not have it anymore.

¶ Death

55   You act astonished, it seems,
Cardinal — up, quickly now,
Let us follow the others together.
Astonishment is of no use.
You have lived grandly
60   And had all the privileges you wanted:
Enjoy the entertainment.
Good sense gets lost amid great privileges.

¶ The Cardinal

I have good reason to be astonished
When I see myself so cornered.
65   Death has come to attack me:

Plus ne vestiray vair ne gris;
Chappeau rouge et chappe de pris
Me fault laissier a grant destresse.
Je ne l'avoye pas aprins:
70   Toute joye fine en tristesse.

¶ Le mort
Venez, noble roy couronné,
Renommé de force et proesse.
Jadis fustes avironné
De grans pompes, de grant noblesse,
75   Mais maintenant toute haultesse
Laisserez. Vous n'estes pas seul.
Peu aurez de vostre richesse:
Le plus riche n'a q'un linseul.

¶ Le roy
Je n'ay point aprins a danser
80   A danse et notte si sauvage.   *(see note)*
Helas, on puet veoir et penser:
Que vault orgueil, force, lignage?
Mort destruit tout — c'est son usage —
Aussi toust le grant que le mendre.
85   Qui moins se prise, plus est saige;
A la fin fault devenir cendre.

fol. 3r   ¶ Le mort
Patriarche, pour basse chiere
Vous ne povez estre quitté.
Vostre double crois qu'avez chiere
90   Un aultre aura — c'est equité.
Ne penses plus a dignité:
Ja ne serez pape de Romme.
Pour rendre compte estes cité.
Fole esperance deçoit l'omme.

¶ Le patriarche
95   Bien parchoy que mondains honneurs
M'ont deceu, pour dire le voir.
Mes joyes tournent en douleurs,
Et que vault tant d'onneur avoir?
Trop hault monter n'est pas savoir.
100   Haulx estas gastent gens sans nombre,
Mais peu le veulent parcevoir:
A hault monter le fais encombre.

Nevermore will I wear gray squirrel trim;
I must, with great distress, give up
The red hat and costly chasuble.
I had not learned it sooner:
70   All joy ends in sadness.

¶ Death
Come, noble crowned king,
Renowned for might and prowess.
Once upon a time you were surrounded
With great pomp and with great circumstance,
75   But now you leave behind
All grandeur. You are not alone.
You will have little of your riches:
The richest man has but a shroud.

¶ The King
I never did learn to dance
80   To such savage steps and melodies.
Alas, one can look and think:
What good is pride, might, lineage?
Death destroys all — that is its custom —
The lofty along with the lesser.
85   He who esteems himself least is the wiser;
In the end one must turn to ash.

¶ Death
Patriarch, your downcast look
Will not acquit you.
Your double cross, which you have prized,
90   Another will have — fair and square.
Think no more about your prerogatives:
You will never be the pope in Rome.
You are summoned to give account.
Foolish hope deceives men.

¶ The Patriarch
95   I clearly do see that worldly privileges
Have deceived me, to be honest.
My joys turn to sorrows,
And what good is having so much privilege?
Climbing too high is not wise.
100   Lofty estates destroy countless people,
But few are willing to realize that:
The burden weighs heavy on him who climbs high.

¶ Le mort
C'est de mon droit que je vous mainne
A la danse, gent connestable.
105   Les plus fors, comme Charlemaine,
Mort prent — c'est chose veritable.
Riens ne vault chiere espoventable,
Ne forte armeure en cest assault.
D'un cop j'abat le plus estable:
110   Rien n'est d'armée quant mort assault.

fol. 3v   ¶ Le connestable
J'avoye encor entencion
D'assaillir chasteaux, forteresses,
Et mener a subjection
En acquerent honneur, richesses.
115   Mais je voy que toutes proesses
Mort met au bas — c'est grant despit.
Tout luy est un, doulceurs, rudesses;
Contre la mort n'a nul respit.

¶ Le mort
Que vous tires la teste arriere,
120   Archevesque? Tires vous pres.
Avez vous peur c'om ne vous fiere?
Ne doubtes: vous venres apres.
N'est pas tousjours la mort empres?
Tout homme elle suit coste a coste.
125   Rendre convient debtes et prests;
Une fois fault compter a l'oste.

¶ L'archevesque
Las, je ne scay ou regarder,
Tant suis par mort a grant destroit.
Ou fuiray je pour moy garder?
130   Certes qui bien la cognoistroit
Hors de raison jamais n'istroit.
Plus ne gerray en chambre painte;
Morir me convient, c'est le droit.
Quant faire fault, c'est grant contrainte.

fol. 4r   ¶ Le mort
135   Vous qui entre les grans barons
Avez eu renom, chevalier,
Obliez trompettes, clarons,
Et me suyvez sans sommeiller.
Les dames souliez resveillier
140   En faisant danser longue piece.

¶ Death
It is in my purview to lead you
To the dance, noble constable.
105   Death captures the mightiest
Like Charlemagne — that is the truth.
A fierce countenance is of no use,
Nor is strong armor against this attack.
With one blow I strike down the steadiest:
110   Military might is nothing when Death attacks.

¶ The Constable
I still had every intention
Of storming and conquering
Castles and fortresses,
While gaining fame and spoils.
115   But I see that Death lays all
Exploits low — that is a great shame.
Gentleness, violence, it is all the same to it;
No one gains reprieve from Death.

¶ Death
Why do you draw your head back,
120   Archbishop? Draw closer.
Are you afraid you will be struck?
Fear not: you will be next.
Isn't Death always closing in?
It sticks by every man's side.
125   You must render debts and dues;
At a certain point one must settle with the host.

¶ The Archbishop
Alas, I do not know where to look,
Death has me in such dire straits.
Where will I flee to protect myself?
130   Surely nobody who recognized Death
Would ever stray from the right path.
Never more will I lie in a painted chamber;
I must die, it is the law.
When one must do it, it is under great duress.

¶ Death
135   You, knight, who among the lofty barons,
Had much renown,
Forget the trumpets and the clarions
And follow me without drifting off.
You used to rouse the ladies
140   By dancing for a good long while.

A aultre danse fault veillier.
Ce que l'un fait, l'autre despiece.

¶ Le chevalier
Or ay je esté auctorisié
En pluseurs fais, et bien famé
145   Des grans, et des petis prisié,
Avec ce des dames amé,
Ne onques ne fu diffamé
A la court de seigneur notable.
Mais a ce cop suis tout pasmé.
150   Dessoubz le ciel n'a riens estable.

¶ Le mort
Tantost n'aurez vaillent ce pic
Des biens du monde et de nature,
Evesque — de vous il est pic,
Nonobstant vostre prelature.
155   Vostre fait gist en aventure.
De voz subgez fault rendre compte;
A chascun dieu fera droicture.
N'est pas aseur qui trop hault monte.

¶ L'evesque
Le cueur ne me puet resjoir
fol. 4v   Des nouvelles que mort m'aporte.
161   Dieu vouldra de tout compte oir:
C'est ce que plus me desconforte.
Le monde aussi peu me conforte,
Qui tout a la fin desherite;
165   Il retient tout: nul riens n'emporte.
Tout se passe, fors le merite.

¶ Le mort
Avancez vous, gent escuier,
Qui savez de danser les tours.
Lance porties et escu hier,
170   Et huy vous finerez voz jours.
Il n'est rien qui ne preigne cours.
Dansez et pensez de suir;
Vous ne povez avoir secours.
Il n'est qui puisse mort fuir.

¶ L'escuier
175   Puis que mort me tient en ses las,
Au moins que je puisse un mot dire:
Adieu, deduis, adieu, soulas,

Now you must stay up late for a new dance.
What one makes, another breaks.

¶ The Knight
Now I used to be honored
For numerous feats, and well reputed
145   Among the lofty, and prized by the lowly,
And also loved by ladies,
Nor was I ever defamed
At the court of a respected lord.
But by this blow I am knocked out cold.
150   Nothing is stable beneath the heavens.

¶ Death
Soon your worldly and natural wealth
Will not amount to this pick-axe,
Bishop — you don't have a single card to play,
Your prelature notwithstanding.
155   Your fate hangs in the balance.
You should take stock of your subjects;
God will dispense justice to all.
He who climbs too high is not secure.

¶ The Bishop
My heart cannot rejoice
160   In the news brought to me by Death.
God will wish to go over all the accounts:
This is what pains me most.
I can get little comfort too from the world,
Which ultimately dispossesses everyone.
165   It keeps all; no one makes off with anything.
Everything fades, save merit.

¶ Death
Come forward, noble squire,
You who know all the dance steps.
You bore a lance and shield yesterday,
170   And today you will end your days.
There is nothing that does not take its course.
Dance and try to keep up;
No one can help you.
There is no one who can flee Death.

¶ The Squire
175   Since Death holds me tight in its snares,
At the very least let me say a word:
Farewell, pleasure, farewell, solace,

Adieu, dames, plus ne puis rire.
Pensez de l'ame qui desire
180   Reppos; ne vous chaille plus tant
Du corps, qui tous les jours empire.
Tout fault pourrir on ne scet quant.

¶ Le mort
Abbé, venez tost, vous fuyez.
fol. 5r   N'ayez ja la chiere esbaye.
185   Il convient que la mort suyez,
Combien que moult l'avez haye.
Commandez a dieu l'abbaye,
Qui gros et gras vous a norry.
Tost pourrierez a peu d'aye:
190   Le plus gras est premier pourry.

¶ L'abbé
De cecy n'eusse point envie,
Mais il convient le pas passer.
Las, or n'ay je pas en ma vie
Gardé mon ordre sans casser?
195   Gardes vous de trop embrasser,
Vous qui vives au demorant,
Se vous voulez bien trespasser.
On s'advise tart en mourant.

¶ Le mort
Bailli, qui savez qu'est justice
200   Et hault et bas, en mainte guise,
Pour gouverner toute police,
Venez tantost a ceste assise —
Je vous adjourne de main mise —
Pour rendre compte de voz fais
205   A grant juge, qui tout un prise.
Un chascun portera son fais.

¶ Le bailly
He, dieu, vecy dure journee.
De ce cop pas ne me gardoye;
Or est la chance bien tournée.
fol. 5v   Entre juges honneur avoye,
211   Et mort fait ravaler ma joye,
Qui m'a adjourné sans rappel.
Je n'y voy plus ne tour ne voye;
Contre la mort n'a point d'appel.

Farewell, ladies, I can laugh no more.
Think of the soul that longs for
180   Eternal sleep; stop worrying so much
About the body that deteriorates with each passing day.
All must rot eventually.

¶ Death
Abbot, come back at once, you are running away.
Do not look so astonished now.
185   It befits you to follow Death,
Much as you have always hated it.
Commend to God the abbey,
Which has turned you out big and fat.
You will rot quickly with little help:
190   The fattest is the first to rot.

¶ The Abbot
I had no desire for this whatsoever,
But I must take the final step.
Alas, did I not in my life
Keep my vows without breaking them?
195   Keep yourself from grasping too much,
You who live in the time that remains,
If you wish to die well.
It is too late to learn on the deathbed.

¶ Death
Bailiff, you who know what justice is
200   Everywhere, in all its forms,
When it comes to governing all administrations,
Come straightaway before this court —
I serve you with a summons —
To account for your works
205   Before the great judge, who assesses everyone alike.
Each and everyone will bear his burden.

¶ The Bailiff
Oh, God, this is a tough day.
I was not on my guard against this blow;
Now my fortunes have truly changed.
210   I used to be honored among judges,
And Death, who has summoned me
Without right of appeal, casts down my joys.
I see no more moves nor routes to take;
Against Death there are no appeals.

¶ Le mort

215 Maistre, pour vostre regarder
     En hault, ne pour vostre clergie,
     Ne povez la mort retarder.
     Cy ne vault riens astrologie.
     Toute la genealogie
220 D'Adam, qui fut le premier homme,
     Mort prent — ce dit theologie:
     Tous fault morir pour une pomme.

¶ L'astrologien

     Pour science, ne pour degres,
     Ne puis avoir provision,
225 Car maintenent tous mes regrez
     Sont morir a confusion
     Pour finable conclusion.
     Je ne scay riens que plus descrive;
     Je pers cy toute advision.
230 Qui vouldra bien morir bien vive.

¶ Le mort

     Bourgoys, hastes vous sans tarder.
     Vous n'avez avoir ne richesse,
fol. 6r Qui vous puissent de mort garder.
     Se des biens dont eustes largesse
235 Avez bien usé, c'est sagesse.
     D'autruy vient, tout a autruy passe.
     Fol est qui d'amasser se blesse:
     On ne scet pour qui on amasse.

¶ Le bourgoys

     Grant mal me fait si toust laissier
240 Rentes, maisons, cens, monteure,
     Mais povres et riches abaissier
     Tu fais, mort, telle est ta nature.
     Sage n'est pas la creature
     D'amer trop les biens qui demourent
245 Au monde et sont siens par droicture.
     Ceulx qui plus ont plus envis meurent.

¶ Le mort

     Sire chanoine prebendez,
     Plus n'aurez distribucion
     Ne gros; ne vous y attendez.
250 Prenez cy consolacion
     Pour toute retribucion:
     Morir vous convient sans demeure.

¶ Death

215 Master, for all your gazing up
     On high and all your clerkly knowledge,
     You cannot delay Death.
     Astrology is worth nothing here.
     The whole lineage
220 Of Adam, who was the first man,
     Gets taken by Death — so says theology:
     All must die for an apple.

¶ The Astrologer
     Despite knowledge, despite degrees,
     I cannot prepare myself for this,
225 For now I regret nothing more
     Than ending up
     Dying in distress.
     I know nothing that might elucidate it more;
     Here I lose all my sight.
230 May he who wishes to die well live well.

¶ Death
     Burgess, hurry up without delay.
     You have neither wealth nor riches
     That might protect you from Death.
     If you have made proper use of the goods
235 That you had in abundance, that is wise.
     What comes from one all passes to another.
     The fool ruins himself through hoarding:
     One does not know for whom one hoards.

¶ The Burgess
     It pains me greatly to give up rents,
240 Houses, revenues, and belongings so soon,
     But you, Death, cast down
     The poor and the rich, such is your nature.
     No creature is wise to love too much
     The goods that remain
245 In the material world and belong to it by right.
     Those who have more are more loath to die.

¶ Death
     Sir Prebendary,
     No more will you have allocation
     Nor revenue; do not count on it.
250 Take consolation in this
     As sole compensation:
     You must die without delay.

Ja n'y aurez dilacion.
La mort vient qu'on ne garde l'eure.

¶ Le chanoine
255   Cecy gueres ne me conforte.
Prebendez fuz en mainte esglise,
Or est la mort plus que moy forte,
Qui tout enmaine — c'est sa guise.
Blanc surplis et aumuce grise
260   Me fault laissier et a mort rendre.
Que vault gloire si tost bas mise?
A bien morir doit chascun tendre.

¶ Le mort
Marchant, regardez par deça.
Plusiers pays avez cerchié
265   A pié a cheval de pieça.
Vous n'en serez plus empeschié:
Vecy vostre desrain marchié.
Il convient que par cy passez;
De tout soing serez despeschié.
270   Tel convoite qui a assez.

¶ Le marchant
J'ay esté amont et aval
Pour marchander ou je porroye
Par longtemps a pié, a cheval,
Mais maintenent pers toute joye.
275   De tout mon povoir acqueroye,
Or ay je asses; mort me contraint.
Bon fait aler moyenne voye:
Qui trop embrasse peu estraint.

¶ Le mort
Alez, marchant, sans plus rester,
280   Ne faictes ja cy resistence.
Vous n'y povez riens conquester.
Vous aussi, homme d'abstinence,
Chartreux, prenez en pacience.
De plus vivre n'ayez memoire;
285   Faictez vous valoir a la danse.
Sur tout homme mort a victoire.

¶ Le chartreux
Je suis au monde pieça mort,
Par quoy de vivre ay moins envie,
Ja soit que tout homme craint mort.

You will get no deferral here.
Death comes when one least expects it.

¶ The Canon
255   This hardly comforts me.
        I had a prebend in many a church,
        But now Death, who carries off everything,
        Overpowers me — that is its way.
        My white surplice and grey amice
260   I must leave and give up to Death.
        What use is glory so soon brought low?
        Everyone should look to dying well.

¶ Death
        Merchant, look over here.
        Once upon a time you roamed through
265   Many lands on foot and in the saddle.
        You will no longer be thus preoccupied:
        Here is your final marketplace.
        You must pass through here;
        You will be discharged of all cares.
270   He who has plenty only covets more.

¶ The Merchant
        For a long time I traveled high and low
        To trade where I could
        On foot and in the saddle,
        But now I lose all joy.
275   I did my utmost to acquire wealth,
        But now I have enough; Death seizes me.
        It is good to take the middle way;
        He who grasps too much grips little.

¶ Death
        Come, merchant, without further delay,
280   Do not put up any more of a fight.
        You can achieve nothing by it.
        You too, man of abstinence,
        Carthusian, have forbearance.
        Forget about living anymore;
285   Put your best foot forward at the dance.
        Death is victorious over all men.

¶ The Carthusian
        I have been dead to the world a long time,
        Wherefore I have less will to live,
        Even though every man fears Death.

290   Puis que la char est assouvie.
      Plaise a dieu que l'ame ravie
      Soit es cieulx apres mon trespas.
      C'est tout neant de ceste vie;
      Tel est huy qui demain n'est pas.

      ¶ Le mort
295   Sergent qui portez celle mace,
      Il semble que vous rebellez.
      Pour neant faictes la grimace;
      Se on vous griefve si, appellez.
      Vous estes de mort appellez;
300   Qui luy rebelle, il se dechoit.
      Les plus fors sont tost ravallez.
      Il n'est fort qu'aussy fort ne soit.

fol. 7v   ¶ Le sergent
      Moy, qui suy royal officier,
      Comment m'ose la mort frapper?
305   Je faisoye mon office hyer,
      Et elle me vient huy happer?
      Je ne scay quelle part eschapper;
      Je suis prins deça et dela.
      Malgre moy me laisse attraper.
310   Envis meurt qui aprins ne l'a.

      ¶ Le mort
      Ha, maistre, par la passez;
      N'ayez ja soing de vous deffendre.
      Plus homme n'espoventerez.
      Apres, moyne, sans plus attendre.
315   Ou pensez vous? Cy fault entendre:
      Tantost aurez la bouche close.
      Homme n'est fors que vent et cendre;
      Vie d'omme est peu de chose.

      ¶ Le moyne
      J'amasse mieulx encores estre
320   En cloistre et faire mon service:
      C'est un lieu devost et bel estre.
      Or ay je, comme fol et nice,
      Ou temps passé commis maint vice,
      De quoy n'ay pas fait penitance
325   Suffisant. Dieu me soit propice:
      Chascun n'est pas joyeux qui dance.

290   Since the flesh has come to term,
        God willing, let my soul be ravished
        To the heavens at my passing.
        This life is but pure naught;
        We are here today and gone tomorrow.

        ¶ Death
295   Sergeant, carrying that mace,
        You seem recalcitrant.
        It is no use at all to make that face;
        If you are being injured so, lodge an appeal.
        You have been called by Death;
300   He who rebels against it deceives himself.
        The strongest are soon felled.
        No man is so strong as to be stronger than Death.

        ¶ The Sergeant
        Me, a royal officer,
        How dare Death strike me?
305   I was carrying out my duties just the other day,
        And today it comes to snatch me?
        I do not know which way to flee;
        I am cornered on all sides.
        Despite myself I let myself get caught.
310   He is loath to die who has not learned to die well.

        ¶ Death
        Ah, master, head on through;
        Do not think to defend yourself.
        You will not frighten anyone anymore.
        You are next, monk, no more dawdling,
315   What are you thinking about? Focus on this:
        Soon your mouth will be shut.
        Man is nothing but wind and ash;
        A human life does not amount to much.

        ¶ The Monk
        I would have preferred still being
320   In the cloister and saying my offices:
        It is a devout place and a beautiful dwelling.
        But, being foolish and senseless, I have
        Committed many a vice in the past,
        For which I have not done sufficient
325   Penance. May God look favorably upon me:
        Not everyone who dances is happy.

¶ Le mort
Usurier de sens desreuglé,
Venez toust et me regardez.

fol. 8r   D'usure estes tant aveuglié
330   Que d'argent gaignier tout ardez.
Mais vous en serez bien lardez,
Car se dieu, qui est merveilleux,
N'a pitié de vous, tout perdez.
A tout perdre est cop perilleux.

¶ L'usurier
335   Me convient il si toust mourir?
Ce m'est grant paine et grant grevance,
Et ne me pourroient secourir
Mon or, mon argent, ma chevance.
Je voys mourir; la mort m'avance.
340   Mais il m'en desplaist somme toute.
Qu'est ce de male acoustumance?
Tel a beaux eulx qui n'y voit goute.

¶ L'omme qui emprunte
Usure est tant mauvais pechié,
Comme chascun dit et recompte,
345   Et cest homme, qui approuchié
Se voit de la mort, n'en tient compte.
Mesmes l'argent qu'en ma main compte
Encor a usure me preste.
Il devra de retour au compte:
350   N'est pas quitte qui doit de reste.

¶ Le mort
Medecin, a tout vostre orine
fol. 8v   Veez vous ycy qu'amender?
Jadis seustes de medicine
Assez pour povoir commander,
355   Or vous vient la mort demander.
Comme aultre vous convient mourir.
Vous n'y povez contremander;
Bon mire est qui se scet guerir.

¶ Le medecin
Longtemps a qu'en l'art de phisique
360   J'ay mis toute mon estudie.
J'avoye science et pratique
Pour guerir mainte maladie.
Je ne scay que je contredie:
Plus n'y vault herbe, ne racine,

¶ Death
Usurer, you with your disordered mind,
Come quick and look at me.
You are so blinded by usury
330   That you burn to rake in wealth.
But it will gouge you,
For if God, who is magnificent,
Does not pity you, you lose everything.
It is a dangerous game in which all can be lost in just one bet.

¶ The Usurer
335   Must I die so soon?
This causes me great pain and great misery,
And not my gold, my silver, nor my wealth
Can possibly help me.
I will die; Death leads the way.
340   But this angers me through and through.
What kind of unfair tax is this?
Sometimes the fairest eyes cannot see a thing.

¶ The Borrower
Usury is such an evil sin,
As everyone says and recounts,
345   Yet this man, who sees his death
Approach, does not take it into account.
He just continues to loan me at interest
The money he counts out into my hand.
He will owe the rest on his account:
350   He who owes still has not settled the debt.

¶ Death
Physician, in all your urine
Do you see here what to cure?
You once knew enough
About medicine to be able to prescribe treatment,
355   But now Death comes to ask for you.
You must die like any other.
You cannot countermand it:
The good doctor knows how to cure himself.

¶ The Physician
For a long time I devoted myself entirely
360   To studying the art of medicine;
I knew both the theory and the practice
Of curing many an illness.
I do not know with what to counter:
Plants and roots and other remedies

365   N'autre remede. Quoy qu'on dye,
       Contre la mort n'a medicine.

       ¶ Le mort
       Gentil amoureux joune et frique,
       Qui vous cuidiez de grant valour,
       Vous estes prins; la mort vous picque.
370   Le monde lairez a doulour.
       Trop l'avez amé — c'est folour —
       Et a morir peu regardé.
       Ja tost vous changerez coulour:
       Beauté n'est qu'ymage fardé.

       ¶ L'amoureux
375   Helas, or n'y a yl secours
fol. 9r Contre mort? Adieu, amourettes.
       Moult toust va jounesse a decours.
       Adieu, chappeaux, bouquez, flourettes,
       Adieu, amans et pucellettes.
380   Souviegnez vous de moy souvent,
       Et vous mirez se saiges estes.
       Petite pluye abat grant vent.

       ¶ Le mort
       Advocat, sans long proces faire,
       Venez vostre cause plaidier.
385   Bien avez sceu les gens attraire
       De pieça, non pas d'uy ne d'ier.
       Conseil si ne vous puet aidier.
       Au grant juge vous fault venir.
       Savoir le devez sans cuidier:
390   Bon fait justice prevenir.

       ¶ L'advocat
       C'est bien drois que raison se face,
       Ne je n'y scay mettre deffense.
       Contre mort n'a respit ne grace;
       Nul n'appelle de sa sentence.
395   J'ay eu de l'autruy, quant je y pense,
       De quoy je doubte estre reprins.
       A craindre est le jour de vengence:
       Dieu rendra tout a juste pris.

fol. 9v ¶ Le mort
       Menestrel qui danses et nottes
400   Savez et avez beau maintien
       Pour faire esjoir sos et sottes,

365   Are no longer any good. Whatever they say,
        There is no cure for Death.

        ¶ Death
        Noble lover, young and elegant,
        You who believe yourself to be of great worth,
        You have been taken; you feel Death's sting.
370   You will leave the world in pain.
        You have loved it too much — how foolish —
        And thought little of dying.
        Soon now your color will begin to change:
        Beauty is but a painted image.

        ¶ The Lover
375   Alas, is there no recourse now
        Against Death? Farewell, dalliances.
        How quickly youth ebbs away.
        Farewell, garlands, bouquets, and blossoms,
        Farewell, lovers and young maidens.
380   May you remember me often
        And mend your ways, if you are wise.
        A little rain can still the strongest squall.

        ¶ Death
        Man of law, without long deliberation,
        Come plead your case.
385   You have well known how to sway folk
        For a long time now, not just since today or yesterday.
        Legal counsel cannot help you.
        You must come before the great judge.
        You should know it for certain:
390   It is meet to uphold justice.

        ¶ The Man of Law
        It is only right that justice be done,
        Nor do I know how to defend myself against it.
        There is no respite nor pardon from Death;
        No one appeals its sentence.
395   I, who took from others, when I think about it,
        Now dread being seized in turn.
        The day of vengeance is to be feared:
        God will pay everything back in full.

        ¶ Death
        Minstrel, who knows dances and
400   Melodies and puts on a good show
        To give delight to fools and ninnies,

Qu'en dites vous? Alons nous bien?
Monstrer vous fault, puis que vous tien,
Aux autres cy un tour de dance.
405   Le contredire n'y vault rien:
Maistre doit monstrer sa science.

¶ Le menestrel
De danser ainsi n'eusse cure;
Certes tres envis je m'en melle,
Car de mort n'est paine plus dure.
410   J'ay mis soubz le banc ma vielle.   *(see note)*
Plus ne corneray sauterelle
N'autre danse; mort m'en retient.
Il me fault obeir a elle:
Tel danse a qui au cueur n'en tient.

¶ Le mort
415   Passez, curé, sans plus songier;
Je sens qu'estes habandonné.
Le vif le mort soliez mangier,
Mais vous serez aux vers donné.
Vous feustes jadix ordonné
420   Mirouer d'autruy et exemplaire.
De voz faiz serez guerdonné:
A toute paine est deu salaire.

¶ Le cure
fol. 10r   Vueille ou nom, il fault que me rende;
Il n'est homme que mort n'assaille.
425   Hee, de mes paroissiens offrande
N'auray jamais, ne funeraille.
Devant le juge fault que je aille
Rendre compte, las, doulereux.
Or ay je grant paour que ne faille:
430   Qui dieu quitte bien est eureux.

¶ Le mort
Laboureur qui en soing et paine
Avez vescu tout vostre temps,
Mourir fault — c'est chose certaine.
Reculer n'y vault, ne contens.
435   De mort devez estre contens,
Car de grant soucy vous delivre.
Approchiez vous, je vous attens:
Fol est qui cuide tousjours vivre.

What do you say? Shall we go?
Since you are in my clutches, you must show
The others here some fancy footwork.
405   It is no use arguing:
The master should show off his expertise.

¶ The Minstrel
I have no desire to dance like this;
I am certainly loath to take part,
For there is no pain worse than Death.
410   I have hung up my hat and packed up my viol,
I will trill no more *sauterelles*
Nor other dances; Death keeps me from it.
I must obey:
A man can dance though his heart is not in it.

¶ Death
415   Come forward, parish priest, without dilly-dallying;
I sense that you have been handed over.
You used to feed off the living and the dead,
But now you will be served up to the worms.
You were once ordained to be
420   A mirror and example unto others.
You will be requited for your works:
All toil is owed its wages.

¶ The Parish Priest
Like it or not, I must turn myself in;
There is no man whom Death does not assail.
425   Ah, never again will I collect
My parishioners' offerings or funeral fees.
I must go before the judge
To give account of myself, wretched and suffering.
Now I fear greatly coming up short:
430   Happy is he whom God fully acquits.

¶ Death
Laborer, you who have lived out
All your days in care and toil,
You must die — that is for certain.
It is no use drawing back or arguing.
435   You should be glad to die,
For Death delivers you from great misery.
Come closer, I am waiting for you:
He is a fool who thinks to live forever.

¶ Le laboureur
La mort ay souhaitié souvent,
440   Mais volentiers je la fuysse.
J'amasse mieux, fist pluye ou vent
Estre es vignes ou je fouysse;
Encor plus grant plaisir y preisse,
Car je pers de peur tout propos.
445   Or n'est qui de ce pas ysse.
Au monde n'a point de reppos.

fol. 10v ¶ Le mort
Faictes voye, vous avez tort,
Laboureur. Apres, cordelier.
Souvent avez preschié de mort,
450   Si vous devez moins merveiller;
Ja ne s'en fault esmay bailler.
Il n'est si fort que mort n'arreste;
Si fait bon a morir veiller.
A toute heure la mort est preste.

¶ Le cordelier
455   Qu'est ce que de vivre en ce monde?
Nul homme a seurte n'y demeure.
Toute vanite y habunde,
Puis vient la mort, qu'a tous court seure.
Mendicité point ne m'asseure;
460   Des meffais fault payer l'amende.
En petite heure dieu labeure;
Sage est le pecheur qui s'amende.

¶ Le mort
Petit enfant naguerez né,
Au monde auras peu de plaisance.
465   A la danse seras mené
Comme autres, car mort a puissance
Sur tous du jour de la naissance.
Convient chascun a mort offrir;
Fol est qui n'en a congnoissance.
470   Qui plus vit plus a a souffrir.

¶ L'enfant
A, A, A, je ne scay parler.
fol. 11r Enfant suy, j'ay la langue mue.
Hyer nasquis, huy m'en fault aler;
Je ne fay qu'entrée et yssue.
475   Rien n'ay mesfait, mais de peur sue.
Prendre en gré me fault — c'est le mieux.

¶ The Laborer
I often wished for Death,
440   Yet now I would flee it willingly.
I would have preferred to be
Hoeing in the vineyards, come rain or wind;
I would enjoy that work more than ever before,
For fear has got me all turned around.
445   But now no one can escape this step.
The world holds no eternal rest.

¶ Death
Get a move on, you are in the wrong,
Laborer. You next, Franciscan,
You have often preached about Death,
450   So you should marvel less at it;
There is no need to act so dismayed.
No one is so mighty as to not get detained by Death;
Thus it is good to be wary of dying.
Death is poised to strike at any time.

¶ The Franciscan
455   What is it to live in this world?
No man resides there in safety.
All kinds of vanity abounds there,
Then comes Death, who attacks everyone.
Being a mendicant protects me not one bit;
460   One must pay amends for one's misdeeds.
God works swiftly;
Wise is the sinner who mends his ways.

¶ Death
Little child newly born,
You will have little joy in the world.
465   You shall be led to the dance
Like the others, for Death has power
Over all from the day of their birth.
Each must make offering unto Death;
He is a fool who does not realize this.
470   The more one lives the more one suffers.

¶ The Child
A, A, A, I do not know how to speak.
Being a child, I am mute.
Born yesterday, today I must depart;
I do nothing but enter and exit.
475   I did no misdeed, but I am wet with fear.
I should take this in stride — that would be best.

L'ordonnance Dieu ne se mue;
Aussi toust meurt joune que vieulx.

¶ Le mort
Cuidiez vous de mort eschapper,
480   Clerc, esperdu pour reculer?
Il ne s'en fault ja desfripper.
Tel cuide souvent hault aler
Qu'on voit a cop tost ravaler.
Prenez en gré, alons ensemble,
485   Car riens n'y vault le rebeller:
Dieu punist tout quant bon luy semble.

¶ Le clerc
Fault il q'un joune clerc servant,
Qui en service prent plaisir
Pour cuidier venir en avant
490   Meure si tost? C'est desplaisir.
Je suis quitte de plus choisir
Autre estat; y fault qu'ainsy danse.
La mort m'a prins a son loisir;
Moult remaint de ce que fol pense.

fol. 11v   ¶ Le mort
495   Clerc, point ne fault faire reffus
De danser; faictes vous valoir.
Vous n'estes pas seul — levez sus —
Pourtant moins vous en doit chaloir.
Venez apres, c'est mon voloir,
500   Homme norry en hermitaige;
Ja ne vous en convient douloir.
Vie n'est pas seur heritaige.

¶ L'ermite
Pour vie dure ou solitaire
Mort ne donne de vivre espace.
505   Chascun le voit, si s'en fault taire.
Or requier dieu q'un don me face:
C'est que tous mes pechiez efface.
Bien suis content de tous ses biens,
Desquelx j'ay usé de sa grace.
510   Qui n'a souffisance, il n'a riens.

fol. 12r   ¶ Le mort luy repond
C'est bien dit, ainsi doit on dire;
Il n'est qui soit de mort delivré.
Qui mal vit, il aura du pire:

God's decree does not change:
The young die along with the old.

¶ Death
Do you think you can escape Death,
480   Clerk, desperate to back away?
You must not struggle so.
Many a man who thinks to climb high
Is seen to be abruptly cast back down.
Take it in stride, let us go together,
485   For it is no use resisting:
God punishes everyone when He sees fit.

¶ The Clerk
Must a young employed clerk,
Who takes pleasure in service,
Thereby hoping to advance himself,
490   Die so soon? That is harsh.
I am released from ever striving
For any other rank: thus must I dance.
Death has taken me at its convenience;
Much of what a fool thinks remains unrealized.

¶ Death
495   Clerk, you absolutely must not refuse
To dance; put your best foot forward.
You are not alone — get up —
Therefore you should be less upset about it.
You are next, that is my will,
500   Man who was raised in a hermitage;
Grief does not befit you.
Life is not granted in perpetuity.

¶ The Hermit
Despite a hard and solitary existence,
Death denies me the opportunity to live.
505   Everyone sees it, thus one must stop complaining.
Now I pray God that He make me a gift:
That is, that He pardon all my sins.
I am fully satisfied with all His goods,
Which I made use of by His grace.
510   He who is unsatisfied with what he has, has nothing.

¶ Death responds to him
That is well said, one should talk thus;
No one may be delivered from Death.
He who lives badly will end up with worse,

Si pense chascun de bien vivre.
515 Dieu pesera tout a la livre;
Bon y fait penser seoir et main.
Meilleur science n'a en livre:
Il n'est qui ait point de demain.

¶ Le roy mort qui vers mignent
Vous qui en ceste pourtraitture
520 Veez danser estas divers,
Pensez qu'est humaine nature:
Ce n'est fors que viande a vers.
Je le monstre, qui gis envers,
Si ay je esté roy couronnez.
525 Telx soiez vous, bons et pervers.
Tous estas sont aux vers donnez.

¶ Machabre docteur
Rien n'est d'omme, qui bien y pense,
C'est tout chose transitoire.
Chascun le voit par ceste danse.
530 Pour ce vous, qui veez l'ystoire,
Retenez la bien en memoire,
Car homme et femme elle amonneste
D'avoir de paradis la gloire.
Eureux est qui es cieulx fait feste.

fol. 12v ¶ Le docteur encor
535 Mais aucuns sont a qui n'en chault,
Comme s'il ne feust paradis
N'enfer. Helas, ilz auront chault.
Les livres que firent jadix
Les sains le monstrent en beaux dis.
540 Acquittiez vous qui cy passez,
Et faictes du bien — plus n'en dis.
Bien fait vault moult aux trespassez.

¶ Angelus et doctor locuntur
Mortales dominus cunctos in luce creavit
Ut capiant meritis gaudia summa poli.
545 Felix ille quidem qui mentem jugiter illuc
Dirigit atque vigil noxia queque cavet,
Nec tamen infelix sceleris quem penitet acti
Quique suum facinus plangere sepe solet.
Sed vivunt homines tamquam mors nulla sequatur,
550 Et velut infernus fabula vana foret,
Cum doceat sensus viventes morte resolui
Atque herebi penas pagina sacra probet

(see note)

So everyone should think to live well.
515 God will weigh everything out exactly;
It is good to think on this night and day.
There is no better wisdom in the book:
We have no tomorrow, none of us.

¶ The dead King eaten by worms
You who in this image
520 See the different estates dance
Consider what is human nature:
It is nothing more than food for worms.
I am the proof, lying before you,
Though I was a crowned king.
525 Good or wicked, you will end up the same.
Every estate will be given to the worms.

¶ Doctor Machabre
When you really think about it, man is nothing,
A mere passing thing.
Anyone can see it in this dance.
530 Therefore you who see the depiction,
Hold it well in your memory,
For it encourages both men and women
To attain the glory of paradise.
He is fortunate who celebrates in the heavens.

¶ The Doctor again
535 But there are some who pay no heed,
As if there were neither heaven
Nor hell. Alas, they will have a very warm welcome.
The books that the saints wrote long ago
Prove it beautifully.
540 Pay off your debts, you who pass through here,
And do good works — I say no more.
Good deeds are worth a great deal to the dead.

¶ Angel and Teacher speak:
The Lord created all mortals in light
So they could seize the greatest joys of heaven through their merits.
545 Happy is that man, at least, who continually directs his mind thither
And wakefully avoids every crime;
Nor is he unhappy, if his evil deed makes him penitent
And if it is his custom to lament for his crime often.
But men live as if no death can pursue them,
550 And as if Hell were a mere fairy tale,
Though the Sacred Page teaches that living sensations are set free by Death
And it shows the punishments of Erebus.

Quas qui non metuit infelix prorsus et amens
Vivit et extinctus sentiet ille rogum.
555 Sic igitur cuncti sapientes vivere certent
Ut nichil inferni sit metuenda palus.

Explicit.

The man who has no fear of them lives utterly unhappily and mad,
And when he is dead, he will feel the pyre.
555 So therefore, let every wise man strive to live
Such that the Lake of Hades may not be feared at all.

The end.

EXPLANATORY NOTES

ABBREVIATIONS: **A version**: Lydgate, *Dance of Death* (Selden); **B version**: Lydgate, *Dance of Death* (Lansdowne); *CT*: Chaucer, *Canterbury Tales*, ed. Benson; **D**: Oxford, Bodleian Library, MS Douce 322 (SC 21896); *DMF*: *Dictionnaire du Moyen Français (1330–1500)*; *DOST*: *Dictionary of the Older Scottish Tongue*; *FP*: Lydgate, *Fall of Princes*, ed. Bergen; **Gray**: "Two Songs of Death," ed. Gray; **Hassell**: Hassell, *Middle French Proverbs, Sentences, and Proverbial Phrases*; *MED*: *Middle English Dictionary*; *ODNB*: *Oxford Dictionary of National Biography*; *OED*: *Oxford English Dictionary*; **Whiting**: Whiting, *Proverbs, Sentences, and Proverbial Phrases*.

JOHN LYDGATE, *DANCE OF DEATH*: A VERSION (SELDEN)

19   *Like the exawmple wiche that at Parys.* Lydgate compares his English translation with its French original. This is an earlier French version of the *Danse macabre*, with accompanying images, that was painted in the early fifteenth century along the walls of the charnel houses that formed the boundaries of the Cemetery of the Innocents in Paris (see Introduction, pp. 5, 17). A contemporary eyewitness, Gilbert de Mets, describes the cemetery as it appeared circa 1430:

> La sont engigneusement entailliés de pierre les ymages des trois vifz et trois mors. La est ung cimitiere moult grant enclos de maisons appellés charniers. La ou les os des mors sont entassés, illec sont paintures notables de la dance macabre et autres avec escriptures pour esmouvoir les gens a devotion.

> In this place there is skilfully sculpted in stone the images of the three living and the three dead. There is a very large cemetery there surrounded by buildings called charnel-houses where the bones of the dead are piled up; there are notable paintings there of the Danse Macabre with writings to move people to devotion. (Guillebert de Mets, *Description de la ville de Paris 1434*, ed. and trans. Mullally, pp. 94–95).

Lydgate, already an established poet and translator by the 1420s, would have encountered this scene when he arrived in Paris in 1426 during the regency of John, Duke of Bedford. He therefore positions himself not only as a translator, but as an eyewitness to the most widely known instantiation of the *danse macabre* at that time.

35   *Daunce at Seint Innocentis.* Even more than the previous reference to "Parys" (line 19), this line identifies Lydgate's source as the St. Innocents *Danse.*

49   *this mirrour.* The idea of a text, especially a didactic one, as 'mirror' or reflection is common in medieval religion; see, for example, Nicholas Love's *Mirror of the Blessed Life of Jesus Christ*, the *Mirror for Simple Souls*, the *Mirror for Holy Church*, etc. The notion of a spiritual or religious mirror combines the idea of a reflection on the world as it is with a more aspirational model for good spiritual conduct and self-evaluation. See also lines 632–40 for the image of Death as a mirror to mankind.

59   *like as Petir had the soverenité.* The apostle Peter is traditionally regarded as the first Bishop of Rome, or Pope, on the basis of Christ's words to him in Matthew 16:18: "And I say to thee: That thou art Peter; and upon this rock I will build my church, and the gates of hell shall not prevail against it." Subsequent popes are said to inherit Peter's authority over the Church (see B version, line 19).

75   *golde your appil round.* The golden apple here recalls the fruit of the Tree of Knowledge of Good and Evil consumed by Adam and Eve in Eden, as recounted in Genesis 3 as well as the golden orb used to represent imperial power from the Roman era onward. The orb is most often depicted surmounted by a cross. When it is depicted this way, it is called the *globus cruciger*. Many Christian rulers are portrayed holding the orb and cross as a symbol of their imperial authority, including the figure of the Emperor in the 1485 Guyot Marchant printing of the French *Danse* and the Kaiser in the 1488 Heidelberger *Totentanz*.

85   *A simple shete — ther is no more to seyne —.* Death informs the Emperor that he will be buried in a simple shroud, or winding sheet, a dramatic contrast to the riches and treasure associated with the Emperor in life. In illustrations to the early printed editions of the French *Danse macabre*, the skeletons (i.e., the speakers identified as "le mort" in the text) are often draped in tattered shrouds. In addition, those viewing the *Dance* in the Pardon Churchyard at St. Paul's in London, or its French analogue at the Holy Innocents in Paris, would have likely had opportunity to see the interment of bodies wrapped in such sheets and witness firsthand the leveling and anonymizing effects of this common form of burial.

94   *Youre hatte of reed.* Cardinals wear a distinctive wide-brimmed red hat, known as a *gallero*, that indicates their high rank within the Church (the College of Cardinals is second in authority only to the Pope himself, a hierarchy that is reflected in the order in which the speakers appear in this poem). The tradition of cardinals wearing a red *gallero* was established by Pope Innocent IV at the First Council of Lyon in 1245.

112   *Shal bere with hym but a sengle shete.* By emphasizing that the King will be buried with a simple shroud, Death reminds the King, like the Emperor before him, that he cannot bring his earthly goods into the afterlife.

121   *Sir Patriarke.* The concept of the patriarch, a cleric assuming the highest position of leadership within ecclesiastical hierarchy, goes all the way back to the Code of Justinian, a collection of works on canon law issued between 529 and 534 CE. The Code (Novellas 123 and 131) stipulated that Christendom be divided into five patriarchates — the Sees of Rome, Constantinople, Alexandria, Antioch,

and Jerusalem. These were known collectively as the Pentarchy (for the head and four limbs of the body of the Church) and arranged in respective hierarchical order. This organizational schema was officially confirmed at the Council of Trullo of 692, though this order was occasionally disputed over the centuries. Thus, although he is traditionally termed "Pope," the head cleric of the See of Rome is one of the original patriarchs, and the other Sees retain the title "Patriarch" for their head clerics. The East-West or Great Schism of 1054 separated the See of Rome from the other four Sees, producing the Roman Catholic and Eastern Orthodox Churches (see further "Patriarch and Patriarchate" in *The Catholic Encyclopedia*). As the "double crosse" at line 123 makes clear, the Patriarch mentioned here is associated with the Eastern Orthodox Church and is, most likely, from the See of Constantinople. The Byzantine Emperor Manuel II Palaiologos visited Western Europe, including a visit to the court of Charles VI in France and a trip to England in the winter of 1400–01 during which he was received by Henry IV at Eltham Palace. Although Matthew I, who was then Patriarch of Constantinople, remained behind (and was in fact temporarily deposed during Manuel's absence), the visit would have been a chance for the English and French alike to become more familiar with Orthodox Christianity. That said, Marchant's editions of the *Danse macabre* depicts the Patriarch as a Catholic bishop, without the distinctive beard and garb of an Eastern Orthodox cleric.

123   *Youre double crosse of gold and stones clere.* The double cross is a variant of the Christian cross in which a smaller cross-bar is placed above the main bar to represent the plaque nailed to Christ's cross, and, sometimes, an additional diagonal cross-bar towards the bottom, symbolizing the foothold for Christ's feet. It is typically associated, as in this case, with the Orthodox Church.

127   *Trustith nevere that ye shal pope be.* The East-West or Great Schism of 1054 saw the division of the Pentarchy (see note to line 121 above) into the Western Roman Catholic and Eastern Orthodox Churches. Subsequent attempts at healing the schism were unsuccessful but raised anew in the 1420s and 1430s as a potential unification strategy before the rise of the Ottoman Empire. These discussions culminated in the Seventeenth Ecumenical Council at Basel convoked in 1431; moved to Ferrara in 1438 and to Florence in 1445, the council achieved a preliminary consensus in unifying the two Churches on the condition that the Eastern Orthodox Churches recognize the primacy of the See of Rome. The agreement immediately faltered due to widespread public opposition on the part of Eastern Orthodox monks and clerics. Thus, for informed mid-fifteenth century audiences, Death's phrase would be a particularly mocking dig at these failed discussions. See further Geanakoplos, *Constantinople and the West*, esp. pp. 224–54, and Jonathan Harris, *The End of Byzantium*.

128   *foly hope deceiveth many a man.* Proverbial. See Whiting H461.

138   *my maister Sir Constable.* The *MED* defines "constable" as the chief executive of a leader, including that of a king or other ruler. This seems to be the sense in which it is being used here, given that the Constable is the first secular figure to appear in the *danse* following the emperor and the king, suggesting that he

ranks above other prominent laymen like the Burgess; the figure is used in the same sense in the French *Danse macabre*. See Oosterwijk, "Of Corpses, Constables and Kings" for the political importance of including this figure in the text, given the ongoing Anglo-French conflict.

139   *Charlemayne*. Charlemagne (742/748–814 CE), king of the Franks who consolidated power and extended Frankish rule across Europe. In 800 he was crowned emperor by Pope Leo III in Rome. He was also one of the medieval "nine worthies," the group of three pagan (Hector, Alexander the Great, Julius Caesar), three Jewish (Joshua, David, Judas Maccabeus), and three Christian (Arthur, Charlemagne, Godfrey of Bouillon) leaders seen to embody the ideals of chivalry and moral virtue.

176   *o man brekith that anothir made*. Proverbial. See Whiting M259.

184   *Undre hevene in erthe is nothing stable*. Proverbial. See Whiting N154.

Before 185   *Lady of Grete Astate*. This is a new character, who does not appear in either the original French *Danse macabre* or in the B version.

204   *goodes of nature*. Goods provided by nature, such as crops; may also include livestock, the elements, minerals, and physical gifts.

215   *He that al withhalt*. Lydgate's odd introduction of a "he" (God?) into the stanza probably has to do with the difficult syntax of his source: "Le monde aussi peu me conforte, / Qui tout a la fin desherite; / Il retient tout: nul riens n'emporte" (see French *Danse macabre*, lines 163–65), in which "il" refers back to "le monde," a masculine noun. Thus, in modern English, the lines read: "I can get little comfort too from the world, / Which ultimately dispossesses everyone. / It keeps all; no one makes off with anything." In Lydgate's defense, the gendering of French nouns can make pronouns extremely tricky in long clauses.

249   *Abbesse*. This is a new character, who does not appear in the original French *Danse macabre*; she corresponds to B version's Abbatissa (before line 193).

265   *Sir Bailly*. A bailiff, or bailly, is "an official of the English crown with delegated administrative or judicial authority; the king's officer in a county, hundred, or town; the keeper of a royal castle, gate, or forest" (*MED baillif*). The name of the Host in the *CT*, Harry Bailly, also presumably derives from this occupation.

288   *And al shal die for an appil round*. This refers to the fruit of the Tree of the Knowledge of Good and Evil, consumed by Adam and Eve in Genesis 3. A similar image appears in line 75 in the description of the Emperor.

296   *Who lyveth aright mote nedis dye wele*. Proverbial. See Whiting L408.

297   *Sir Burgeis*. The *MED* (*burgeis*) defines a burgess as "a freeman of a town, a citizen with full rights and privileges; also, an inhabitant of a town; — usually used of city merchants and master craftsmen in the guilds." His appearance here reflects the specifically urban context of the *danse macabre*.

313   *Sir Chanoun, with many grete prebende*. A canon is a clergyman serving at a church or cathedral (*MED canoun* [n.2]), such as St. Paul's or the church associated with

the Cemetery of the Holy Innocents in Paris. A prebend is "an estate or portion of land belonging to a cathedral or collegiate church, the revenues from which are used as the stipend of a canon or member of the chapter; also, the tenure of such an estate" (*MED prebende*).

321   *My benefices with many a personage*. In the Middle Ages, the Church obtained major revenue through rents and other profits gained from donations or bequests, such as land willed to the church. Benefice holders within the church would receive a portion of the income derived from these assets in exchange for performing their duties. A parsonage might refer to either a dwelling for such a cleric, or the benefits of his office more broadly (*MED personage* [n.2]). In theory, a cleric could only hold a single benefice at one time, but the system was easily exploited. It appears Lydgate's canon is one of many who obtained special dispensation to collect the revenues of multiple benefices.

325   *Amys of grys*. An amice is a cloth, usually white, with two ribbons going over the shoulders, that is draped over a priest's vestments during Mass.

326   *Surplys*. Lydgate appears to be punning on the term "surplice," a clerical vestment, used in his source (compare *Danse macabre*, l. 259) and "surplus" in the sense of "additional income" (see *MED, surplus*, sense 2).

347   *Sir Chartereux*. A Chartereux is monk of the Carthusian order. Founded at La Grande Chartreuse near Grenoble in 1084, the order was noted (as Death's response here indicates) for its asceticism. The Carthusian appears in the French text as well, and there were Carthusian houses in both London and Paris in the early fifteenth century.

361   *Sir Sergant with youre statly mace*. A sergeant is a serving man or attendant (*MED sergeaunt* [n.1]), but more specifically "an officer of a city, the royal household, etc. usually charged with collecting debts and arresting offenders" or an equivalent officer in a court of justice (sense 3). The mace he carries is a ceremonial club and a mark of his office.

374   *And may not flee, though I hadde it sworn*. In a poetic reversal of fortune, the Sergeant finds himself on the wrong side of the law, "arrested" by Death. Death will not release him despite his willingness to swear that he will appear as expected for future legal proceedings, which is equivalent to being released on bond in contemporary U.S. and Canadian legal systems. Given the Sergeant's haughty attitude in the previous stanza, he seems unlikely to have extended this clemency to offenders in his jurisdiction.

377   *Sir Monke also, with youre blak habite*. Members of the Benedictine Order, one of the largest monastic orders in medieval Europe, were distinguished by their black habits and were sometimes known simply as black monks (compare this with line 580 (1:16) of the English translation of Guillaume Deguileville's *Pilgrimage of the Life of Man*, attributed to Lydgate, which describes "monkys greyë, whyte, and blake"). As a monk of the Abbey of Bury St. Edmunds, John Lydgate himself was a member of this order. The Monk appears in the French *Danse* as well, but

without reference to the color of his habit — this detail, perhaps a personal one, is added by Lydgate.

393   *Thou Usurer.* Usury, the lending of money at interest, was necessary to the growth of a capitalistic system, but was forbidden to medieval Christians; Jews, however, were not under similar religious proscriptions. Because of this, negative attitudes toward usury (such as those presented here) often coincide with expressions of anti-Semitism, although Lydgate does not specify the religion of the usurer in his poem. See Le Goff, *Your Money or Your Life*. The non-believer, whether Jew or Muslim, is often depicted as a blind man, as in line 406.

417–18   *on youre uryne . . . stare agein the sonne.* Examination of urine, by holding it up to light, was a common diagnostic technique in medieval medicine. Some medical manuscripts contain illustrations of urine in a range of colors, with accompanying explanations of what medical conditions the hues indicate, to aid in diagnosis. In the Heidelberger *Totentanz*, Marchant's *Danse macabre*, and Hans Holbein's woodcuts, the physician is shown gazing at a flask of urine. Chaucer's Physician, in the Ellesmere manuscript drawing, also examines a flask of urine.

424   *Good leche is he that can himsilfe recure*. Proverbial. See Whiting L170.

429   *To finde oute agens pestilence.* "Pestilence" often refers to the bubonic plague or Black Death, which swept across Europe in the fourteenth century. It arrived in 1348 in England, where it killed as much as half the population. The scale of its impact and rapidity with which it advanced (many victims died within a few days of falling ill) naturally led to a disruption of normal customs surrounding death, funerals, and burial. Scholars have traditionally seen the *danse macabre* as a response to the Black Death, but Elina Gertsman challenges this assumption; she ties the tradition instead to preoccupations with death and the afterlife arising out of generalized anxieties over spiritual life engendered by the ecclesiastical crisis of the Western Schism (1378–1416), whereby the papacy moved from its seat in Rome to Avignon (Gertsman, *Dance of Death in the Middle Ages*, pp. 42–44).

448   *windes grete gon doun with litil reyn*. Proverbial. See Whiting R15. The sense is that Death, like a bit of rain, can stop even the great winds of life.

Before 449 *Gentilwomman Amerous.* This is a new character, who does not appear in the original French *Danse macabre*; she corresponds to B version's Generosa (before line 353).

451   *As faire as yee was somtyme Polycene.* Polyxena, in myth, was the daughter of King Priam of Troy and his queen, Hecuba. She does not appear in Homer's *Iliad* but in other sources is depicted as accompanying her brother Troilus when he is ambushed and killed by the Greek warrior Achilles. Achilles was later killed by two of Polyxena's other brothers, and, according to the Greek playwright Euripides, at the end of the Trojan War Achilles' ghost demanded Polyxena's sacrifice in exchange for fair winds for the returning Greek ships. For a modern edition and translation, see Euripedes, *Hecuba*, ed. Kovacs. This version of the story also appears in section 33 of Boccaccio's *De mulieribus claris* (see Boccaccio, *Famous Women*, trans. Brown, pp. 132–33).

452   *Penolope, and the quene Eleyne.* Penelope was the wife of Odysseus and mother of Telemachus. In Homer's *Odyssey*, she spends twenty years faithfully awaiting her spouse's return from war, deferring the attentions of numerous suitors, until she reunites with Odysseus. She is considered a model of fidelity and prudence. Helen was the beautiful Greek woman, the wife of Menelaus, whose abduction by the Trojan prince Paris instigated the Trojan war.

453   *Yit on this daunce thei wente bothe tweine.* Although this reading is consistent across manuscripts, there is a contradiction between the three women (Polyxena, Penelope, and Helen) to whom the Gentlewoman Amorous (equivalent to the Generosa, or Rich Woman, in the B text) is compared and "both tweine," which clearly refers to two figures.

465   *Sir Advocate.* An advocate is a professional pleader in courts of law, e.g., an attorney; compare with Chaucer's Man of Law. Compare also the Explanatory Note to line 383 of the French *Danse macabre* for a discussion of the verbal play in this line, which Lydgate maintains in his English translation.

Before 481   *Jourrour.* In medieval England, jurors were required to hold property, meaning that the speaker's identification here as a juror reflects on his socio-economic class as well as on his legal responsibilities. This is a new character, who does not appear in the original French *Danse macabre*; he corresponds to B version's Juror (before line 417).

513   *Maister John Rikele, sometyme Tregetour.* This is the only instance in the poem in which Lydgate appears to refer to a real historical personage. It is also the only reference to this John Rikele, and his apparent role of court magician in the court of Henry V, in the historical record. As Sophie Oosterwijk notes, "it is usually assumed that the inclusion of the 'some tyme tregetowre' Rikelle in Lydgate's poem means that he was already dead, but nobody of that name has so far been identified in the accounts of Henry V" ("Dance, Dialogue and Duality," p. 37). This is a new character who does not appear in the original French *Danse macabre* or in the later B version.

521   *What may availe magik natural.* "Magik natural" refers to sorcery or divination designed to manipulate the forces of the natural world, such as planetary influence (as opposed to calling on supernatural forces such as demons).

529   *Sir Curat.* A curate is a parish priest, directly responsible for the spiritual welfare of his parishioners. Unlike the idealized Parson in the *CT*, the Curate appears to display the same greed and self-interest that mark most of the ecclesiastical figures in this poem.

536   *to eche labour dewe is the salarie.* An allusion to 1 Corinthians 3:8: "Now that he planteth, and he that watereth, are one. And every man shall receive his own reward, according to his own labour."

543   *And for my shepe make a just rekenyng.* The sheep are the people in the care of the Parson. See Matthew 18:12–14, Luke 15:3–7, and John 10:1–18, as well as John 21:17, when Jesus says to Peter, "feed my sheep." Compare with Chaucer's description of the virtuous Parson in the General Prologue to the *CT* I(A) 496–506.

561   *Sir Cordeler.* A cordeler is a Franciscan friar, so called for their practice of wearing a cord as a belt, in imitation of the order's founder, St. Francis of Assisi.

574   *nothing . . . that may fro Dethe defende.* Proverbial. See Whiting D78.

584   *Who lengest lyveth moost shal suffre woo.* Proverbial. See Whiting L407.

596   *Of benefices or some greet prebende.* See note to line 313 above.

Before 601   *Clerke.* This character does not appear in the B version of the *Dance of Death*.

609   *Ye that have lived longe in wildernesse.* The Hermit, who has voluntarily left society to practice religious devotion, and the Child (see lines 577–92), who has not had time to be integrated into society, are the only two speakers who willingly accompany Death on his dance.

624   *No man is riche that lackith suffisaunce.* Proverbial. For an inversion, see Whiting S867.

Before 633   *The Kyng ligging dead and eten of wormes.* This stanza breaks the dialogic form of the preceding section of the poem. A similar stanza, with analogous heading, appears in Lydgate's French source (*Danse macabre*, lines 519–26). Although the speaker is identified as a king, he also presents himself as a model for all estates, reinforcing the hierarchical structure of the poem.

633   *Ye folke that lokyn upon this portrature.* "Portrature" can refer to verbal or pictorial representation, but, in this case, it is evidently something that apparently directs readers to contemplate the accompanying images. This is an intriguing choice on Lydgate's part, since none of the early manuscripts of Lydgate's *Danse* include pictures, although the same injunction to look at the "pourtraiture" occurs in the French *Danse* at line 519. Interestingly, the B version replaces "portrature" with "scripture" (line 561), although it was this version that was painted at St. Paul's Cathedral (see Introduction, pp. 16–18).

640   *wormes food.* Proverbial. See Whiting W675.

666   *Not worde by worde but folwyng the substaunce.* This commonplace discussion of best translation practices goes back to St. Jerome's meditations on his work in translating the Latin Vulgate text of the Bible from its original Hebrew, which itself has precursors, as Rita Copeland argues, in Late Antique discussions of grammar and rhetoric by figures such as Cicero. See her *Rhetoric, Hermeneutics*, pp. 42–55.

669   *Rude of langage (I was not born in Fraunce).* Lydgate here takes a performative and conventional position of humility, making claims for the insufficiency or roughness of his work. Lydgate knew French (he made numerous translations from French beyond the *Danse macabre*), but here he contrasts the French of England with the higher-prestige French of France. Lydgate's self-deprecating assessment of his Anglo-French recalls Chaucer's caustic remarks about the Prioress in the General Prologue to the *CT*: "And Frenssh she spak ful faire and fetisly, / After the scole of Stratford atte Bowe, / For Frenssh of Parys was to hire unknowe" (*CT* I[A] 124–26). This is also a well-known posture of late medieval

English writers seeking to emulate their French contemporaries: Chaucer similarly lamented his own lack of "suffisaunce" in treating the French poetic subject of the daisy in lines 66–67 of the F version of the Prologue to the *Legend of Good Women* (c. 1385–86), while Gower asks to be excused for his lack of "faconde" or "eloquence" in French due to his Englishness in the final lines (XVIII.24, trans. Yeager) of his *Traitié pour essampler les amantz mariez* (early 1390s).

672   *Her corious metris in Englisshe to translate.* "Meters" in this instance should be taken in the broad sense of 'verses' or 'poems', a usage typical of the late fourteenth and fifteenth centuries, especially in Lydgate. The *MED* defines "corious" as "carefully, skillfully, artistically, or elaborately designed or made; artistic, exquisite, fine; costly, sumptuous" (sense 2). Like Lydgate's claim to be "rude of language," this phrase is another example of a humility topos, often deployed with regard to translation in this period, as there is nothing especially "corious" about Lydgate's source from the perspective of prosody. Written in octosyllabic eight-line stanzas and *ababbcbc* rhyme, the *Danse* is typical of French poetry produced in the first half of the fifteenth century (for a good overview, see Laidlaw, "The *Cent Balades*"). If anything, Lydgate's ability to maintain his source's rhyme scheme and stanza length, albeit with a longer, decasyllabic line, testifies to his own "corious metre." Compare Chaucer's *Complaint of Venus*, in which he laments that "rym in Englissh hath such skarsete, / To folowe word by word the curiosite / Of Graunson, flour of hem that make in Fraunce" (lines 80–82: rhyme in English is so insufficient / to translate word by word the elegance / of [Othon de] Granson, chief of those who write poetry in France); notice Chaucer's use of "curiosite" in line 81.

JOHN LYDGATE, *DANCE OF DEATH*: B VERSION (LANSDOWNE)

Before 1   *Incipit Macrobius.* Three manuscripts of the B version of the poem (Lansdowne, Lincoln, and Leiden) include an attribution to Macrobius at the beginning of the poem, probably a misunderstanding or corruption of "Macabre" (the note in Leiden is in a later hand). Macrobius Ambrosius Theodosius was a fifth-century Roman author whose *Commentary on the Dream of Scipio*, a treatise on the interpretation of dreams, was widely read in the Middle Ages; the ascription to Macrobius might also represent an attempt to associate the text with a known textual authority rather than the more mysterious "Macabre" (see Introduction, pp. 4–6). Two other manuscripts of the B version (Bodleian and Corpus Christi) identify it in their incipits as the "Dance of Pauls," referring to the murals painted in the Pardon Churchyard of St. Paul's Cathedral in London. None of the A text manuscripts include references to either Macrobius or the St. Paul's location.

Before 9   *Angelus.* The French *Danse* concludes, in some manuscripts, with a Latin stanza rubricated as "Angelus et doctor locuntur" (The Angel and the doctor speak) at line 543. Marchant's edition opens and closes with woodcuts showing an angel hovering over an author figure (identifiable by his pose of reading at a lectern); this angel is holding scrolls containing the Latin texts that open and close the

French work. If an angel was included at the beginning of the Parisian mural, it could explain the B version's decision to give the second stanza to this character, who does not otherwise speak in the poem.

9   *this myrrour.* See A version's note to line 49 above.

19   *And lik to Petir have the sovereynté.* See A version's note to line 59 above.

35   *Ye must forsake of gold your appill round.* See A version's note to line 75 above.

45   *A symple shete — ther is no more to seyn —.* See A version's note to line 85 above.

54   *Your hatt of red.* See A version's note to line 94 above.

Before 65 *Imperatrix.* This is a new character, who does not appear in the original French *Danse macabre* or in the A version.

77   *Deth seith chekmat.* The concept of a match of chess or a similar game played against Death or another supranatural figure is an ancient one. W. L. Nash writes, "[t]he ancient Egyptian game, which we call the game of draughts, has been the subject of many myths and legends. Plato quotes an ancient tradition that the game was invented by Thoth. Herodotus (II, 122) repeats the legend related to him by the Egyptian priests, that Rhampsinitus (Rameses III) descended into the lower world, there played at draughts with Isis, and returned, a victor, to Earth. Plutarch (de Isis, 12), probably referring to the same legend, says that Hermes (Thoth) played at draughts with the moon, and won five lunar days, which he added to the solar year" (341). In Chaucer's *Book of the Duchess*, the Man in Black, lamenting his love, states that "fals Fortune hath pleyd a game / Atte ches with me" (lines 618–19). Several examples survive in visual art, most notably a large painting of a man playing chess with Death in Täby Church outside of Stockholm, painted by Albertus Pictor c. 1480–90, which is said to have inspired the similar scene in Ingmar Bergman's 1957 film *The Seventh Seal*.

81   *Sir Patriarch, ful sad and humble of cheere.* See A version's note to line 121 above.

83   *Your dowble cros.* See A version's note to line 123 above.

Before 129   *Princeps.* In A (line 145), this speaker is identified as the Constable.

131   *Carlemayn.* See A version's note to line 139 above.

132–33   *worthy Arthour of . . . . the Rounde Table.* A central figure in medieval romance, King Arthur was a legendary ruler of England who was also understood as a historical figure in the later Middle Ages due to his central role in works like Geoffrey of Monmouth's *History of the Kings of Britain* (c. 1136). Arthur was said to have gathered the knights in his service around a round table at his court at Camelot, which served as their base in their search for the Holy Grail, the chalice used by Jesus at the Last Supper. Many of the Knights of the Round Table, including Lancelot, Galahad, and Gawain, appear as the protagonists of their own romance narratives.

151   *brouht to lure.* The phrase is used in hawking to mean "to bring somebody under control" (*MED lure* [n.1], sense 1c).

Before 161   *Comes et Baro*. In A (line 177), this speaker is identified as "the Baroun or the Knyht."

Before 177   *Abbas et prior*. In A (line 223), this speaker is identified only as the Abbot. B adds the Prior.

188   *somwhat the lesse grevaunce*. In A, this line reads "passinge grete grevaunce" (line 244), a somewhat stronger statement of dismay than the revised line.

Before 193   *Abbatissa*. This is a new character, who does not appear in the original French *Danse macabre*; she corresponds to the A version's Abbesse (line 249).

Before 209   *Iudex*. This is a new character, who does not appear in the original French *Danse macabre* or in the A version.

216   *Weel is hym that alwey weel doth*. Proverbial. See Whiting D278.

225   *Doctour of Canon and Cyvile*. In medieval Europe, two legal systems operated alongside one another: canon law, which was made and enforced by ecclesiastical authorities and used throughout Europe, and civil law, which was made and enforced by local secular authorities. Medieval universities taught both systems of law; the doctor whom Death addresses in this stanza is a scholar of both, as indicated by his terminal degree (*doctor utrisque juris*). This is a new character, who does not appear in the original French *Danse macabre* or in the A version.

235   *No man of his liff hath charter nor seele*. A charter is a formal document granting certain rights or privileges; a seal attached to such a document would give it legal effect. Using legal language, Death asserts here that no one has authority over his or her own life.

Before 241   *Miles et armiger*. In A, both the speaker marker and line 217 name only the Squire. B adds the Knight.

Before 257   *Maior*. This is a new character, who does not appear in the original French *Danse macabre* or in the A version.

273   *Sir Chanon Reguler*. The *MED* (*canoun* [n.2], sense 2a) defines a canon regular as "a canon living under a quasi-monastic rule, a regular canon, an Augustinian or a Premonstratensian canon." Such canons would have lived on the grounds of St. Paul's during the time the *Dance of Death* was present in the Pardon Churchyard. This is a new character, who does not appear in the original French *Danse macabre* or in the A version.

289   *Sir Dean or Chanon, with many gret prebend*. See A version's note to line 313 above. The B version adds the reference to a dean, the head of a chapter of canons associated with a cathedral or collegiate church (*MED den* [n.2]), which would be particularly appropriate for the *Dance of Death*'s setting at St. Paul's.

297   *My divers cures, my riche personages —*. See A version's note to line 321 above.

305   *ye be barbid and claad in clothis blaake*. See A version's note to line 377 above. Although the Monk appears in both the French *Danse macabre* and the A version, his stanzas here are substantially revised.

306   *Chastly receyved the mantil and the ryng.* The mantle (a sleeveless overgarment worn by monks and nuns) and the ring were outward symbols of a vow of perpetual chastity typically bestowed by a bishop.

323   *Sir Chartreux.* See A version's note to line 347 above.

337   *Sir Sergeant.* The Sergeant-at-Law is equivalent to the Man of Law in the A version of the text (lines 465–80) and is distinct from the Sergeant who appears in the B text from lines 401–16.

348–49   *Tescape awey from . . . . nor gret prudence.* In A (lines 476–77), these lines appear in the opposite order.

Before 353   *Generosa.* This is a new character, who does not appear in the original French *Danse macabre,* but her exchange with Death corresponds to the A version's Gentilwomman Amerous (line 449).

355   *As fair as ye was whilom Polliceene.* See A version's note to line 451 above.

356   *Penolope and the queen Eleyn.* See A version's note to line 452 above.

357   *Yit on this daunce thei went bothe tweyn.* See A version's note to line 453 above.

376   *And alle shul deie for an appyll rounde.* See A version's note to line 288 above. A similar image appears in line 35, in the description of the Emperor.

401   *thou Sergeant with thi stately maas.* See A version's note to line 361 above.

414   *And may nat flee, thouh I hadde it sworn.* See A version's note to line 374 above.

417   *Maister Jurour.* See A version's note to before line 481 above.

433   *Gentil menstral.* Although the Minstrel appears in the A version (line 497), his stanzas here are substantially revised.

440   *Bettir late than nevyr.* Proverbial. See Whiting L89.

448   *alle be nat mery that othirwhyle daunce.* Proverbial. See Whiting A88.

Before 449   *Famulus.* This is a new character, who does not appear in the original French *Danse macabre* or in the A version.

456   *the tyde abidith no man.* Proverbial. See Whiting T318.

465–80   *Ye phisiciens . . . . fynaly no boote.* Death's dialogue with the Physician in B seems closer to the French *Danse* (lines 351–66) than the corresponding section in A (lines 417–32). Where the *Danse* reads: "Comme aultre vous convient mourir" (line 356: You must die like any other), the A version omits this, while the B version has: "For Deth comyng sodeynly doth assaile / As weel lechis as othir" (lines 469–70). Similarly, only B reproduces the *Danse*'s "Plus n'y vault herbe, ne racine, / N'autre remede" (lines 364–65: "Plants and roots and other remedies / Are no longer any good") with "Wherfore shal helpe nothir herbe nor roote, / Nor no medycine . . ." (lines 478–79), while the A version omits the line. It is not clear why Lydgate may have gone back to his French source in revising this specific section.

465–66   *that loken so fast / In othir mennys watris what thei eyle.* See A version's note to line 417–18 above.

472   *al men shal repe as thei have sowe.* Proverbial. See Whiting S542.

480   *For ageyns Deth is fynaly no boote.* Proverbial. See Whiting D78.

Before 497   *Artifex.* This is a new character, who does not appear in the original French *Danse macabre* or in the A version.

509–12   *She pershith sheeldis . . . . be no deffence.* In this passage, Death is referred to as feminine. In French, Death is feminine (*la mort*), but there is no section that corresponds to the Artifex stanzas in the *Danse macabre*.

544   *For as sone deieth a yong sheep as an olde.* The usage of "sheep" here is metaphorical; see A version's note to line 543 above.

545   *Ye that have lived long in wildirnesse.* See A version's note to line 609 above.

552   *this liff heer is but a pylgrymage.* The idea of a life as a pilgrimage is present in a variety of late medieval devotional texts, perhaps most notably in Guillaume de Deguileville's *Le pèlerinage de la vie humaine*, which was translated twice into Middle English, once in prose as *The Pilgrimage of the Life of the Manhood* (dated to the 1420s) and once in verse as *The Pilgrimage of the Life of Man* (1426/27); the latter text is attributed to Lydgate, although the attribution remains questionable. Compare also Chaucer's Knight's Tale: "This world nys but a thurghfare ful of wo, / And we been pilgrymes, passynge to and fro. / Deeth is an ende of every worldly soore" (*CT* I[A] 2847–49). See also Whiting P201.

561   *Ye folk that loken upon this scripture.* "Scripture" seems to refer specifically to the written word; the A text uses "portrature," a word with visual connotations, in the equivalent passage at line 633.

569–70   *What is mannys liff but . . . a puff of wynde.* See James 4:15. See also Whiting L242.

JOHN LYDGATE, "DEATH'S WARNING TO THE WORLD" (DIMEV 4905)

This work boasts an especially intriguing textual history and visual presentation. Of its eight stanzas, five come from Lydgate's *Fall of Princes*, itself a translation of Boccaccio's *De casibus virorum illustrium*. Thus, lines 15–21 correspond to *FP* I.764–70; lines 29–35 to *FP* I.806–12; lines 36–42 to *FP* I.918–24; lines 43–49 to *FP* I.925–31; and lines 50–56 to *FP* I.960–66 (see Textual Notes for variants). This is one of several extracts from *FP* to circulate independently (see DIMEV 1904). In all three extant manuscripts, this poem precedes an extract on the *ars moriendi* from *The Seven Points of True Love and Everlasting Wisdom*, an early-mid-fifteenth century Middle English prose translation of a section of Henry Suso's *Horologium sapientiae* (not to be confused with Hoccleve's *Lerne to Die*, which is a verse translation of the same section of Suso's *Horologium*).

The resulting text itself has an element of hybridity to it: stanzas 1–4 (lines 1–28), out of which only stanza 3 comes from *FP*, treat familiar themes from the death poetry tradition. The speaker, Death, emphasizes his own unrelenting and violent nature, noting that he is armed with a fearsome weapon (lines 8–9). In what seems like a twist on the Signs of Death theme, this poem's Death points out that he scores his victims with a particular mark (line 11), as in "A Mirror for Ladies at Their Toilet" (DIMEV 3454, line 6). Like that poem, this work also addresses itself to a female who is emphatically young, fragile, and ephemeral in her beauty (lines 15–18) and whom Death menaces with a sharp weapon (lines 8–11). However, she is also presented in a relation with Death we have not seen before: she is his "hostesse" (line 1), welcoming Death into her own abode. By presenting the female addressee as Death's hostess, Lydgate adduces an aura of both intimacy but also mutual obligation and social convention into the interaction between Death and the female addressee.

In addition to being characterized as a hostess, the female addressee is also presented as a book owner and perhaps even compiler, when Death mentions that she has "in [her] book . . . set [his] image" (line 2). This detail firstly speaks to the rise in female book ownership, especially of devotional material, in the fifteenth century (see, in particular, Erler, *Women, Reading*). It also bears on this work's particular material context. Its earliest manuscript, Oxford, Bodleian Douce 322, fol. 19v (dated 1450–75), features an ink drawing of a skeleton holding a spear and a bell, which matches Death's description in lines 7–8. The image immediately prefaces the work, taking up thirteen lines of the 33-line text block. Enclosed in a double blue frame, the black-inked skeleton with brown ink shading looks away to the right as it stands on a grassy green surface, with a long spear with a red handle in its right hand and a large bell in the left, against a background decorated with red vegetal flourishes. The word *death* (variously spelled "dethe," "deþe," and "deþ") is written 19 times in a thick black formata hand all around the skeleton, with a cluster of eight renditions of the word around the bell, as if the illustrator imagines the line "I my belle rynge" (line 7) as the word "death" coming out of the bell itself. Meanwhile, the spear emerges from the blue frame into the blank space between the folio's dual-column layout, pointing to the word "declyneth" across the page (line 18). A similar presentation is found in London, British Library, MS Harley 1706, fol. 19v (dated 1475–1500). Here the image — comprising sixteen lines of the 40-line text block — is rendered more simply with no outline, or decorative background, and just a black line indicating the ground. The skeleton (also in black outline with brown shading) has been redrawn to match the stance of the figure in Douce; faint lines below the image show that originally the skeleton faced forward and held the spear at a sharper downward angle. There is no color besides red outlining for the handle of the spear and for the bell, and "deth" is written just five times in red in a circle around the skeletal figure. "Deth" is also added in black across the skeleton's chest, identifying it as Death itself. As in Douce, the spear extends into the space between the text columns, here pointing to "dye of nature" in line 28. Thus, like the *Dance of Death* itself, the manuscript context of this work is also designed to function as an image-text.

Stanzas 5–8 of the poem, which are all taken from *FP*, demonstrate a marked shift in the work's tone, moving away from the vivid personification of Death into a more standard devotional register of the *ars moriendi* tradition. Here the poem stresses the expulsion from Eden and Christ's redemptive sacrifice in the context of preparing one's soul for the afterlife through contrition and repentance. Thus, the hybrid work fuses two dominant strands of the late medieval death poetry tradition. This hybridity is underscored by the presence of a rubric in the Douce and Harley manuscripts, reading: "Thyese balades that thus ben wrytenne here be tak owte of the book of Johnne Lucas and sayde to the peple that shall see thys lytell tretyse in tyme to come." Although it occurs in the middle of the work, the rubric seems to refer, by the phrase "[t]hyese balades," both to the four stanzas preceding and the four stanzas following it. In the later Cambridge manuscript, however, produced 1475–1500, this rubric is omitted so that the works appear as a coherent whole.

2   *And in youre book to set myn ymage.* For MS illustrations, see the corresponding Textual Note.

4   *mortall usage.* Word-play here on two senses of *mortal,* meaning "as pertaining to death" and "as pertaining to mortals," thus: "it is my custom and deadly tendency" and "it is my custom and tendency when it comes to mortals . . ."

7   *my belle.* See note to line 2 above.

21   *patent.* This is a plate which holds the sacramental bread during the celebration of the Mass.

23   *For of my commyng there is no tyme sette.* Compare Matthew 24:36.

28   *Adams synne.* This refers to the consumption of the fruit of the Tree of the Knowledge of Good and Evil, for which Adam and Eve were expelled from the Garden of Eden in Genesis 3.

Before 29   *the book of Johnne Lucas.* The attribution of these works to "John Lucas" remains unclear. Henry MacCracken reads it as a scribal slip for "John Bochas," the Middle English rendering of Giovanni Boccaccio, Lydgate's source for the *Fall of Princes,* from which this poem is extracted: see *Minor Poems,* ed. MacCracken, 2:656n28.

39   *do almes.* The practice of distributing alms, in the form of material recompense to the poor and needy, is a core Christian virtue and stands at the heart of Christian penitential practice. Sharing goods within a community for the benefit of the common people is discussed in Acts 4:32 and 11:29 and prescribed by Paul in 1 Corinthians 16:1–2 and Galatians 2:10.

"THREE MESSENGERS OF DEATH" (DIMEV 5387)

This narrative poem is found in the monumental and closely related Vernon and Simeon manuscripts (both dated c. 1390–1400), enormous collections of devotional poetry, romance, and other works, mainly in the vernacular; for a discussion of their contents see, in particular, the new facsimile edition *Facsimile of the Vernon Manuscript,* ed. Scase and Kennedy; and Scase, *Making the Vernon Manuscript.* The poem, like the rest of the Vernon Manuscript, is written in the West Midlands dialect, thus reminding us of the spread of death-related poetry through England.

The poem presents Death as having three trusty messengers: "Aventures" (literally "Adventure" but better translated in the sense of *chance, diversion, fortune,* or *hazard*), Sickness, and Old Age. Chance, the poem relates, steals people away like a thief in the night (lines 61–62), a description that, like many of the other works in this volume, uses the figure of the violent criminal to characterize the suddenness of Death's approach. This thief, not choosy in his victims, steals a child that is but one day old (line 37–38), an image also seen in the *Danse macabre* and Lydgate's *Dance of Death*. The poem compares the blithely unaware to a "foul in the lift" (bird in the air, line 98), playing on the notion of the dying person's ephemeral beauty and fragility, as we also see in "A Mirror for Ladies at Their Toilet" (DIMEV 3454) and in "Warning Spoken by the Soul of a Dead Person" (DIMEV 3624). The second messenger, Sickness, treats the dying with greater honesty: Sickness "apertely" (line 73) announces Death's approach, unlike his compatriot Chance who steals up unawares. Sickness also moves people to contrition, although the speaker sneers that such emotion is often short-lived once the illness is cured (lines 85–96). The poem thus critiques the hypocrisy of human religiosity when it flares up only in times of distress and emergency. Finally, Old Age, in the poem's longest section, is characterized as a servant, forever at the gate and barred from entering into Death's domain but pointing the way inside (lines 117–24). This detail is reminiscent of the metaphor for death in Chaucer's Pardoner's Tale, in which the Old Man is ever knocking "on the ground, which is [his] moodres gate" without ever being let in (*CT* VI[C] 729) and speaks to the broader significance of architectural motifs to the death poetry tradition. This section also elaborates the trope, familiar from the *danse macabre* tradition, of Death's inevitability and relentlessness in going after people of all social ranks, including the pope and the emperor (lines 139–40).

The Old Age section brings a few more generic motifs into play that we have not seen as much in other works in this edition. It cites learned authorities — St. Paul and Augustine — to bolster its claims concerning death's inevitability and the importance of repentance and briefly paraphrases St. Paul's "thorn in the flesh" passage from 2 Corinthians 12:1–10 when discussing Sickness. The poem also features a brief *ubi sunt* moment concerning the passing of wealthy nobility that once amused themselves with hunting and hawking (lines 141–44), which we also see in "The Dawnce of Makabre" (DIMEV 4104). The poet goes on to present an Everyman figure at a churchyard, in which decorated tombs cover rotting bodies with wealth and finery. This stark image reminds the reader both of the physical presence of *danse macabre* imagery in churchyards, as well as of the vogue for *transi* tombs and their elaborate representation upon their valuable surfaces of the decomposing flesh within.

From here, the poem seamlessly moves into a brief vision of hell, which it chillingly and rather brilliantly imagines as a "pore halle" (line 157) with a low ceiling and close sides, filled with naked bodies, fittingly reminding us of a charnel house. Here the poem showcases some vivid turns of phrase, describing the dead as wrapped "in cloth of colde" (in a cloth of the chill of death, line 156) and highlights its characterization of hell as a cramped building by punning on the terms "helewowe" (end wall of a building) and "hell woe" (line 163). In this way, the poem builds up the architectural motifs introduced with the figure of Old Age as the servant at Death's door. At this point, it also delves into the Signs of Death tradition, as it asserts the necessity of contemplating the visual spectacle of the body's decomposition and consumption by maggots (lines 165–72). It thus also offers the mangled, rotting body as a paradoxical object of veneration and contemplation as we also see in "Warning Spoken by the Soul of a Dead Person" (DIMEV 3624).

This work is further enlivened by its macaronic quality: it intercalates two short Latin quatrains (lines 21–24, 89–92), which are roughly paraphrased in the English text in a manner reminiscent of Langland's intercalation of Latin devotional verses and biblical citations, with vernacular translation and paraphrase, in *Piers Plowman*.

3   *Job*. Protagonist of the Book of Job in the Old Testament, Job is a paradigmatic figure of human suffering and perseverance. To disprove Satan, who maintains that humans only love God when in good fortune and prosperity, God chooses a wealthy and happy man, Job, and tests his faith by sending him a series of cataclysmic misfortunes. Job loses his livelihood, his family, is afflicted with disease, but, though embittered, ultimately maintains his faith and gains insight into the mysterious and, from the human perspective, arbitrary workings of the divine.

7   *And seide his lyf nas bote a breth*. Compare Job 7:7: "Remember that my life is but wind, and my eyes shall not return to see good things."

10   *For his righte wol he not lete*. The subject of this line is Death.

45   *dedly synne*. The Christian church recognizes two classes of sin: venial and mortal. Venial sins are a violation of the moral law that merit punishment on earth but do not break the covenant with God, although their repeated occurrence may predispose one to graver infractions. Mortal sins break the covenant with God through a severe violation of Christian precepts and, without full repentance and divine forgiveness, ratified through the Church, result in eternal exclusion from the kingdom of Heaven.

46   *veyghe*. An alternate spelling of ME *weien*, this word literally means, according to the *MED*, "To weigh (somebody, a soul, one's deeds, etc. in or as in a balance) to determine worthiness of divine punishment or reward, damnation or salvation; weigh (the soul) on the divine balance at the Day of Judgment" (sense 1b(a)).

47   *ginne*. *Ginne* has the same wide semantic field as the French *engin*: thus, according to the *MED*: "Inventive talent, ingenuity, cleverness; an expedient, scheme; strategy; trickery, treachery; ruse, wile; an ingenious device or contrivance, machine; an instrument; a machine or structure used in assaulting or defending fortifications, a siege machine or tower." The semantic breadth of the word lends richness to the characterization of Aventures.

53   *Seint Poul bit we schulden awake*. An allusion to 1 Thessalonians 5:6: "Therefore, let us not sleep, as others do; but let us watch, and be sober."

68   *hende*. Literally "handsy," the same adjective applied to Nicholas in Chaucer's Miller's Tale. See *CT* I (A) 3199.

100   *Bereveth hem bothe hosel and schrift*. The consequence of dying without repenting and receiving forgiveness for mortal sin is, according to the Christian church, eternal damnation. Compare note to line 45 above.

100   *hosel*. The Eucharist is a Christian rite that goes back to the biblical New Testament, when Jesus instructed His followers during the Last Supper, on the

night before His Crucifixion, to eat bread and drink wine in remembrance of His body and blood. Still practiced today, the rite consists of parishioners imbibing wine and bread blessed by a priest at the conclusion of a church service.

105   *ure Lordes kniht*. This phrase is apposite to *Seynt Poul*. On St Paul's illness, compare 2 Corinthians 12:1–10 and Galatians 4:12–14.

141–44   *Wher ben heo . . . . uppon heore steeden*. This passage represents a well-known medieval motif known as *ubi sunt*, a lament for the death of revered figures from the past and for the inexorable passage of time that draws us, in the present, further from an imagined Golden Age. The convention of using the Latin phrase *ubi sunt* (meaning "where are they?") goes back to an early use of the motif in the Book of Baruch 3:16–19. Modern readers may recognize the well-known phrase "But where are the snows of yester-year?" as exemplifying this motif; the phrase comes from Dante Gabriel Rossetti's 1870 translation of the medieval French poet François Villon's *Ballade des dames du temps jadis* (1461). In addition to invoking the general *ubi sunt* motif, this stanza in *Three Messengers of Death* is a textual allusion to the *Sayings of Saint Bernard*, a popular Middle English poem composed c. 1275: see Furnivall's edition of the *Sayings* in *Minor Poems*, pp. 511–22, especially lines 181–86 (p. 521).

163   *Me may reche the helewowe*. Surely there is wordplay here on *helewough* (end wall of building), continuing the architectural motif earlier in the stanza, and *hell woe*, or the suffering found in hell.

172   *him*. The antecedent of "him" is Death in line 160.

180   *that is wormes mete*. Proverbial. See Whiting W675.

186   *Matussalé*. Methuselah is mentioned in Genesis 5:21–27 as the longest-living person in the Hebrew Bible, dying at the age of 969 years old; he is also an important member of the genealogy connecting Adam and Noah, as the son of Enoch and father of Lamech. His name also comes up in passing in 1 Chronicles 1:3 and Luke 3:37.

191   *prime*. This indication of time refers to one of the set times for prayer, by which Christian clergy structure their day; this practice is known as the Liturgy of the Hours, the Divine Office, or the canonical hours.

194   *seynt Austyn*. St. Augustine of Hippo (354–430 CE) was a Christian theologian and church father (that is, a founding figure for Christian thought) living in a Roman province of Northern Africa, where he served as bishop of Hippo Regius. His writings, such as *The City of God*, *On Christian Doctrine* and his autobiographical *Confessions*, have been enormous influences on the development of the Western theological and philosophical traditions. The author seems to be invoking Augustine in this moment to lend his words additional authority.

208   *Ne scholden him of pyne bringe*. The antecedent of "him" in this line is the man in line 201.

222   *Trinité.* The Christian doctrine of the Trinity holds that the Christian God is one God in three coequal and coeternal manifestations that are distinct from one another but of one substance: the Father, the Son (Jesus Christ), and the Holy Ghost. A useful popular comparison is to consider the physical properties of water, whereby ice, water, and vapor are three different manifestations of the same substance.

"A WARNING SPOKEN BY THE SOUL OF A DEAD PERSON" (DIMEV 3624)

Found in a devotional miscellany dating to the first quarter of the fifteenth century, this poem is exemplary of the Signs of Death genre (see Introduction, p. 2), in which the speaker imagines his or her body in its multiple stages of decomposition by contrast with its formerly beautiful state in life. In this lyric the body's dissolution is accentuated by the work's replacement of internal physiological structures, like the spine, for the external forces of decomposition, such as the adder, as we see in line 17. In this way the poem creates an opposition between the body's internal dissolution and the external forces of destruction visiting it in death. In its spatial codification of the body's destruction and emphasis on gory detail, furthermore, this poem insists on its memorability for the purpose of contemplation, not unlike that required of the viewer in Man of Sorrows iconography, which depicts Christ's wounded body for the purposes of devotional contemplation. Although this body's state is quite different from that of Christ crucified, it similarly presents as a spectacular object, inciting meditation on its fragility through the emphasis on its beleaguered condition.

24   *stynke foulere than an hounde.* Proverbial. See Whiting H592.

"A MIRROR FOR YOUNG LADIES AT THEIR TOILET" (DIMEV 3454)

This short lyric is extant in a single manuscript dated after 1461 to 1500 (based on its inclusion of a chronicle mentioning Edward IV: see "Detailed Record for Harley 116" in the British Library's online manuscript catalogue), which also includes Hoccleve's *Regiment of Princes*, a frequent manuscript companion to Lydgate's *Dance of Death*.

The poem is an address by Death to young women who pay attention to their good looks. To underscore the transitory quality of their beauty, Death implicitly compares the young women to ephemeral creatures, whose time on earth is fleeting ("Sone shalte thu flytte . . . Shorte is thy sesoun here . . . ," lines 4–5). In the second and third stanzas, Death's relentlessness emerges in stark contrast to the fragile beauty evoked in the opening stanza, as Death describes his actions and attributes in increasingly violent terms: "I marke thee with my mace . . . I manace . . . my lace [snare] . . . I smyte, I sle . . . " (lines 6–14), which we also see in the *danse macabre* tradition. The use of "pray" in line 9, in address to the young women, further underscores Death as a predator or hunter stalking after defenseless animals about to be caught in his trap. In this way, articulating the familiar characterization of women as prey before a predator, the lyric evokes connotations of sexual violence, suggesting that Death here is being gendered male. The lyric goes on to exhort the young women to "awake" from their vanity and pay heed to their eternal salvation (line 15).

The lyric's French rubric is noteworthy given its explicit address to a female audience. Its use of French speaks to the preponderance of French-language conduct literature aimed at women that was composed and consumed during the fourteenth and fifteenth centuries, of which Watriquet de Couvin's *Miroer as dames* (1324), *Le Livre du Chevalier de la Tour Landry* (1371–72), and *Le Menagier de Paris* (c. 1393) are prime examples. For discussions of these and other texts see, in particular, *Medieval Conduct*, ed. Ashley and Clark; and Burger, *Conduct Becoming*.

The French rubric of our English poem also points to the French cultural context of the *danse macabre* tradition. As Francis Utley notes, the French rubric to this poem evokes a French poem on similar themes, which opens with the lines, "Mirez vous cy, dames et damoiselles, / Mirez vous cy et regardés ma face. / Helas! pensez, se vous estes bien belles, / Comment la mort toute beauté efface" (lines 1–4: Behold yourselves here, ladies and maidens, / Behold yourself here and look at my face. / Alas! consider, if you are very beautiful, / How death effaces all beauty) (*Crooked Rib*, pp. 190–91, for full text of poem see Söderhjelm, "Le miroir des dames," pp. 31–35, translation our own). This similar French poem features a female speaker mourning the imminent progressive decomposition of her body in a French iteration of the Signs of Death genre. It is, furthermore, found in a manuscript (Paris, Bibliothèque nationale, naf. 10032) that also contains the *Danse macabre* and the *Danse macabre des femmes*, which opens with almost the same wording.

Our English work is further distinguished by its formal complexity. Unusually, the lyric inverts its rhyme scheme in the second stanza, thus *abbba-baaab-abbba* (see further Cutler, "A Middle English Acrostic," pp. 88–89). Through this inversion, the lyric fosters a sense of the middle stanza's being caught by the tight framing of stanzas 1 and 3, thus formally mirroring the lyric's claustrophobic theme of Death as a hunter seizing his prey. In keeping with the notion of catching or binding and its formal reflection within the lyric's structure, the entire work itself is an acrostic evidently intended to spell out MORS SOLVIT OMNIA, or "death loosens all," although the lyric's only manuscript substitutes a "B" for the necessary "N" in OMNIA. Cutler notes that this phrase is also associated with the well-known lyric "Erthe upon Erthe," similarly a work that treats the transitory and fleeting nature of earthly possessions ("A Middle English Acrostic," p. 89). Thus, this lyric's content emphasizes the capture of living creatures in the tight grip of Death, as mirrored on the metapoetic level by the lyric's internal rhyme structure. Meanwhile, in contrast, the lyric's superstructure of the acrostic highlights the notion of death as the ultimate release from earthly bonds.

Rubric	*C'est le myrroure . . . testes bealment adressere.* There seems to be a play on words here as *adressere* can have both a literal meaning of arranging something, such as hair, as well as a more figurative meaning of moral rectitude, apt for a work suggesting leaving behind worldly vanity for spiritual progress. Thus, we could gloss the second half of the rubric as "instructing/rectifying their heads (i.e., minds) virtuously."
13	*Ne.* The text seems somewhat corrupt here, as the only manuscript reads "Be" for "Ne", which ruins the acrostic (see Textual Note to this line).

lace. The poem's use of the imagery of a snare seems to be playing with the idiomatic expression *dethes las*, which the *MED* defines as "death's grasp" (*las* (n.), sense 4).

"The Ressoning betuix Deth and Man," Ascribed to Robert Henryson (DIMEV 4000)

This short poem, composed in Middle Scots (the Anglic language used in the Scottish Lowlands between 1400 and 1700, as distinct from the Gaelic language of the Scottish Highlands), presents the narrator's dialogue with a personified figure of death. The poem appears in two places in the famous Bannatyne Manuscript; in one of these, the poem is scribally attributed to Robert Henryson (c. 1430–1500), one of the most well-known poets writing in Middle Scots. The language of this work and its attribution to a Scottish poet highlights the spread of death poetry in the British Isles. The Bannatyne Manuscript (Edinburgh, National Library of Scotland, Advocates MS 1.1.6) is a massive, nearly 400-folio sixteenth-century anthology of works by, among others, Henryson and Dunbar and some Chauceriana, copied by George Bannatyne (1545–1606). The manuscript is divided into two parts: the Draft, itself comprised of several individual manuscripts dated 1565–67, and the much longer Main, internally dated 1568, in which the works from the Draft are recopied and greatly augmented with new ones (see MacDonald, "The Bannatyne Manuscript"). In the Main, the poem is ascribed to "Hendersone," which is understood to be "Henryson" due to the other Henryson poems copied around it; given the uniqueness of the copy, however, the attribution is considered weak. Although it appears twice in one manuscript copied by a single scribe, the two versions in Bannatyne seem to be copied from different exemplars (see Textual Notes).

In terms of its contents, the work intersects in several ways with other late medieval death poetry. In keeping with the *danse macabre* tradition, the work is organized as a dialogue between Death and an Everyman figure. It similarly offers a diverse catalogue of representatives of social strata, who will all become equal in their death, from the pope and the emperor onwards (lines 4–5). Like other poems on similar themes, this poem also characterizes Death as violent force, here inflicting damage with a dart (line 6), Furthermore, like the "Three Messengers of Death" (DIMEV 5387), it relies on architectural imagery to emphasize Death's all-consuming power (lines 7–8), which speaks to the presence of death imagery on numerous architectural structures in the late medieval period. Like Signs of Death poetry, it also briefly reminds the reader of the body's imminent decomposition and consumption by vermin (line 38).

Title *The Ressoning betuix Deth and Man.* That is, the discussion between Death and Man. See *MED resoun* (n.2), sense 8: "speech, talk, discourse."

2 *Quhilk sowld thy myrrour be.* Compare Lydgate's *verba translatoris* to the *Dance of Death* (A text, lines 31, 637 and B text, line 565) where he counsels his audience to have his words as a mirror before their mind. The same image reappears in this poem at line 10.

24 The subject of this line ("he" in the gloss) is "nane" (no one) in line 21.

"THE DAWNCE OF MAKABRE" (DIMEV 4104)

Although this poem does not contain the characteristic features of the *danse macabre* such as social satire and a dialogue between Death and the living, it is identified in its manuscript, British Library Additional MS 37049, as "The Dawnce of Makabre." The poem, written in a Northern dialect, is one of a large number of death-related texts included in British Library MS Additional 37049, a Carthusian miscellany produced in Yorkshire during the second half of the fifteenth century. The allusion in this context shows that the *danse macabre* was recognized in monastic as well as lay contexts and circulated in England, well outside of London, where most of the surviving manuscripts of Lydgate's poem were made.

It is representative of a popular genre of late medieval and early modern epitaphs in verse, although here (as in many other examples of the genre) the length of the poem calls into question whether or not this was ever actually inscribed on a tombstone or other monument. While in the Additional MS the poem is titled "The Dawnce of Makabre" and at line 63 enjoins its readers to "remembyr of the dawnce of makabre," it does not contain the catalogue of figures or elements of estates satire found in Lydgate's poem and characteristic of the Dance of Death tradition more broadly. It does, however, emphasize the inevitability and universality of death throughout, as well as the transitory nature of earthly life and achievements.

While, despite the title it is given in manuscript, the text is not closely aligned with the *danse macabre* tradition, it contains a number of other interesting literary features. The poem is framed as an epitaph, in which the memorial itself speaks to passersby. The second stanza is carefully structured to include each of the seven deadly sins, while the fourth and fifth stanzas feature an extended meditation on the great men of the past, an example of the *ubi sunt* trope borrowed from classical literature, which we also find in "Three Messengers of Death" (DIMEV 5387) included in this edition. The direct address to the reader, maintained throughout the poem, asks the reader to directly confront issues related to death, packing both vivid description and emotional intensity into the poem's 83 rhyme royal lines. In the manuscript, a large, colored drawing of a skeleton wearing a crown, facing the reader and with one hand upraised, further heightens the sensation of direct address. This visual addition evokes the "image-text" quality of the larger *danse macabre* tradition, and resembles the visuals accompanying Lydgate's "Death's Warning to the World" (DIMEV 4905).

1   *O ye al whilk that by me cummes and gothe.* This poem presents itself as an epitaph or memorial inscription, addressing itself to passersby. For more on the 'speaking' tombstone, see the notes to lines 76 and 78 below.

8–14   *Why art thou . . . . has sone pasayge.* This second stanza touches on each of the seven deadly sins: pride ("prowde elacyon"), avarice ("wordly covetyse"), anger ("wrathe"), envy ("invyos swellyng"), gluttony ("glotony"), sloth ("Brynnyng in slomer and slawly in corayge"), and lust ("to be lycheros").

22–27   *Wher is Salomon . . . . Jonathas ful amyabyll.* This 6-line stanza with an *ababbb* rhyme scheme breaks from the poem's regular 7-line *ababbcc* stanza form. This stanza is an example of the *ubi sunt* (where are they?) trope, which reflects on the greatness of departed figures from the past. See also the note to lines 141–44 in "Three Messengers of Death" (DIMEV 5387) in this edition.

22   *Salomon . . . with al his prudence.* Solomon is the Old Testament Israelite king known for his wisdom and traditionally considered the author of the biblical books of Proverbs, Ecclesiastes, and the Song of Songs.

23   *myghty Sampson duk invyncybyll.* In the Old Testament Book of Judges 13–16, Samson is a leader of the Israelites who possesses extraordinary physical strength. His strength failed after his long hair was cut by his mistress Delilah, in violation of his Nazarite vow.

24   *Tullyus the retrysciane with al his eloquence.* Marcus Tullius Cicero, (106 BCE–42 BCE), is a Roman politician and rhetorician whose letters were an important stylistic model for medieval writers.

25   *Arystotil.* Ancient Greek philosopher Aristotle (384–322 BCE) is considered one of the founders of the Western philosophical tradition.

26   *Or this emprour Octavy mest pessybyll.* Gaius Octavius Augustus is the first Roman emperor, grand-nephew of Julius Caesar. His reign (27 BCE–14 CE) coincided with a period of relative peace known as the *pax romana.*

27   *swete Jonathas ful amyabyll.* Jonathan is considered a model of loyalty, whose friendship with King David is described in 1 Kings 18.

30   *twynkillyng of ane ee.* Proverbial. See Whiting T547.

38   *As Job says in his funerall obsequye.* The protagonist of the biblical book of Job is considered a model of devout and patient suffering; see also the note to line 3 in "Three Messengers of Death" (DIMEV 5387) above. The more specific reference here may be to *Pety Job,* a popular poetic meditation on the Office of the Dead, written in the mid-fifteenth century. *Pety Job* quotes from and imaginatively expands upon a series of verses drawn from Job's speeches, as well as material from the Book of Psalms. As the *Dawnse of Makabre* says, the purpose of *Pety Job* is that readers "may lerne to dye." The "tretys" mentioned in line 40 refers to the biblical Book of Job.

42–43   *O erthly man . . . sal to erth.* An allusion to Genesis 3:19: "In the sweat of thy face shalt thou eat bread till thou return to the earth, out of which thou wast taken: for dust thou art, and into dust thou shalt return." This theme also reappears in line 58. See also Whiting E22.

51   *Into powdyr we sal fall.* The phrase evokes the Order for the Burial of the Dead in the 1549 Book of Common Prayer ("I Commende thy soule to God the father almightie, and thy bodye to the grounde, earth to earth, asshes to asshes, duste to dust, in sure and certayne hope of resurreccion to eternall lyfe, through our Lorde Iesus Christe" sig. T6v; STC 16272) which itself alludes to Genesis 18:27: "And Abraham answered, and said: 'Seeing I have once begun, I will speak to my Lord, whereas I am dust and ashes.'"

63   *Man remembyr of the dawnce of makabre.* This is the only explicit reference to the *danse macabre* in the poem. The injunction for the reader to remember echoes line 18 of the A version of Lydgate's *Dance of Death*, which suggests that readers imprint the Dance in their "memorial" or memory.

76   *ite venite.* Literally, "go, come" (e.g., come from here), this Latin phrase was a common inscription on tombstones. The phrase evokes the address to those who "by me cummes and gothe" in the first line of the poem.

78   *this litterall scripture.* A pun. The poem is literally inscribed on the tombstone.

"CAN YE DANCE THE SHAKING OF THE SHEETS" (DIMEV 956)

The poem is found in British Library MS Additional 15225, a miscellany of mostly Catholic ballads compiled in the first quarter of the seventeenth century. Although the date of the manuscript is late, the language of many of the poems, including the one printed here, is earlier. (The contents of the entire manuscript are described in Rollins, *Old English Ballads*, p. xxvii–xxx). The poem draws on several familiar dimensions of the medieval *danse macabre* tradition, including its emphasis on Death's leveling power across all levels of society ("Bringe away the beggar and the king, / And everie man in his degree," lines 8–9). While Lydgate's poem contains a more or less equal representation of clerical and secular occupations, most of the figures named here are laypeople and the more explicitly "Popish" figures found in Lydgate's version, like the Pope and the Friar, are absent.

This version of the *danse macabre* engages with religion in other ways, however. The fourth stanza references the "solempe syses last" in Oxfordshire. This is an allusion to the so-called "Black Assize" of the summer of 1577. As many as 300 people died in an outbreak of "gaol fever" (typhus) that coincided with the trial of a recusant (Catholic) bookseller, Roland Jenkes (see *ODNB*, "Barham, Nicholas"). The dead included Sir Robert Bell, chief baron of the exchequer, and Nicholas Barham, a sergeant-at-law, as well as several members of the jury — Puritans who were perceived to be biased against Jenkes. The event is described by Holinshed in the expanded and revised 1587 version of his *Chronicle* (p. 1270) and, in addition to the English ballad here, was the source for a Welsh carol by the recusant priest and martyr Richard White (see *English Martyrs*, ed. Pollen, p. 99).

The references to the "solempe syses last" suggest this version of the poem was composed shortly after the events of 1577, although this stanza — the only one in the poem to contain topical references — may be an interpolation into an older text. The text was printed numerous times as a broadsheet ballad in the seventeenth century. Like other broadsides in the *danse macabre* tradition, these later printings often feature woodcuts of Death armed with a spear (also a feature of the fifteenth-century illustrations to Lydgate's "Death's Warning to the World" [DIMEV 4905]).

1   *the shakinge of the sheetes.* Of this allusion, Gray writes, "According to Chappell, *Popular Music of the Olden Time*, I, 84ff., the name of a country dance" (p. 71). See also *OED shaking* (n.), sense 1d, which notes that the phrase "shaking of the sheets" was "in the 16–17th centuries very often used jocularly for sexual intercourse."

5   *Make readie then your winding sheete*. The burial shroud, or winding sheet, is a
           frequent motif in poems of the *danse macabre* tradition. See, for example, the
           Emperor's comment at lines 85–86 in the A version of Lydgate's *Dance of Death*,
           where he acknowledges his worldly wealth will pass away and he will be left with
           "a simple shete — ther is no more to seyne — / To wrappe in my body and
           visage."

14   *the banker with his beating hookes*. This allusion is untraced. The later printed
           editions emend it to "baiting hookes" (see Textual Note to this line), an image
           that suggests a desire to lure unsuspecting clients into disadvantageous financial
           arrangements.

23   *How sodenlie in Oxfordshire*. An allusion to the "Black Assize" at Oxford in 1577,
           an outbreak of "gaol fever" (likely typhus) that coincided with the trial of a
           recusant bookseller by a largely Puritan jury. See *ODNB*, "Barham, Nicholas."

26   *And tooke both Bell and Baram away*. Sir Robert Bell, chief baron of the exchequer,
           and Nicholas Barham, a sergeant-at-law, were two of the dead during the "Black
           Assize." While Sir Robert Bell was a judge and chief baron of the exchequer, it
           is not clear why Barnham is singled out here among the more than a dozen
           figures named in Holinshed's *Chronicle*.

37   *peltinge*. This word is likely of Scots origin. See *DOST pelt* (n.2).

Explicit   *Thomas Hill*. None of the printed versions of the poem are signed. Gray suggests
           this may be Edmund Hill (1564–1644), an English Benedictine monk whose
           name in religion was Thomas St. Gregory (*ODNB*, "Hill, Edmund"). Hill
           published several devotional works, but there is no evidence to connect him
           directly to this text.

LA DANSE MACABRE, TRANSLATION BY ELIZAVETA STRAKHOV

CHOICE OF BASE MANUSCRIPT

The French *Danse macabre* is extant in fifteen manuscripts, the earliest dating from 1426–27 (see Headnote in Textual Notes) and the rest falling between the mid-late fifteenth century, nineteen incunabula printed from 1485 to 1500 alone, and one sixteenth-century manuscript that is a copy of an incunabulum (Paris, Bibliothèque Mazarine, MS 3896, copying Marchant's edition of 1490). Authorship of the *Danse* remains uncertain, but several scholars have pointed to the fact that in Paris, Bibliothèque nationale de France lat. 14904, dated to c. 1440 by Gilbert Ouy (*Les manuscrits de l'Abbaye de Saint-Victor*, 2.327–28), the *Danse* is specified in the contemporary table of contents as being the text as copied from the Cemetery of the Holy Innocents and is collocated with texts by Jean Gerson (1363–1429) and Nicolas de Clemanges (1360–1437). Meanwhile, a Catalàn translation of the *Danse*, made at the end of the fifteenth century by Pedro Miguel de Carbonell, ends with a *verba translatoris* (words of the translator) alleging his source to have been penned by "un sant home doctor e Canceller de Paris en lengua francesa apellat Joannes Climachus sive Climages" (a devout man, a doctor and clerk of Paris in French named Joannes Climachus or Climages) (Saugnieux, *Les danses macabres de France et d'Espagne*, p. 25). This coincidence has suggested to Maya Dujakovic ("The Dance of Death, the Dance of Life," pp. 222–27) that the work was or was believed to come from the circles of Jean Gerson (who was a chancellor at the University of Paris) and Nicolas de Clemanges. However, Jöel Saugnieux (*Les danses macabres de France et d'Espagne*, pp. 54–55) and Sophie Oosterwijk ("Of Dead Kings," pp. 153–54) advance objections to this argument, citing the circumstantial quality of the evidence.

The *Danse macabre* is clearly Lydgate's direct source for the *Dance of Death*, as he alleges in his opening *verba translatoris* in the A version, in which he describes seeing "Machabres Daunce" (A version, line 24) at "Seint Innocentis" (A version, line 35). In most manuscripts of the *Danse*, the opening and closing stanzas of the work are spoken by an authority figure variously named "docteur," "l'acteur," or "maistre." In Paris, Bibliothèque nationale de France, fr. 14989, a manuscript belonging to Philip the Good, Duke of Burgundy, however, this speaker is explicitly identified as "Machabre Docteur." (According to Kurtz [*Dance of Death and the Macabre Spirit*, p. 23], the same speaker marker occurs at the end of the text in Paris, Bibliothèque nationale de France, naf. 10032; we have not, unfortunately, been able to verify this through consultation of the original manuscript.) Lydgate calls the same character "Machabre the Doctour" (A version, before line 641). Hanno Wijsman dates the French manuscript of the *Danse* containing the "Machabre docteur" speaker marker to 1426 or 1427 on the basis of its watermark; he further shows that it was once bound with the *Division des Orleanois contre les Anglois*, which treats the death of Thomas Montacute, Duke of Salisbury, who died in 1428. These details place BNF MS fr. 14989 in Paris right after the *Danse macabre* mural was finished and during or just after Lydgate's visit in 1426. Wijsman goes on to argue that the unique level of visual detail in this manuscript version's speaker markers suggests that it may have been copied directly from the mural, which the scribe aimed to verbally describe in his otherwise unillustrated copy (see "Un manuscrit de Philippe Le Bon"). In addition, the order of speakers in the A version of Lydgate's *Dance* matches the order of speakers in this and other manuscripts of the *Danse*; Marchant's 1485 and subsequent editions follow a slightly altered order, suggesting he was working from a different recension. This manuscript, BNF MS fr. 14989, thus seems closest to Lydgate's source for his *Dance of Death*, and we have therefore chosen to edit and translate its contents to accompany Lydgate's text.

LYDGATE'S TRANSLATION OF THE *DANSE*

In the A version's final two stanzas, titled "Lenvoye de Translator" or "translator's envoy," Lydgate adopts the well-known pose of the humble translator, professing his lack of "suffisaunce" (fluency, line 671) in French due to being an English native. He also invites his readers to correct his translation where it is wanting and notes that he translates "[n]ot worde by worde but folwyng the substaunce" (not word by word but following the content, line 666). This is a familiar posture of proclaimed English deference before the cultural might of literary French that mirrors Lydgate's fellow Francophile English predecessors: see the note to line 671 of the A version of Lydgate's *Dance*. Lydgate's professed difficulties with French are belied, however, by the translation itself. Lydgate's close attention to the language of his original yet simultaneous impulse to adapt and rewrite to vivid effect are already visible from the opening stanzas of his work. The opening stanza of the original *Danse*, for example, is as follows:

O, creature raisonnable,	O, creature endowed with reason,
Qui desires vie eternelle,	You who long for eternal life,
Tu as cy doctrine notable	You have before you an important precept
Pour bien finer vie mortelle.	For properly ending your mortal life.
La danse macabre s'appelle	It is called the *Danse macabre*,
Que chascun a danser apprant.	Which everyone learns to dance.
A homme et femme est mort naturelle;	Death is natural to men and women;
Mort n'espargne petit ne grant.	Death spares neither the lowly nor the lofty.
(lines 7–14)	

In Lydgate's rendition, we find:

O creatures ye that ben resonable	*who are reasonable*
The liif desiring wiche is eternal,	
Ye may se here doctrine ful notable,	*see*
Youre lif to lede wich that is mortal,	
Therby to lerne in especial	*in particular*
Howe ye shul trace the Daunce of Machabre,	*follow*
To man and womman yliche natural,	*alike*
For Deth ne spareth hy ne lowe degré.	*does not spare*
(lines 41–48)	

Here Lydgate's heavy reliance on cognates has the double advantage of gesturing extensively to his French source while rendering the text into a flowing English idiom. But by adding "ye shul trace" in line 46 he subtly highlights the dynamic performative quality of the *Danse macabre*, whereas the French original just presents the phrase as the text's title. These processes — of relying on cognates but also insisting on alterations that emphasize, in particular, the active participatory quality of Death's dance — are characteristic of Lydgate's whole text.

In our own translation, we have remained as faithful as possible to the original French *Danse*, and we note especially syntactically and linguistically challenging moments in our Explanatory Notes. Since the A version of Lydgate's text is closer to the *Danse* than the later B revision, all references to Lydgate refer to this version unless otherwise noted. Furthermore, this translation was intentionally done without consulting Lydgate's own in the process, lest his word choices unduly influence the modern English renderings and thus taint the modern English with Middle English usage and, more importantly, leave a distorted impression of the closeness of Lydgate's translation. Yet the final results, we think, speak for themselves: for all the distance between Middle and modern English, our new translation helps show that Lydgate offers a remarkably precise rendering of his French original in his instances of close translation.

Within our own translation, one particularly difficult decision has revolved around naming the *Danse*'s representation of its deadly interlocutor. The French text renders this character as "le mort," literally "the dead man," a figure clearly intended to double the living persons, all male, to whom it speaks. That "le mort" is the terrifying double of the *Danse*'s all-male characters is also suggested by widespread *danse macabre* iconography, in which each living person is represented in conversation with his or her own emaciated and decomposing figure. In the later *Danse macabre des femmes* the figure is, fittingly, "la morte," "the dead woman." The French term for the abstract concept of death, meanwhile, is "la mort," gendered female. We have nevertheless chosen to translate "le mort" as "Death" for several reasons: firstly, "the dead man" seemed aesthetically clunky; secondly, this is the term used throughout the Middle English death poetry that forms the subject of this collection, suggesting that contemporary English readers, like Lydgate, would have understood "le mort" as the abstract concept of death, despite the gendering of the term (see, for example, the illustration of Death in MS Douce 322, discussed in the Headnote to the Explanatory Notes for Lydgate's "Death's Warning to the World" [DIMEV 4905]). We have therefore chosen to render "le mort" by the more efficient and historically pertinent "Death," while cognizant that there is no good method for underscoring the way in which "le mort," in the spirit of late medieval death poetry as a whole, neatly combines the idea of death as universalized abstraction with that of death as a particularized humanoid figure that inversely mirrors the living bodies of its interlocutors.

Given the similarity in content between this text and Lydgate's adaptation thereof, the reader is referred to the Explanatory Notes accompanying Lydgate's *Dance of Death* (both A and B versions) for any overlapping material. The Explanatory Notes that follow here concern details specific to this text and to this translation. The Latin here and at the end of the poem has been translated by C. J. Lambert (Columbia University), whose accompanying notes are reproduced and marked accordingly. We also thank Lucas Wood for his invaluable assistance in helping us work through some of the thornier sections of the text.

1–2   *Nec pictura decus . . . . ducere festa monet.* This and several other manuscripts open with this line in Latin that draws attention to the idea of a painting representing dancing, which speaks to the "image-text" quality of the *Danse* painted at the Holy Innocents; compare lines 519–20.

2   *In que* is being taken with *festa* here, according to Lambert.

14   *Mort n'espargne petit ne grant.* Proverbial. See Hassell M200.

17   *Cilz est eureux qui bien s'i mire.* Pursuant to the complex semantic field of "mirouer" (see Explanatory Note to Lydgate, A version, line 49 above), "bien s'i mire" evokes both the literal sense of seeing one's reflection as well as the more figurative notions of contemplating and meditating on that reflection and the curative sense of taking care of oneself.

22   *Tout est forgié d'une matiere.* Proverbial. See Hassell M98.

70   *Toute joye fine en tristesse.* Proverbial. See Hassell J23.

78   *Le plus riche n'a q'un linseul.* Proverbial. See Hassell L59.

80   *sauvage.* The poet's choice of this term in the context of a terrifying dance, as spoken by the character of the king, would surely have reminded contemporary readers of the devastating "Bal des ardents" (The Dance of the Burning Men), also known as the "Bal des sauvages" (The Dance of the Wild Men) of 1393. At the dance, King Charles VI, who had suffered his first attack of madness the year

before, disguised himself and several other courtiers as shaggy wildmen, or creatures of the forest, for the purposes of a masque. Although attendees were warned to keep candles away from the highly flammable costumes, fire broke out, and multiple courtiers died, while the king himself barely escaped a similar fate. Some contemporary chroniclers suspected an assassination attempt by Louis of Orléans, the king's brother. These suspicions fueled political opposition to Louis that resulted eventually in his assassination in 1407 and the outbreak of the Armagnac-Burgundian Civil War. See further Veenstra, *Magic and Divination*, pp. 89–95. Lydgate reproduces the term "savage" in his translation at line 114 of the A version, though it is not clear if he is picking up on this reference or simply using a cognate.

86   *A la fin fault devenir cendre*. Proverbial. See Hassell C19.

94   *Fole esperance deçoit l'omme*. Proverbial. See Hassell E76.

118   *Contre la mort n'a nul respit*. Proverbial. See Hassell M193. See also lines 366, 375–76, and 393.

142   *Ce que l'un fait, l'autre despiece*. Proverbial. See Hassell F6.

150   *Dessoubz le ciel n'a riens estable*. Proverbial. See Hassell R39.

151–53 *pic . . . . pic*. The author is punning here on two meanings for the word "pic": pick-axe as well as an idiomatic expression derived from *jeu de piquet*, a type of card game, in which "pic" refers to a situation where one player dominates the game so thoroughly that his opponent cannot even score a single point. This expression also occurs as a metaphor for death contemporaneously in the lyric *Mourir me voy* by Reginaldus Libert (fl. c. 1425–35) and in an untitled lyric found in the Bayeux manuscript (Paris, Bibliothèque nationale de France, fr. 9346), a collection dating to c. 1500. See further, *Oxford Music Online*, "Libert, Reginaldus" and Gérold, *Manuscrit de Bayeux*, p. 44 (Chanson XXXIX).

155   *Vostre fait gist en aventure. Aventure* is a semantically laden word in French, similar to the association of the Middle English *aventure* with the ideas of chance and risk as well as 'adventurous journey' (compare "Aventures" in "The Three Messengers of Death" [DIMEV 5387], lines 13, 44, 47, 61, and 99). We have selected a looser translation to get at this sense of the exciting, unexpected, and potentially dangerous.

174   *Il n'est qui puisse mort fuir*. Proverbial. See Hassell M195.

190   *Le plus gras est premier pourry*. Proverbial. See Hassell G52.

214   *Contre la mort n'a point d'appel*. Proverbial. See Hassell M191.

230   *Qui vouldra bien morir bien vive*. Proverbial. See Hassell M231.

238   *On ne scet pour qui on amasse*. Proverbial. See Hassell A86.

247   *chanoine prebendez*. See note to Lydgate's *Dance of Death* A version, line 313.

254   *La mort vient qu'on ne garde l'eure*. Proverbial. See Hassell M201.

262   *A bien morir doit chascun tendre*. Proverbial. See Hassell M224.

270   *Tel convoite qui a assez*. Proverbial. See Hassell C291.

278   *Qui trop embrasse peu estraint*. Proverbial. See Hassell E23.

298   *appellez*. From *appeller*, to shout and, figuratively, to lodge an appeal; both would
        be fitting actions for an officer of the law who was in the process of being
        violently attacked.

310   *Envis meurt qui aprins ne l'a*. Literally, "he is loath to die who has not learned it,"
        wherein the referent to "it" is not fully clear. We have taken this as referring to
        the whole idea of the *ars moriendi*, or learning to die.

318   *Vie d'omme est peu de chose*. Proverbial. See Hassell V97.

327   *sens desreuglé*. This phrase has a dual sense of both a troubled mind (as in,
        troubled by fear) but also in the sense of mental breakdown or disorder. In this
        way, the poet seems to be suggesting that usury is such an unnatural way of
        making a living that it will literally drive its practitioner mad.

334   *A tout perdre est cop perilleux*. This elliptic phrase appears to be a French proverb
        derived from gambling. An eighteenth-century proverb dictionary explains as
        follows: "A tout perdre il n'y a qu'un coup perilleux: se dit, lorsque'en risquant
        tout, on se resout à tout ce qui peut arriver" (It takes but one dangerous play to
        lose everything: this is said when, in risking everything, one resigns oneself to
        anything that may happen); see *Dictionnaire des proverbes françois*, ed. Backer,
        perdre. The general sense seems to concern the precariousness of one's fortunes
        in games of chance; we have therefore chosen a slightly looser translation to get
        at the full dimensions of the proverb. Lydgate, it should be noted, opts for a
        more literal rendition: "O perillous strook shal make thee lese al" in line 400 of
        the A version.

342   *Tel a beaux eulx qui n'y voit goute*. Proverbial. See Hassell Y4.

350   *N'est pas quitte qui doit de reste*. Proverbial. See Hassell Q12.

358   *Bon mire est qui se scet guerir*. Proverbial. See Hassell M154.

374   *Beauté n'est qu'ymage fardé*. Proverbial. See Hassell B35.

382   *Petite pluye abat grant vent*. According to the *DMF*, *pluie* (n.), this phrase is
        proverbial: "Idée de changement rapide (en partic. entre joie et tristesse, entre
        vantardise et abattement . . .). 'Il faut peu de chose pour que tout change, pour
        que l'effet soit important.'" (The notion of swift change (esp. between joy and
        grief, between boastfulness and comeuppance . . .). 'It takes just a little bit to
        change everything, to have an enormous effect.') See also Hassell P201. Lydgate
        opts for a similar rendition, writing, "And windes grete gon doun with litil reyn"
        in line 448 of the A version.

383   *sans long proces*. This is an expression literally meaning with no delay but clearly
        playing on "proces" in the sense of trial or juridical proceeding, which befits
        Death's addressee in this stanza. We have chosen to translate this as "deliberation"

to evoke the idea of delay within a legal context. Lydgate also picks up on this pun, rendering the phrase with a neat "short processe for to make" in line 465 of the A version.

390   *Bon fait justice prevenir.* Proverbial. See Hassell J53.

398   *Dieu rendra tout a juste pris.* Proverbial. See Hassell D82.

406   *Maistre doit monstrer sa science.* Proverbial. See Hassell M28.

410   *J'ay mis soubz le banc ma vielle.* An idiomatic expression that literally means, "I have placed my viol under the bench" this phrase figuratively denotes the idea of fully and with finality abandoning a project or activity. Hence, we have translated the phrase a bit loosely, to get at both senses implied.

411   *sauterelle.* The *sauterelle* is an animated dance characterized by high leaps and skips. See Taylor, "Que signifiait 'danse,'" pp. 265–67 on the particular association in medieval iconography of the *danse macabre* with fast dancing, featuring high leaps, characteristic of contemporary representations of folk dancing. Compare also the king's laments concerning the "savage" nature of the dance in the *Danse macabre*, line 80, as well as in Lydgate's *Dance* (A version, line 114, and B version, line 106).

430   *Qui dieu quitte bien est eureux.* Proverbial. See Hassell D94.

438   *Fol est qui cuide tousjours vivre.* Proverbial. See Hassell C352.

446   *Au monde n'a point de reppos.* Proverbial. See Hassell R29.

454   *A toute heure la mort est preste.* Proverbial. See Hassell M186.

461   *En petite heure dieu labeure.* Proverbial. See Hassell D87.

478   *meurt joune que vieulx.* Proverbial. See Hassell M226.

486   *Dieu punist tout quant bon luy semble.* Proverbial. See Hassell D81.

494   *Moult remaint de ce que fol pense.* Literally, "much remains of what a fool thinks," which we have chosen to clarify with the addition of "unrealized." Lydgate seems to have understood the phrase similarly in his translation: "For moche faileth of thing that foles thinke" in line 608 of the A version.

502   *Vie n'est pas seur heritaige.* Proverbial. See Hassell V98.

517   *livre.* I.e., the Bible.

519–20   *Vous qui . . . danser estas divers.* The text's injunction to look upon the accompanying "pourtraitture" reminds us that the *Danse* was apprehended by many contemporaries, Lydgate included, as a visual image as well as text; compare *Danse macabre*, line 1. Lydgate also has his king speak to readers "that lokyn upon this portrature" in line 633 of the A version. In the B version, however, he replaces the word with "scripture" (line 561), a curious change given that it is the B version that seems to have been painted at St Paul's Cathedral (see Introduction, pp. 16–17).

522   *est . . . viande a vers.* Proverbial. See Hassell V86.

535–37   *Mais aucuns sont . . . . ilz auront chault.* The French text is punning here on "n'en chault" (do not care) in line 535 and "auront chault" (will be warm, i.e., in the fires of hell) in line 537. Since English does not allow for the same pun, we have chosen instead to use the phrase "warm welcome" to lend the passage a similarly satirical tone.

542   *Bien fait vault moult aux trespassez.* Proverbial. See Hassell B97.

548   *plangere.* Stronger than merely lamenting or bewailing, this word can refer to beating or striking the body or chest, according to Lambert.

552   *herebi.* According to Lambert, this refers to classical Erebus and the realm of the Erinnyes (the Furies), from Greek 'Ερεβος' the lower world or god of darkness.

           pagina sacra. This refers to the text of Scripture, i.e., Christian teaching/doctrine, according to Lambert.

TEXTUAL NOTES

ABBREVIATIONS: A1: London, British Library Additional 37049 fols. 31v–32r (basis for "Dawnce of Makabre"); **A2**: London, British Library Additional 15225, fols. 15r–16r (basis for "Shaking of the Sheets"); **BD**: Edinburgh, National Library of Scotland, Advocates' 1.1.6 (Bannatyne MS Draft), pp. 43r–44r; **BM**: Edinburgh, National Library of Scotland, Advocates' 1.1.6 (Bannatyne MS Main), fols. 56r–57r (basis for "Resoning betuix Death and Man"); **Brown**: *Religious Lyrics of the XVth Century*, ed. Brown, p. 241; **Brunner**: "Mittelenglische Todesgedichte," ed. Brunner, pp. 27–28, 30; **C**: Cambridge, Cambridge University Library Ff.5.45, fols. 13r–14r; **Cov**: Coventry, Coventry Archives Acc. 325/1, fols. 70rb–74vb; **Cutler**: Cutler, John L. "A Middle English Acrostic," p. 88; **D**: Oxford, Bodleian Library Douce 322 (SC 21896), fols. 19vb–20ra (basis for "Death's Warning to the World"); **Doty**: "An Edition of British Museum MS Additional 37049: a Religious Miscellany," ed. Doty, pp. 206–11; **Dufour**: *La dance macabre peinte sous les charniers des Saints Innocents de Paris*, ed. Dufour; **F**: Bibliothèque nationale de France fonds français 14989, fols. 1r–12v (basis for French *Danse macabre*); **Fein**: *The Danse Macabre Printed by Guyot Marchant*, ed. Fein; **Furnivall**: "Of Þre Messagers of Deeth," ed. Furnivall, 2:443–48; **H1**: London, British Library Harley 1706, fols. 19v–20r; **H2**: London, British Library, Harley 116, fols. 128r–v (basis for "A Mirror for Young Ladies at their Toilet"); **Horstmann**: "Nachträge zu den Legenden 5: The Messengers of Death," ed. Horstmann, pp. on 432–34; **L**: British Library MS Lansdowne 669, fols. 41v–50v (basis for Lydgate, *Dance of Death*, B version); **Lincy**: "La danse macabre reproduite textuellement d'apres l'unique exemplaire connu de l'édition princeps de Guyot Marchant," ed. Le Roux de Lincy, pp. 291–317; **N**: New Haven, Beinecke Library MS 493, fols. 51v–60v; **P**: Cambridge, Magdalene College, Pepys Library, Pepys Ballads 2.62; **R**: Oxford, Bodleian Library 4o Rawl. 566 (203); **RV**: Rome, Venerable English College (AVCAU) MS 1405, fols. 111r–21r; **S**: Oxford, Bodleian Library MS Selden Supra 53, fols. 148r–58v (basis for Lydgate, *Dance of Death*, A version); **Saugnieux**: "*La danse macabre* française de Guyot Marchant (1486)," ed. Saugnieux, pp. 143–64; **Silverstein**: "Cest le Myrroure pur les Iofenes Dames," ed. Silverstein, pp. 121–22; **Sim**: London, British Library Addit. 22283 [Simeon MS], fols. 88vb–89ra; **V**: Oxford, Bodleian Library Eng. poet. a.1 (SC 3938) [Vernon MS], fols. 297vc–98rb (basis for "Three Messengers of Death"); **Warren**: *The Dance of Death*, ed. Warren and White; **W1**: Oxford, Bodleian Library Wood 401 (60) (Wing H2013A); **W2**: Oxford, Bodleian Library Wood 402 (48) (Wing H2013B).

JOHN LYDGATE, *DANCE OF DEATH*: A VERSION (SELDEN)

This version of the *Dance of Death* survives in nine manuscripts: Rome, Venerable English College MS 1405; New Haven, Beinecke Library MS 493; Oxford, Bodleian Library MS Selden Supra 53 (SC 3441); Oxford, Bodleian Library MS Laud Misc. 735 (SC 1504); Oxford, Bodleian Library MS Bodley 221 (SC 27627); London, British Library MS Harley 116; Coventry, Coventry Archives Acc. 325/1; San Marino, Huntington Library MS EL 26 A 13; and Cambridge, Trinity College MS R.3.21. It is also the version of the poem appended to Tottel's 1554 edition of Lydgate's *Fall of Princes* (STC 3177).

Bodleian Library MS Selden Supra 53 is the base text for our edition. It has been collated with Florence Warren's critical edition for the Early English Text Society, which takes as its base text the closely related but later manuscript Huntington Library MS EL 26 A 13. Readers are referred to the critical apparatus of the EETS edition for further information on the source of these variants. We have also noted variants found in the Beinecke, Rome (AVCAU), and Coventry manuscripts of the poem, since these were unknown to Warren and are not included in her edition.

MANUSCRIPTS:

Oxford, Bodleian Library, MS Selden Supra 53, fols. 148r–58v
Oxford, Bodleian Library, MS Bodley 221, fols. 53v–62r
Oxford, Bodleian Library, MS Laud misc. 735, fols. 52r–61r
Cambridge, Trinity College, MS R.3.21, fols. 278v–84r
London, British Library, MS Harley 116, fols. 129r–40v
Coventry, Coventry Archives, Acc. 325/1, fols. 70rb–74vb
San Marino, Huntington Library, MS EL 26.A.13, fols. 1r–12v
Rome, English College, AVCAU MS 1405, fols. 111r–21r (82 stanzas only, omits 7 and 52)
New Haven, Yale University, Beinecke Library, MS 493, fols. 51v–60v

EARLY PRINT EDITION:

Lydgate, John. *The fall of prynces. Gathered by John Bochas, fro[m] the begynnyng of the world vntyll his time, translated into English by John Lidgate monke of Burye Wherunto is added the fall of al such as since that time were notable in Englande: diligently collected out of the chronicles.* Londini: in aedibus Johannis Waylandi, cum priuilegio per sepatennium, [1554?], Appendix. [STC 3177]

EDITIONS:

Hammond, Eleanor Prescott, ed. "The Dance Macabre." *English Verse between Chaucer and Surrey: Being Examples of Conventional Secular Poetry, Exclusive of Romance, Ballad, Lyric, and Drama, in the Period from Henry the Fourth to Henry the Eighth.* Durham, NC: Duke University Press, 1927. Pp. 131–42.

Warren, Florence, and Beatrice White, eds. "The Daunce of Death." In *The Dance of Death, Edited from MSS. Ellesmere 26/A.13 and B.M. Lansdowne 699, Collated with the Other Extant MSS.* EETS o.s. 181. London: Oxford University Press, 1931; Rpt. New York: Klaus Reprint Co., 1971. Pp. 1–77.

Incipit   *Verba translatoris.* All speaker markers in S are written in red. In RV this heading appears at line 17.

2   *the.* RV: *this.*

      have. RV: *yeue.*

5   *se.* Cov: *seene.*

      aforn. RV: *afore*; Warren: *aforne.*

6   *Of.* Cov: *O.*

      ben. So Warren. Cov: *art*; S, RV: *be.*

8   *yong and olde.* RV: *olde and younge.*

      lowe and hy. RV: *high nor low.*

9   *not.* Cov: *nothir.*

      lowe ne hy. RV: *hie and low.*

10   *Popes.* N: *Pepes.*

      emperours. N: *emprours.*

11   *thei.* RV: *thay.*

      in felicité. RV: *in thaire felicite.*

12   *fresshnes of her flours.* Cov: *fressheness of her flouris.*

13   *The.* Warren: *ther.*

      clipsen with his shours. Cov: *clipsinge with her shoures.*

14   *Make.* Cov: *Maken.*

      her. Warren: *theire.*

17–25   *Considerith this . . . . Machabres Daunce.* In RV and in Huntington Library MS EL26 A 13 (the base text for Warren), this stanza is marked *verba translatoris.*

      Considerith this. Cov: *Considereith*; RV: *Consideryng this.*

      ben. So Warren. Cov, N, S: *be.*

18   *enprentith.* RV: *emprenteth.*

19   *the exawmple.* So Warren. Cov: *to þe ensaumple*; S, N: *thensaumple.*

20   *in.* RV: *vpon*; Warren: *on.*

21   *notably.* Cov: *notable*; Warren: *notabely.*

22   *takyng.* Cov: *taken.*

23   *translatyn.* Cov: *translate.*

24   *Machabres.* Warren: *Macabrees.*

25   *whos.* N: *what.*

      avys. Cov: *avice*; RV: *advis.*

      atte the leste. Cov, W: *atte leste*; RV: *at the leste.*

26   *Thorugh.* Cov: *Through*; N: *Thurght*; RV: *Thurgh*; N: *Thurh.*

      her₂. RV: *thaire.*

      steryng. Cov: *strength.*

27   *her.* RV: *thaire.*

28   *playn.* W: *pleyne.*

30   *that ben.* So Cov, Warren. N, S: *þat be*; RV: *ben.*

31   *toforn.* So Cov, RV, Warren. N: *to fer*; S: *tofor.*

      in. Cov: *ne.*

32   *Her.* RV: *Theire.*

      cleerly. Cov: *clerkli*; RV: *clerely.*

33	*By.* Cov: *Bi her*; RV: *By this.*
	exaumple. RV: *ensample.*
	her. RV: *thaire.*
34	*her.* RV: *thaire.*
36	*Portreied.* N: *portreyd.*
	surplusage. So Cov, RV, Warren. S, N: *surpluage.*
38	*Yeven.* So Warren. Cov, RV: *youen*; N: *yove*; S: *ȝove.*
	lyves. Cov: *lifis.*
39	*declare.* RV: *deliuer.*
40	*wille.* So RV, Warren. Cov, S: *wole.* N: *woll.*
41	*ben.* N, S: *be.*
42	*desiring.* Cov: *deservinge.*
	wiche is. Cov: *whiche*; RV: *whiche that is.*
43	*se.* Warren: *sene.*
46	*shul.* Warren: *schulle.* Cov, RV: *shal.*
48	*ne₂.* RV: *nor.*
49–56	This stanza is absent in RV.
50	*goo.* Cov: *gone.*
51	*toforn.* Cov: *to fore.*
53	*eche.* Cov: *euery.*
	lowly. Cov: *loweli*; Warren: *lowely.*
54	*not.* Cov: *noþere.*
	royal. Cov: *riall.*
55	*Eche.* Cov: *euerie.*
56	*o.* N: *a.*
Before 57	*Deeth to the Pope.* Cov, Warren, RV, and S all include speaker markers. Cov, S, and W all follow the same format throughout, e.g. "Dethe to the Pope" and "The Pope" (although the word "pope" has been expunged from Cov by a later reader in both speaker markers, as well as at line 10); in RV the speaker markers give the identity of the speaker only in the response stanza, as in line 73: *Dethe* and line 81: *The Emperour.*
57	*O yee.* Cov, N: *Ye.*
	ben. So RV, Warren. Cov, N, S: *be.*
	dignité. Cov: *degree.*
58	*alle estatis.* N: *astates.*
59	*soverenité.* Cov, RV: *soverainte.* Warren: *soverente.*
61	*ye firste.* Cov: *ye*; RV: *firste.*
64	*of lordship.* RV: *lordship.*
	honour. Warren: *honowre.*
65	*First.* Cov: *Frist.*
67	*perillous.* RV: *perlious.*
	ho. RV: *who.*
68	*dignité.* Cov: *dingnite.*
69	*al for.* Warren, RV: *for all.*
70	*other.* N: *oþer odyr.*

71   *honour.* Warren: *honoure.*

        who. Cov: *he.*

        prudently. Warren: *prudentely.*

72   *dothe.* Warren: *doth.*

75   *must.* RV, Warren: *most.*

        your. Cov: *the.*

77   *Behinde.* RV: *behynde you.*

        ricchesse. Cov: *your richesse.*

79   *Agein.* Warren: *Aȝens*; Cov: *Ayenst.* N: *Aȝen.*

        is worth. RV: *worth is.*

80   *Adamis.* RV, N: *Adams*; Cov, Warren: *Adames.*

        mosten. So Cov, RV, Warren. N: *must*; S: *moste.*

81   *not.* So Warren. Cov, S: *note.*

        may. RV: *may me.*

83   *gein.* Cov: *gynne*; RV: *bote.*

86   *visage.* Cov: *my vesage.*

87   *Therupon sore I may compleine.* RV: *And thervpon I may me sore compleyn.*

88   *have.* Cov: *han.*

        litel. RV: *so litel.*

89   *ben.* So Cov, Warren. N, S: *be*; RV: *been.*

90   *shewith.* Cov, RV: *semeth.*

        by. W: *be.*

91   *shulle.* Cov, RV: *shal.*

93   *bileven.* RV: *ye leue*; Warren: *beleue.*

95   *rekenyd.* Cov: *I rekened.*

        yfere. N: *I fere*; RV: *in fere.*

96   *honour.* Warren: *honowre.*

98   *ben.* So Warren. Cov, S: *bene*; RV: *be.*

        greetly. Cov: *greteli*; W: *gretli.*

99   *Sithen.* So Warren. Cov: *sethen*; S: *seth*; N, RV: *sith.*

100   *That I shal nevere heraftir clothed be.* This line omitted in RV.

101   *ne.* W: *ner.*

        RV inserts an additional line after line 101, replacing its missing line 100.
          This inserted line reads: *alle myn aray to leue behynde me.*

102   *My.* RV: *myn*; Cov: *myne.*

103   *lerned.* So Warren. Cov: *levid*; N, S: *lyved*; RV: *conceyued.*

104   *Howe that al.* RV: *That worldly.*

107   *somtyme had.* RV: *had somtyme.*

        enviroun. Warren: *envroun.*

109   *al youre grete.* RV: *for all your.*

        hynes. Cov: *hevinesse.*

110   *shul.* Cov, RV: *shal.*

113   *aforn.* Cov, RV: *afore.*

114   *in sooth.* Cov: *of sothe.*

        footyng. Cov: *fote*; N: *foot.*

116   *or.* Cov: *ne.*

118   *Greet.* RV: *Bothe grete.*

119	*Who.* So Cov, RV, Warren. S: *ho*; N: *He.*
	he is. Cov: *hym.*
120	*we.* So RV, Warren. Cov, N, S: *he.*
	asshes. Cov: *asshen.*
121	*alle.* RV: *with al.*
122	*quite.* Cov: *quiteth.*
	ne. RV: *for.*
124	*al youre dignité.* Cov: *youre dingnite.*
127	*shal.* S: *shulle*; Warren: *shul.*
130	*Have.* So RV, Warren. S: *han*; Cov: *hath.*
131	*ben.* So RV, Warren. Cov, S: *be.*
	to. Cov: *into.*
132	*vailith it.* RV: *availleth.*
	suche. N: *shull.*
134	*oute of.* Cov: *without.*
136	*berthen.* Cov: *berden*; RV: *birthen*; Warren: *burdoun.*
	hym. Cov: *hem.*
	ofte. Cov: *offten.*
Before 137	*Constable.* RV: *Knyght constable.*
137	*my right.* RV: *right.*
	to. Cov: *you to.*
	reste. Cov: *areste.*
	yow constreine. Cov: *constrene.*
138	*Sir.* W: *sire.*
	Constable. Warren: *Conestable.*
139	*strong.* RV: *strenger.*
	Charlemayne. Cov: *Chalemain.*
140	*aforced.* Cov, RV: *enforced.*
141	*ne.* Cov: *and*; RV: *nor.*
	this is. RV: *is.*
142	*armure.* N: *arm[ou]re.*
	plates. Cov: *plate.*
143	*folkes.* Cov: *folke.*
144	*luste.* So Cov, RV, Warren. S, N: *lest.*
Before 145	*The Constable answerith.* RV: *knyght constable.*
146	*To assaille.* RV: *to haue assailed.*
	mighty forteresses. RV: *forteresses.* Cov: *myghtilie to recesse*; N: *myghty to recesse.*
147	*unto.* Cov: *to.*
148	*seke.* Cov: *seche.*
	fame. So RV, Warren. Cov, N, S: *and fame.*
149	*worldly.* Warren, N: *wordli.*
	prowesses. Cov, N, RV: *prowesse.*
151	*him.* N: *hym hym.*
	sorwe. Cov, N, Warren: *sorowe*; RV: *sorow.*
	swetnesses. Cov, RV: *swetnesse*; Warren: *swetenesses.*
152	*agein.* Cov: *ayen*; RV: *ayenst*; Warren: *aȝeyne.*
	founded. Cov, N, S, Warren: *founden*; RV: *founde.*

153	*yow.* RV: *so.*
155	*muste.* RV, Warren: *most.*
	to. RV: *vnto.*
156	*contrarie.* Cov: *constreine.*
	were. So RV, Warren. Cov: *neve*; S: *nere*; N: *ware.*
	not but. RV: *but.*
157	*for day by day.* Cov: *ffro daie to daie.*
	is noon othir geyn. Cov: *is nis noo noþer.*
158	*at.* So RV, Warren. Cov: *atte*; S, N: *at the.*
159	*mote.* RV: *moste.*
	agein. RV: *ayene;* Warren: *aʒeyne.*
160	*counten.* RV: *compten.*
	her. RV: *thaire.*
161	*woote.* N: *wate.*
	partie. N: *p[ar]tis.*
162	*For drede of Dethe I have so grete distresse.* Cov: *Dethe hath in erþe noo ladie me maistresse.*
163	*ascape.* Cov: *escape.*
167	*chaumbres.* Cov: *chambir.*
168	*must.* Warren: *mote.*
169	*lordis.* RV: *ladyes.*
	barouns. Cov: *barones.*
170	*Hav.* Cov, S: *han.* RV: *haue.*
171	*trumpetis.* RV: *trompette.*
	youre clariouns. Cov: *clariones*; N: *youre clairons*; RV: *youre clarion.*
174	*daunce.* Cov: *dauncen.*
176	*o.* N: *a.*
177	*sithe.* RV: *tymes.*
	auctorised. N: *aucorised.*
179	*thanke.* N: *thonke.*
181	*Ne.* Cov: *no.*
182	*court.* Cov: *courtes.*
Before 185	*Lady of Grete Astate.* RV: *Princesse.*
186	*muste.* RV, Warren: *most.*
	goo. Cov: *gone.*
187	*Nowt.* So Warren. Cov, S: *not.* RV: *noght.*
188	*beauté.* Cov: *grete beaute.*
	greet plesaunce. Cov: *plesaunce.*
190	*so many holde.* RV: *holde so many.*
	on. So Cov, RV, Warren. S: *an.*
192	*Ye.* So Cov, RV, Warren. S: *þe.*
	mote. RV: *most.*
Before 193	*The Lady answerith.* RV identifies this speaker as *princesse.*
194	*Deeth hath in erthe no lady ne maistresse.* Cov: *ffor drede of dethe I haue so grete distresse.*
	lady ne. N: *lady no.*
195	*his.* Cov: *this.*

           muste. Cov: *mot*; RV, Warren: *moste*.

           I. So RV, Warren. Cov, S: *ye*.

196   *nys*. RV: *is*.

           contesse ne duchesse. Cov: *duchesse ne Countesse*.

197   *beauté*. So RV, Warren. Cov, N, S: *bounte*.

198   *Deeth*. RV: *right*.

           mote. RV: *moste*.

199   *youre*. RV: *our*.

           countirfeet. Cov, Warren: *counterfete*. RV: *contrefete*.

           fresshnesse. Cov: *fairnesse*.

200   *Owre*. So Warren. Cov, S: *youre*.

           rympled. RV: *riveled*.

           age. Cov: *face*.

202   *I ensure*. Cov: *I you ensure*.

203   *For al*. RV: *Alle*.

205   *the*. N: *ȝe*.

           gostli dredeful. So RV, Warren. Cov, S, N: *dredly goostly*.

207   *acounte*. RV: *accompte*.

           shulle. Cov, RV: *shal*.

209   *My*. Cov: *Myne*.

           is. Cov: *nys*.

           nouther. RV: *nothing*; N: *nowether*.

210   *tidinges*. N: *tithings*.

           ye bring. RV: *ye me bringe*.

211   *festis*. Cov, RV: *feste is*.

           into. So Cov, Warren. RV, S: *into a*.

           ferye. N: *fayres*.

212   *list nothing syng*. Cov: *lust noo lenger sing*.

           syng. RV: *to syng*.

213   *contrarie nowe*. Cov: *is contrarie*.

           to. So RV, Warren. Cov, S, N: *unto*.

           me in. RV: *my*.

215   *parting*. Cov: *departing*.

216   *And al*. RV: *Alle*.

217   *right fresshe of*. Cov: *fresshe in*. RV: *right fressh in*.

222   *wil*. Cov: *wol*.

224   *fro*. Cov: *from*.

225   *Sithen*. RV: *Sith*.

           that Dethe. RV: *dethe*.

           his. N: *þis*.

226   *pace*. RV: *passe*.

227   *adieu nowe*. RV: *adieu*.

228   *Adieu*. Cov: *Adewe nowe*.

229   *beuté*. Cov: *now*.

           solace. Cov: *all solace*.

231   *Thinketh*. Cov, RV: *Thenke*.

232   *wote*. N: *wate*.

234	*abaisshed*. N: *abasshed is*.
	though. N: *is þogh*.
235	*hede*. So RV, Warren. Cov, N, S: *hood*.
236	*mote*. RV: *moste*.
237	*Leveth*. So RV, Warren. Cov, N, S: *leve vp*.
239	*Who*. Cov: *he*.
	that is fattest. RV: *is moste fatte*.
	have hym. Cov: *have hit hym*.
240	*In his grave shal*. RV: *Shal in his graue*.
	putrefie. Cov: *purify*.
241	*thretis*. Cov: *tretis*.
	have I. RV: *I have*.
242	*nowe leve*. N: *leve now*.
	al. Cov: *all þe*.
245	*nor*. Cov: *ne*.
247	*axe I*. RV: *I ask*; N: *aske I*.
248	*Though*. Cov: *For*.
	too late men. Cov: *men to late*.
	hem avise. N: *avyse*.
249	*lady gentil*. Cov: *gentil ladie*.
250	*mantels*. Cov: *mantelle*.
251	*Youre veile, youre wymple passing of greet richesse*. This line is inserted in the margin in N.
	passinge of. Cov: *of*.
252	*mote*. RV: *most*.
	leie. Warren: *leyne*.
	aside. N: *on syde*.
253	*shal*. RV: *moste*.
255	*provide*. Cov: *purveie*.
256	*man*. RV: *wight*.
258	*it not*. Cov: *nat*.
262	*to walke atte large*. In Selden, this line breaks off after *ful ofte* and space is left for the remainder, along with absent lines 263 and 264, which are supplied here from Warren's edition.
	to. Cov, N: *for to*.
263	*Thus cruel Dethe dothe al estates fyne*. This line is omitted in N. Cov: *To make þe worlde to me encline*.
264	*mote*. RV: *moste*.
265	*knowen*. Cov: *knowest*; RV: *know*; Warren: *knewe*.
266	*rightwisnes*. Cov: *of right wisnesse*; RV: *rightwisnesse*.
267	*must*. RV, Warren: *moste*.
269	*ben*. So RV, Warren. Cov, S: *be*.
	somonyd. Cov: *somned*; N: *somenyd*; RV: *somond*; Warren: *sommened*.
	bit. Cov: *bytte*; RV: *biddeth*.
270	*yelde*. RV: *yeue*; Warren: *ȝefe*.
	acountes. RV, Warren: *accomptes*.
	wole. RV, W: *wil*.

272   *owne.* RV: *oune.*
273   *this.* RV: *that.*
274   *whiche.* So RV, Warren. Cov, N, S: *suche.*
               aforne. So RV, Warren. Cov: *a forme*; N, S: *a fourme.*
               tooke. Cov: *take*; Warren, RV, N: *toke.*
275   *chaunge.* Warren: *chaunce.*
276   *list.* Cov, RV: *lust.*
277   *by.* Cov, RV: *for.*
               for. N: *be.*
278   *rescuse.* So Cov, RV, Warren. N, S: *rescws.*
               by. RV: *ne.*
280   *Agein.* Cov: *Ayenne*; RV: *Ayenst*; Warren: *Aȝen.*
               vaille. Cov, RV: *availle.*
281   *loken.* Cov: *lokest.*
282   *instrumentis.* RV, N: *Instruments.*
285   *Sethen of.* Cov, N, S: *Sethen.* RV: *Sith that of*; Warren: *Sith of.*
               alle. So RV, Warren. Cov, S: *and alle.*
286   *ferst.* Cov: *frist.*
               walke. Cov: *walken.*
287   *dooth areste.* RV: *aresteth.*
               seith. Warren: *seieth.*
               theologie. S: *Thelogie.*
289   *or.* RV: *and.*
291   *serche oute no.* Cov: *serche oute ne*; RV: *seche no.*
292   *domefiynge.* Cov: *doome feynynge*; RV: *demonstring.*
               ne. Warren: *nor.*
293   *Safe.* Cov, RV: *saue.*
296   *Who.* Cov: *He þat*; RV: *But who.*
               mote. RV: *most.*
298   *aver.* Cov: *honour*; N: *haver*; RV: *haueur.*
               youre greet. Cov: *greet.*
299   *straunge.* N: *stronge.*
300   *mote yow.* Cov: *mote*; RV: *moste you.*
302   *cam.* N: *com*; RV: *come.*
303   *bysynes.* Cov: *a besynes.*
305   *Certis.* Cov: *Sertes.*
306   *not.* Cov: *nat.*
308   *fordothe.* RV: *destroieth.*
309   *wys is.* Cov: *right wise is*; N: *is wise.*
310   *moot.* RV: *moste.*
311   *The worlde it lente.* Cov: *To the worlde is lent*; N: *þe worldus lente.*
               wille. So RV, Warren. Cov, N, S: *mot.*
               recovere. Warren, RV: *recure.* Cov: *rekeuere.*
Before 313   *Chanoun.* RV: *The Canon prebended.*
313   *many.* RV: *many a.*
               grete prebende. Cov: *prebende.*
316   *For there.* RV: *There.*

319	*dilacioun*. Cov: *delacioun*.
320	*ay*. RV: *euer*.
321	*benefices*. Cov: *benefice*.
	a personage. So Cov, RV, Warren. N: *personages*; S: *personage*.
322	*lite*. RV: *litel*.
	comforte. N: *conforth*.
323	*of*. N: *on*.
324	*not*. Cov: *nat nowe*.
325	*Amys of grys*. Cov: *amyses of greie*.
	wille. So RV, Warren. Cov, S: *wole*.
	agein. Cov, RV: *ayen*; Warren: *aȝen*.
328	*shulde*. Cov: *sholde*.
329	*marchaunt*. N: *marchand*.
	mote. RV: *moste*.
330	*ful many*. So RV, Warren. Cov, N, S: *many*.
	divers. RV: *a divers*.
333	*mote*. RV: *moste*.
	yeve. RV: *ye*; N: *ȝefe*.
334	*now*. So RV, Warren. Cov, S: *yow*.
336	*No more coveite*. So Cov. In S, a superscript *y* is inserted between *more* and *coveite*. RV: *Nomore covet*; Warren: *None more coueite*; N: *No more covytt*.
	than. Cov: *I þan*.
	have. Cov: *han*.
338	*my marchandise*. In S, *my* is inserted in superscript. Cov, N: *marchandise*.
340	*iles*. Cov: *londis*.
341	*My*. Cov: *mennes*; RV, Warren: *myn*.
	herte. Cov: *hertis*.
	fret. Cov: *freteth*.
342	*doth me*. So W. Cov, N: *me*; RV: *me dothe*; S: *doith me*.
	constreine. Cov: *constreineth*.
343	*seie*. RV: *see*.
344	*enbraceth*. RV: *embraceth*.
	shal restreine. Cov: *he restreineth*.
345	*Yeve*. W: *Gefe*.
346	*longe*. Cov: *of longe*.
347	*Chartereux*. Cov: *Chartereus*.
	and youresilfe. Cov: *and your selue*; N: *ȝoursilf*.
349	*agein*. RV: *ayen*; N, Warren: *aȝen*.
350	*not*. Cov: *nat*.
351	*as in*. Cov, RV: *in*.
353	*the*. RV: *this*.
354	*my*. RV: *myn*.
357	*flesshly*. Cov: *flossheli*.
359	*from dampnacioun*. RV: *dampnacion*.
360	*bene*. RV: *men ben*.
	today. RV: *this day*.

	shulle. RV, Cov: *shal*.
	be. N: *ben*.
363	*Not*. Cov: *nat*; RV: *Noght*.
365	*pele*. Cov, RV: *appele*.
367	*champioun*. Cov: *a champioun*.
368	*another*. RV: *dethe*.
369	*dare this Dethe*. Cov: *dare thus dethe*; RV: *durst thou sette*.
370	*That am*. Cov: *That*.
371	*west and este*. RV, Warren: *este and weste*.
372	*ful surquidous of*. RV: *with surquidous*.
374	*though I*. N: *y*.
375	*and*. RV: *or*.
377	*Sir Monke*. Catchword *ir monke* appears in bottom right-hand corner of fol. 153v.
378	*no*. RV: *not*.
	sojour. N: *ʒour soiour*.
379	*is*. RV: *may*.
	that may yow here. RV: *here you*.
380	*Agein*. Cov: *Ayen*; N: *Aʒen*; RV: *Ayenst*; Warren: *Aʒein*.
	for to do. So Warren. S: *for to*. Cov: *to*. RV: *to doo*.
381	*mote acounte*. RV: *moste accompte*.
382	*have spent it*. Cov: *han spent it*; RV: *haue spendid*.
	in dede worde. RV: *worde dede*.
384	*of nought*. N: *noʒt*.
385	*the*. RV: *my*.
	be. RV: *to be*.
388	*vice*. Cov: *wise*; Warren: *vise*.
389	*dissolut*. Cov, RV: *desolate*.
391	*to*. Cov: *is to*.
392	*be*. Warren: *ben*.
	se. Warren: *seen*.
393	*Thou*. RV: *O thou*.
394	*you*. Cov, N: *þu*; RV: *that*.
	thi. Cov, RV: *thy*.
396	*thrust*. Cov: *therst*; RV: *thurst*; N: *thursse*.
397	*you*. RV, Warren: *thou*; Cov, N: *þu*.
402	*greet grevaunce*. Cov, RV: *greuance*.
404	*ne*. Cov: *and*.
	chevesaunce. Cov: *cheveshance*; RV: *chevissance*; Warren: *cheuisshaunce*.
405	*thorugh*. Cov: *through*; N: *thrught*; RV: *thurgh*; Warren: *thrugh*.
	abit. RV: *abideth*; N: *habit*; Warren: *abitte*.
	parveaunce. Cov: *paruiance*; RV, Warren: *purviance*.
406	*look*. RV: *see*.
407	*happith*. RV: *it happeth*.
408	*have*. Cov: *han*.
	see. Warren: *seen*.
409–16	*Usuré to God . . . . bihinde of dette*. This stanza is omitted in RV. N misidentifies this stanza as *Deth to þe poor man*.

411	*borwith.* Cov: *boroweth*; N: *borowith.*
412	*lent.* Cov: *leueth.*
414	*acountes.* Warren: *accomptes.*
	sette. Cov, Warren: *fette.*
416	N has rubric in margin apparently anticipating an additional stanza following poem's usual dialogue format: *The poor man aswerith.*
	man. N: *man man.*
417	*on.* RV: *in.*
418	*agein.* Cov, N: *aȝen*; RV: *ayenst*; Warren: *aȝenne.*
419	*medicine.* N: *medcyne.*
420	*Al.* RV: *And alle.*
422	*Agein.* Cov: *Ayen*; N: *Aȝene*; RV: *ayenst*; Warren: *Aȝeyne.*
423	*have.* Cov: *han.*
424	*Good.* Cov: *A goode.*
	recure. Cov: *cure.*
425	*agon.* So RV, Warren. Cov, N, S: *agoo.*
427	*also in.* RV: *in.*
428	*gete.* Cov: *geten.*
	thorugh. Cov: *through*; RV, Warren, N: *thurgh.*
429	*agens.* Cov: *ayenst*; RV: *aenst*; N, Warren: *aȝens.*
430	*Preservatives.* N: *Preseruatykes.*
432	*Agens.* Cov, RV: *Ayenst*; N: *Aȝens.*
Before 433	*Amerous Squire.* Cov: *Þe Squier*; RV: *the Galant Squyer.*
433	*be.* RV: *ben.*
	gentil. Cov: *so gentil.*
	amerous. Cov: *so amerous.*
434	*grene.* Cov: *yonge.*
435	*free of herte.* RV: *free and of hert.*
	and eke desirous. So Cov, W. RV: *desirous*; N, S: *eke desirous.*
437	*of visage.* RV: *visage.*
438	*asshes.* Cov: *asshen.*
439	*bewté.* RV: *youre beaute.*
442	*Agens.* Cov, RV: *Ayenst*; N: *Aȝens.*
	provide. Cov: *purveie.*
445	*service.* Cov: *the service.*
446	*so fressh so wel besein.* N: *so flessh so well beseyn*; RV: *so wele and fressh beseyn.*
447	*agein.* Cov, RV: *ayen.*
448	*gon.* So Cov, RV, Warren. S: *goo*; N: *go.*
Before 449	*The Gentilwomman Amerous.* Cov: *þe Gentilwoman.*
450	*holde.* Cov: *ye holde.*
451	*Polycene.* Cov: *Pollicene*; RV: *Pollixene.*
452	*Penolope.* N, RV, Warren: *Penelope.*
453	*wente.* Warren: *wenten.*
454	*shulle.* Cov, RV: *shall.*
	youre. Warren: *ȝow.*

455–56	*Though daunger longe . . . . chaunge of doubilnesse.* Lines 455 and 456 are transposed in N. This error is corrected in the margin.
	hath. RV: *haue.*
456	*Arestid.* RV: *Arest.*
459	*hast.* Cov: *has.*
	yseide. Cov, N, RV: *seid.*
462	*a man.* RV: *man.*
	to have. RV: *have*; W: *to a.*
463	*fool.* RV: *fole.*
	sentement. RV: *sentence.*
464	*assurid.* Cov: *ensured.*
Before 465	*the Man of Lawe.* RV: *the Advocate.*
466	*Ye.* N: *I ȝe.*
	highe Iuge. RV: *Iuge.*
470	*availe may.* RV: *may availle.*
472	*Tofore.* RV: *Before.*
474	*cannot.* RV: *can.*
	agein. Cov, RV: *ayen*; N: *aȝen.*
475	*me kepe.* Cov: *kepe me.*
	ne. N: *and*; RV: *nor.*
478	*Nothing.* RV: *man.*
479	*Ageins.* Cov: *Ayenst*; N: *Aȝens*; RV: *Ayen*; Warren: *Aȝeyne.*
	resistence. RV: *no resistence.*
480	*quite.* Cov: *quiteth*; RV: *quyteth.*
481	*that at.* Cov: *that atte.* N: *þat.*
	assise. RV: *assises.*
482	*atte.* N: *had.*
	doste. RV: *diddest.*
483	*londe.* Cov: *londis*; RV: *land.*
	devise. RV: *devises.*
486	*cowdest.* RV: *kewde.*
	folkes. Cov, Warren: *folke.*
487	*lete.* RV: *lat.*
488	*thou canst.* Cov: *canst thou*; Warren: *thou cannest.*
490	*bellewedir.* Cov: *bellwethir*; N: *belwedur*; RV: *belwether.*
	was. Cov, RV: *is.*
491	*Nought.* Cov, N, RV, Warren: *Not.*
	lowe and hie. Cov, RV: *hie and low.*
492	*list.* Cov, RV: *lust.*
493	*And hange.* Cov: *And honge*; RV: *Hange.*
	respite. Cov: *acquite.*
494	*lad.* Cov, RV: *ledde.*
497	*mynstral.* RV: *ministral.*
	canst. Warren: *cannest.*
498	*do.* Cov: *done.*
499	*I shal anoone.* RV: *soone I shal.* Warren: *anoone I shal.*
	thee. N: *þi.*

500	*other.* N: *oder.*
	goo. Cov: *gone.*
501	*neither avoidaunce.* Cov: *noo voidaunce*; Warren: *nowther avoydaunce.*
504	*maister.* Cov: *þat maister.*
	shewe. RV: *shal shew.*
	science. So Cov, RV, Warren. S: *sentence.*
505	*newe.* RV: *new.*
506	*passingly.* Cov: *passinge.*
508	*sithes.* RV: *tymes.*
509	*to me is.* Cov: *is to me.*
511	*tarie.* Cov: *vary.*
512	*Ofte.* RV: *Ofte tyme.*
	of. RV: *at.*
513	*Rikele.* Cov: *van rikell*; RV: *Rykel.*
514	*Harry.* Cov, N: *herry*; RV: *Henry.*
	Engelond. N: *ynglong.*
516	*sleightes.* N: *slightnes.*
517	*must.* RV, W: *moste.*
	this. Cov: *and this.*
	to undirstond. Cov: *undirstond.*
518	*Nought.* Cov: *Nat.*
519	*nouther.* RV: *neith.*
	on. Cov: *in.*
	ne. RV: *and.*
520	*nought.* Cov: *nat*; RV, Warren, N: *not.*
	none. N: *noo.*
522	*Or any.* N: *Of my.*
524	*of the hevene.* RV: *of heven.*
	al the influence. Cov: *the influence.*
525	*Ageins.* Cov, RV: *Ayenst*; N: *Aȝens.*
	stonde at defence. Cov: *stonden atte defence.*
526	*Legerdemeyn.* N: *Largerdemeyn.*
528	*Deth moo.* Cov: *dethe yitte moo*; RV: *dethe hath moo.*
	yit than. Cov, RV: *than.*
	hath. Cov, RV: *haue.*
529	*bene.* Cov: *art.*
	nowe here. RV: *here*; Warren: *here now.*
535	*Like.* Cov: *Like to.*
536	*And.* RV: *As.*
537	*must.* Cov: *mot*; RV: *most*; Warren: *moste.*
538	*lifly.* N: *lufly*; Cov: *liffeli*; RV: *lyvely.*
541	*tithis and.* RV: *my tithe.*
542	*mote.* RV: *moste.*
	counte. Cov: *account*; RV: *compte.*
543	*make.* Cov: *to make.*
544	*he is.* Cov: *hym.*
545	*Thou.* RV: *O thou.*

546   *lad.* RV: *ladde.*

547   *Thou.* N: *ȝow.*

           moste. Cov, N: *must.*

           eke. RV: *now.*

548   *if.* Cov, RV: *thogh.*

550   *oonly.* Warren: *wonli.*

           this from thee. Cov: *for me the*; RV: *this the.*

551   *The.* RV: *ffro the.*

           that can so folke. Cov: *that so folke*; RV: *that can folkes.*

           faile. N: *failly.*

552   *fool.* RV: *foole.*

553   *wisshed.* Cov: *wesshid.*

554   *be that.* Cov: *be it.*

           have. Cov: *han.*

555   *have.* Cov: *han.*

           leyn. Cov: *leien.*

556   *reyn.* Cov: *in reine.*

           and. RV: *to*; Cov: *I.*

           at. RV: *at the*; Cov, Warren: *atte.*

557   *and*₂. RV: *have.*

558   *Dolve.* Cov: *Delfe.*

           diched. Cov: *dike*; RV: *dyked.*

           the carte. Cov, W: *atte carte.*

561–68   *Sir Cordeler . . . . present and redy.* Ink fading at bottom of fol. 156v.

561   *myn.* RV, Warren: *my.*

563   *have.* Cov: *han.*

           itaught. RV: *taught.*

564   *Howe that.* RV: *how.*

           am. N: *may.*

           gastful. RV. *gastly.*

           forto drede. Cov: *in dede.*

566   *is ther.* Cov: *þer is.*

           ne. N: *nor.*

567   *dare reste.* Cov, RV: *areste.*

570   *sureté.* RV: *seurte*; Warren: *seuerte.*

571   *Strengthe.* Warren: *strengh.*

           what so. RV: *what.*

572   *Worldly.* Warren: *wordly.*

574   *fro.* Cov, RV: *from.*

Before 577 *the Childe.* RV: *the younge Childe.*

           borne. So RV, Warren. Cov: *ibore*; S: *yborn.*

579   *must.* RV, Warren: *most.*

           here toforn. Cov: *heretofore.*

580   *Be lad.* Cov, RV: *Be ledde.*

           fatal. Cov: *sharper.*

581   *goo.* Cov: *gone.*

           on. Cov, RV: *vpon*; N: *to.*

582	*in soth.* Cov: *for soth.*
583	*every.* Cov: *oueri.*
584	*moost.* RV: *moste.*
585	*o.* RV: omitted; Warren: *a.*
	I cannot. Cov: *can I nat.*
586	*bore.* Cov, RV: *born.*
587	*be.* Cov: *ben.*
	wreke. RV: *awreke.*
588	*list.* Cov, RV: *lust.*
	lenger. Cov: *longer.*
589	*cam.* RV: *come.*
590	*no tale.* Cov: *tales.*
591	*wil.* RV: *wille.*
Before 593	*the Clerke.* RV: *The younge beneficed Clerk.*
593	*O ye Sir.* Cov: *O sir*; RV: *O ye.*
594	*or.* Cov: *on.*
	defende. Cov: *to defende.*
595	*wende have.* Cov: *wend han*; RV: *haue.*
	unto. Cov: *up onto.*
596	*benefices.* RV: *benefice.*
	or. Cov: *of.*
	greet prebende. Cov: *prebende.*
597	*hiest.* RV: *hie.*
598	*agens.* Cov: *ayens*; N: *aȝens*; RV: *ayenst.*
600	*ponissheth.* RV: *punysshet.*
602	*bettir.* N: *bett*; Warren: *bette.*
603	*no$_1$.* Warren: *noon.*
	geyn. Cov: *gynne.*
	ne. Cov: *no.*
	bettir. Cov: *lenger.*
604	*sure.* RV: *seure.*
606	*bene.* RV: *be.*
611	*Atte.* So Cov, Warren. N, RV; S: *At the.*
	mote. RV: *most.*
	Signature in left margin: *Thomas Holt.*
613	*agein.* Cov: *aȝenne*; N: *aȝen*; Warren: *aȝeyne.*
	is. RV: *may be.*
615	*this.* Cov: *his.*
616	*this.* RV: *in this.*
	here is. RV: *is.*
618	*agein.* Cov: *ayenne*; N: *aȝen*; RV: *ayenst*; Warren: *aȝeyne.*
	no respite. RV, Warren: *respite noon.*
619	*our.* RV: *steven.*
	doth. RV: *deth.*
	not. Cov: *nat.*
620	*welcome be.* Cov: *welcome.*
627	*al his herte.* RV: *hert.*

628	*Seth*. Cov: *Sethen*.
629	*deserve*. Cov: *disserueth*; RV: *serue*.
	quit. Cov: *quiteth*.
630	*To*. RV: *The*.
632	*sure to*. RV: *seure*.
	N has rubric: *þ(e) armytt answerith*.
Before 633	*The Kyng ligging dead and eten of wormes*. Cov: *A kynge lienge deede and eten with wormes*; RV: *A kyng liggyn in his grave*; N: *þe kyng liggyng ded & eten with wormes*.
633	*folke*. Cov: *folkis*.
	portrature. Cov: *portatrure*.
634	*the estates*. So Cov, Warren. RV: *estates*; S: *the states*.
635	*Seeth*. Cov, RV: *Sethe*.
636	*not*. Cov: *& nat*.
638	*I*. So Cov, RV, Warren, N. S: *ȝe*.
	kyng. RV: *a king*.
640	*fyne*. Cov: *ende*.
Before 641	*Machabre the Doctour*. RV: *The wordes of the Doctour Machabre*.
641	*not*. Cov: *nat*; Warren: *nowght*.
642	*wiche*. Cov: *that*.
643	*whether*. N: *wedur*.
	he. Cov: *ye*.
645	*Remembringe ay*. Cov: *remembreth*.
	bet. Cov, RV: *better*.
646	*at the*. Cov, Warren: *atte*.
647	*shul*. RV: *shal*.
648	*that maketh in hevene*. RV: *in heuen that maketh*.
651	*helle none ne*. So Cov, RV, Warren. S, N: *hell none nor*.
655	*lyve wel*. N: *lyve*.
	take this. RV: *take*.
	best. So Warren. Cov, RV, N: *the best*.
656	*Is*. Cov: *It is*.
	shul. Cov: *shullen*.
	pace. RV: *passe*.
Before 657	*Lenvoye de Translator*. RV: *Verba Translatoris*.
657	*my lordis*. RV: *maisters*.
	maistres. RV: *folkes*.
659	*myn*. RV, N: *my*.
661	*aske*. So RV, Warren. N, Cov, S: *axe*.
662	*goodly*. RV: *godely*.
	this. N: *his*.
663	*to sowpouaile drede*. Cov: *subhope away drede*; N: *sowpowayle*; RV: *suppowel drede*; Warren: *soupewaile*.
664	*Benignely*. So RV; Cov: *Benyngli*; Warren: *Benyngneli*.
665	*drewe*. Cov: *drowe*; RV: *drow*; Warren: *drowe*.
666	*by*. RV: *for*.
667	*Engelonde*. RV: *England*.

670   *my name is John Lidgate.* In Cov, the name of the author is omitted and a
                   blank space is left.
             Have. RV: *Holde.*
671   *her.* RV: *thare.*
672   *Her.* RV: *thaire.*
Explicit   *Here endith the Daunce of Deeth.* N: *Laus tibi sit christe etc Finis*; RV: *Explicit.*

John Lydgate, *Dance of Death*: B Version (Lansdowne)

This version of the *Dance of Death*, which appears to have been derived from the earlier
Selden version of the text, survives in six manuscripts: Bodleian Library MS Bodley 686 (SC
2527), Corpus Christi College Oxford MS 237, British Library MS Cotton Vespasian A.XXV,
British Library Lansdowne MS 699, Lincoln Cathedral Library MS 129, and Leiden
University Library MS Vossius Germ. Gall. Q.9.

Lansdowne MS 699 is the base text for our edition, collated with Florence Warren's critical
edition for the Early English Text Society. Warren also records the many variant readings
from Cotton Vespasian, a late manuscript (c. 1600) that describes the poem as "writen in the
cappell of Wortley of Wortley Hall" (fol. 172r) and thus may represent a transcription from
an otherwise unattested set of paintings, similar to those created for the Pardon Churchyard
at St. Paul's.

Manuscripts:
Oxford, Bodleian Library, MS Bodley 686, fols. 209r–16r
Oxford, Corpus Christi College, MS 237, fols. 147r–57r
London, British Library, MS Cotton Vespasian A. XXV, fols. 172r–77v (49 stanzas only)
London, British Library, MS Lansdowne 699, fols. 41v–50v
Lincoln, Lincoln Cathedral Library, MS 126, fols. 79v–86r
Cambridge, Harvard University, Houghton Library, MS Eng. 752, fol. 44r (one stanza only,
        inserted in the text of Lydgate's *Troy Book*)
Leiden, Leiden University Library, MS Vossius Germ. Gall. Q.9, fol. 29v

Early Print Edition:
Lydgate, John. *Hore beate marie virginis ad vsum insignis ac preclare ecclesie Saru[m] cu[m] figuris
        passionis mysteriu[m] representa[n]tibus recenter additis.* [Parisius: Per J. bignon pro R. fakes
        Lodoii [sic] librario, [1521?]] (20 stanzas only). [STC 15932]

Edition:
Warren, Florence, and Beatrice White, eds. "The Daunce of Death." In *The Dance of Death,
        Edited from MSS. Ellesmere 26/A.13 and B.M. Lansdowne 699, Collated with the Other Extant
        MSS.* EETS o.s. 181. London: Oxford University Press, 1931; Rpt. New York: Klaus
        Reprint Co., 1971. Pp. 1–77.

1   *O creatures ye.* So Warren. L: *O creatures.*
7   *yliche naturall.* So Warren. L: *that be naturall.*
27   *Thestat ful perilous.* So Warren. L: *thestat perlious.*

39	*Ageyn my myth*. So Warren. L: *ageyn myth*.
46	*visage*. So Warren. L: *my visage*.
52	*daunce for to leer*. So Warren. L: *daunce to leer*.
56	*avys*. So Warren. L: *amys*.
58	*gretely*. So Warren. L: *grisly*.
60	*That I shall*. So Warren. L: *that shal*.
	hereaftir. So Warren. L: *aftir*.
62	*Myn hat of*. L: *myn ~~of~~ hat of*
63	*Bi which*. So Warren. L: *bi the which*.
72	*ye*. So Warren. L: *I*.
73	*or*. So Warren. L: *os*.
75–76	*Or what availeth . . . . porte or straungenesse*. These lines are transposed in L. A note in red in the outer margin indicates the correct order.
76	*or₂*. So Warren. L: *os*.
82	*with me*. So Warren. L: *withynne*.
86	*possessid*. So Warren. L: *possedid*.
89	*grete tresour*. So Warren. L: *tresour*.
90	*Have*. So Warren. L: *hath*.
92	*availeth it*. So Warren. L: *availeth*.
96	*ofte*. So Warren. L: *often*.
113	*Sir Archebishop whi*. L: Rubricated caesura after *Archebishop*.
115	*my*. So Warren. L: *your*.
124	*that*. So Warren. L: *that ~~it~~*.
126	*adieu*. This word is underlined in red and written with a red initial *a* wherever it appears in L. See also lines 251–53 and 487.
127	*my tresour*. So Warren. L: *tresour*.
130	*This*. So Warren. L: *The*.
	not eschewable. So Warren. L: *mysschevable*.
133	*of*. So Warren. L: *at*.
136	*Deth availe*. So Warren. L: *deth*.
Before 137	*Nicholas Munston (?)*. Abraded signature in a later hand above this stanza in L.
138	*assege*. So Warren. L: *asseged*.
	forteresses. So Warren. L: *porterresses*.
140	*worship*. So Warren. L: *worshepis*.
	grete rychesses. So Warren. L: *worthynessis*.
141	*prowesses*. So Warren. L: *prowessis*.
143	*eke swetnesses*. So Warren. L: *& swetnesses*.
151	*acounte*. So Warren. L: *counte*.
157	*world*. So Warren. L: *word*.
161	*thourh*. L: *r* inserted above *thouh* indicating correction.
164	*This*. So Warren. L: *ther*.
172	*Cherishid*. So Warren. L: *chershid*.
182	*your state*. So Warren. L: *~~yo~~ thestat*.
Before 193	*Abbatissa* written in red ink in another hand in the top left corner of fol. 44v.
200	*no good*. So Warren. L: *good*.
201	*for me so*. So L. Warren: *so for me*.
203	*this daunce*. So Warren. L: *this*.

220	*deferrid.* So Warren. L: *differrid.*
240	*shade.* So Warren. L: *slade.*
242	*gise.* So Warren. L: *gises.*
244	*devise.* So Warren. L: *devises.*
245	*emprise.* So Warren. L: *emprises.*
249	*Sith.* So Warren. L: *But sith.*
	Deth me. L: Rubricated caesura after *deth.*
262	*on.* So L. Warren: *out.*
274	*ysworn.* So Warren. L: *I sworn.*
282	*to.* So Warren. L: *the.*
	of verry. L: *of ~~to~~ verray.*
301	*Amys.* Underlined in red in L; it is possibly misrecognized as the French *amis* (friends).
318	*helpe more at.* So Warren. L: *helpe at.*
323	*and doth.* So Warren. L: *doth.*
329	*ded.* L: *de~~th~~.*, with *d* inserted above the deleted letters.
331	*Thowgh every.* So Warren. L: *euery.*
332	*Dredith.* So Warren. L: *dredith hym.*
334	*the Lord.* So Warren. L: *my lord.*
338	*Juge.* So Warren. L: *Iustise.*
341	*foly.* So Warren. L: *hihe.*
345	*Natures lawe.* So Warren. L: *natures of lawe.*
350	*in.* So Warren. L: *on.*
352	*God qwyteth al men lyke as they deserve.* So Warren. L: *but god quyteth men bettir than thei deserve.*
355	*ye was.* So Warren. L: *thei were.*
	Polliceene. L reads *pollixene*, which is underlined in red; *Polliceene* is added in red in the outer margin in another hand.
356	*Penolope.* L: underlined in red.
	and. So Warren. L: *or.*
357	*thei went.* So Warren. L: *went thei.*
369	*mayster.* So Warren. L: *ye.*
372	*astrologye.* L: *astroulogye* with a punctus under *u*, indicating correction.
374	*walke upon the.* So Warren. L: *walkyn vpon.*
379	*in the sterris.* So Warren. L: *in sterris.*
380	*nor.* So Warren. L: *or.*
382	*descrive.* So Warren. L: *descriven.*
384	*Who livith aryght.* So Warren. L: *but he that weel livith.*
387	*prechyng.* So Warren. L: *techyng.*
	ofte. So Warren. L: *often.*
395	*Strengthe richesse.* So Warren. L: *strengthe nor richesse.*
	what so that. So Warren. L: *what that.*
396	*Of.* So Warren. L: *or.*
401	*forth thou Sergeant.* So Warren. L: *forth sergeant.*
413	*arrested.* So Warren. L: *arrest.*
416	*for to.* So Warren. L: *to.*
428	*whom.* So Warren. L: *as.*

433	*shewe me now.* So Warren. L: *shewe now.*
436	*unto.* So Warren. L: *to.*
460	*profites that long.* So Warren. L: *profites long.*
474	*plyed.* So Warren. L: *plye.*
482	*thorow many.* So Warren. L: *many.*
489	*strong.* So Warren. L: *a strong.*
490	*my.* So Warren. L: *many.*
508	*ther may nothyng.* So L. Warren: *which that may.*
518	*fro.* So Warren. L: *for.*
524	*gon.* So Warren. L: *go.*
	at the plouh. So Warren. L: *at plouh.*
530	*world.* Warren, L: *word.*
533	*gon.* So Warren. L: *pleyen.*
542	*Of me no more.* So Warren. L: *on me more no.*
547	*mote.* So Warren. L: *mete.*
550	*hermitage.* So Warren. L: *heritage.*
554	*space.* So Warren. L: *grace.*
561	*Ye.* So Warren. L: *ye ye.*
570	*Or as a.* So Warren. L: *or a.*

JOHN LYDGATE, "DEATH'S WARNING TO THE WORLD" (DIMEV 4905)

MANUSCRIPTS:
Oxford, Bodleian Library MS Douce 322 (SC 21896), fols. 19vb–20ra (basis for this edition)
London, British Library MS Harley 1706, fols. 19v–20r
Cambridge, Cambridge University Library MS Ff.5.45, fols. 13r–14r

EDITIONS:
MacCracken, Henry Noble, ed. "Death's Warning." In *The Minor Poems of John Lydgate, Edited from all Available MSS., with an Attempt to Establish the Lydgate Canon. Part II: Secular Poems.* EETS o.s. 192. London, Oxford University Press, 1934. Rpt. 1961: 2.655–57.

Rubric	None in D, H1. C: *Dictamen. Vel lugubre carmen terribilissimi mortis.* (Letter. A very grievous song of most frightful death.)
1	*hostesse.* So C. D, H1: *costes.* We have chosen *hostesse* since it is an existing manuscript reading that fits in with the trope of female addressees found elsewhere in contemporary death poetry.
2	*And in youre book to set myn ymage.* In Douce 322 and Harley 1706 (fol. 19v in both), the poem is immediately preceded by an ink-drawn image of a skeleton holding a bell and spear (see Explanatory Note to line 7 and Headnote to the Explanatory Notes) with the words "deth" written in profusion around the skeleton's form, evoking the pealing of the bell as well as naming the figure.
3	*with gret avyses.* So D, H1. C: *by gret avisenesse.*
4	*mortall.* So D, H1. C: *my mortal.*

5	*to spare.* So D. H1: *spare.*
	nether. So D, H1. C: *neither.*
	ne. So D. C: *ner.*
7	*Afore.* So D, H1. C: *Aforn.*
8	*y grounde.* So D. H1: *sharpe I grounde.* C: *whet and grounde.*
9	*thys.* So D, H1. C: *thus.*
10	*withstande.* So D, H1. C: *withstonde.*
11	*Ne whomme I merke.* So D, H1. C: *Nor whan I marke.*
	other. So D, H1. C: *othir.*
12	*of day oure ne space.* So D, H1. C: *a day houre or space.*
14	*Yef.* So D, H1. C: *Though.*
15	*past.* So D, H1. C: *passed.*
16	*lasteth but.* So D, H1. C: *lastyng.*
17	*ey.* So D. H1: *eye.* C: *yhe.*
18	*blossom falleth.* So D, H1. C: *blosmes falle.*
20	*elde unwarly crepyng.* So D, H1. C: *age unwardly in crepyng.*
21	*purely thanne.* So D, H1. C: *pouerly you.*
22	*The gospell byddeth than wake and prey.* So D. H1: *The gospel than wake and pray.* C: *The gospel bit you for to wake and prey.*
24	*Ne no manne knoweth whenne.* So D, H1. C: *Nor no man wote the houre whan.*
	dye. So D, H1. C: *dey.*
26	*kynde.* So D, H1. C: *kynge.*
	knot unknyt. So D, H1. C: *knot upknet.* These readings point to opposite understandings of the relationship between death and creation. C emphasizes how tightly bound death is with the very idea of life, while D and H1 instead speak to the theme, seen in other death-related works of this period, of death loosening all bonds. Compare the acrostic in *A Mirror for Young Ladies at their Toilet* (DIMEV 3454), spelling out MORS SOLVIT OMNIA ("death loosens all").
27	*every.* So D, H1. C: *eche.*
28	*For.* So D, H1. C: *Fro.*
	Adams. So D, H1. C: *Adames.*
Rubric	*Thyese balades that . . . tyme to come.* So D, H1. Not in C. This omission is especially interesting since all three manuscripts then continue with an extract from Henry Suso's *Seven Points of True Love and Everlasting Wisdom,* entitled "Orologium Sapientie," suggesting some textual relationship between their contents, despite the differences in their presentation.
29	*worldely.* So D, H1. C: *wordly.*
31	*be.* So D, H1. C: *bene.*
33	*breke.* So D, C. H1: *breken.*
	preceptys. So H1. D: *preceprt*; C: *preceptes.*
	ayenst. So D, H1. C: *ageyn.*
35	*he dyed.* So D, H1. C: *he shedde it.*
36	*hate.* So D, H1. C: *hateth.*
37	*offens.* So D, H1. C: *offences.*
38	*mokry.* So D. H1: *mokey*; C: *mockery.*

39	*Ayenst.* So D, H1. C: *ageyn.*
	do. So D, H1. C: *doth.*
40	*for to have.* So D, H1. C: *to have.*
	souveranly. So D, H1. C: *soffevenly.*
42	*exampelere.* So D, H1. C: *exemplary.*
43	*redempcioun.* So D, H1. C: *redempcion.*
44	*nayled to.* So D, H1. C: *nayled on.*
45	*Suffred.* So H1, C. D: *suffird.*
	passioun. So D, H1. C: *cruel passyon.*
46	*asketh.* So D, H1. C: *axed.*
47	*ayenward.* So D, H1. C: *ageyn.*
48	*that we sette.* So D, C. H1: *we sette.*
	all holy. So D, C. H1: *alonly.*
52	*entre.* So D, H1. C: *entre ageyn.*
53	*From.* So D, H1. C: *For.*
55	*so brynge.* So D. H1: *brynge.* C: *do bryng.*
56	*by thy dethe had.* So D, H1. C: *by dethe haddest.*
	Amen. So D, H1. Absent in C.

"Three Messengers of Death" (DIMEV 5387)

Manuscripts:

Oxford, Bodleian Library, MS Eng. poet. a.1 (SC 3938) [Vernon MS], fols. 297vc–98rb (basis for this edition)

London, British Library, MS Additional 22283 [Simeon MS], fols. 88vb–89ra

Editions:

Horstmann, Carl, ed. "Nachträge zu den Legenden 5: The Messengers of Death." *Archiv für das Studium der neueren Sprachen und Literaturen* 79 (1887), 432–34.

Furnivall, Frederick James, ed. "Of Þre Messagers of Deeth." In *The Minor Poems of the Vernon MS., Part II (with a few from the Digby MSS. 2 and 86).* EETS o.s. 177. London: Kegan Paul, Trench, Trübner & Co., 1901. Pp. 443–48.

Doyle, I. A., ed. *The Vernon Manuscript. A Facsimile of Bodleian Library, Oxford, MS. Eng. Poet.a.1, with an introduction by A.I. Doyle.* Cambridge: D. S. Brewer, 1987. Fols. 297vc–98rb.

Scase, Wendy, and Nick Kennedy, eds. *A Facsimile Edition of the Vernon Manuscript: Oxford, Bodleian Library, MS. Eng. Poet. A. 1.* Oxford: The Bodleian Library, 2011. Fols. 297vc–98rb.

Title	*Three Messengers of Death.* This title is derived from the Vernon Manuscript's rubric to the work (fol. 297vc).
Rubric	*Her biginneth . . . iwis.* So V. Not in Sim.
6	*sore he.* So V. Sim: *Sore al he.*
21	*vetat.* So V. Horstmann, Furnivall amend to *necat.*
23	*Inter.* So Horstmann, Furnivall. V, Sim: *iter.*
24	*quelibet.* So V. Sim: *quilibet.*

29	*this messagers.* So V. Sim: *the messagers.*
38	*Theih.* So V. Sim: *þauh.*
	o. So V. Sim: *on.*
39	*and.* So V. Sim: *an.*
50	*Withouten.* So V. Sim: *Withoute.*
64	*mowe.* So V. Sim: *mowen.*
77	*beoth.* So V. Sim: *ben.*
82	*habben.* So V. Sim: *habbe.*
84	*wolen.* So V. Sim: *wolleþ.*
97	*ben.* So V. Sim: *beoþ.*
98	*in the lift.* So V. Sim: *doth in the lift.*
101	*heore.* So V. Sim: *her.*
110	*messagers.* So V. Sim: *messager.*
114	*bekneth.* So V. Sim: *bekeneþ.*
120	*porter.* So Sim, Horstmann, Furnivall. V: *poter.*
123	*atte yate.* So V. Sim: *at the yate.*
142	*weore.* So V. Sim: *weoren.*
144	*An.* So V. Sim: *And.*
183	*doth us.* So V. Sim: *doth him.*
205	*alle men.* So V. Sim: *al the men.*
206	*Weore prestes masses to synge.* So V. Sim: *Weore prestes and masses dude singe.*
210	*in atte helle.* So V. Sim: *in at the helle.*
217	*he falleth.* So V. Sim: *thu falles.*

"A WARNING SPOKEN BY THE SOUL OF A DEAD PERSON" (DIMEV 3624)

MANUSCRIPT:
Oxford, Bodleian Library Bodley 789 (SC 2643), fols. 149r–50r (basis for this edition)

EDITIONS:
Woolf, Rosemary, ed. "Mi Leeve Liif." In *The English Religious Lyric in the Middle Ages.* Oxford: Clarendon Press, 1968. Pp. 317–18.

Hirsh, John C., ed. "*Index of Middle English Verse* No. 2255." In "Prayer and Meditation in Late Mediaeval England: MS Bodley 789." *Medium Ævum* 48 (1979), 61–62.

"A MIRROR FOR YOUNG LADIES AT THEIR TOILET" (DIMEV 3454)

MANUSCRIPT:
London, British Library, MS Harley 116, fols. 128r–v

EDITIONS:
Brown, Carleton Fairchild, ed. "A Mirror for Young Ladies at their Toilet." In *Religious Lyrics of the XVth Century.* Oxford: Clarendon, 1939. P. 241.

Cutler, John L., ed. "No. 2136, A Mirror for Young Ladies at their Toilet." In "A Middle English Acrostic." *Modern Language Notes* 70.2 (1955), 88.

Silverstein, Theodore, ed. "Cest le Myrroure pur les Iofenes Dames." In *Medieval English Lyrics*. London: Edwin Arnold Ltd., 1971. Pp. 121–22.

Title	*A Mirror for Young Ladies at their Toilet*. This title was coined by Brown in his edition of the work.
11	*Wel thee*. H2, Brown, Cutler: *welthe*. We have chosen to emend for clarity, agreeing with Silverstein.
13	*Ne lengthe*. H2, Brown, Silverstein, Cutler: *Be lengthe*. We emend to *Ne* given the acrostic.

"The Ressoning betuix Deth and man," ascribed to Robert Henryson (DIMEV 4000)

Manuscripts:

Edinburgh, National Library of Scotland, Advocates MS 1.1.6 (Bannatyne MS Draft), pp. 43–44

Edinburgh, National Library of Scotland, Advocates MS 1.1.6 (Bannatyne MS Main), fols. 56r–57r (basis for this edition)

Edinburgh, National Library of Scotland, Advocates' 18.5.14, fol. ii (fragment)

Editions:

Dalrymple, Sir David, ed. "The Ressoning betwixt Deth and Man." *Ancient Scottish Poems. Published from the MS. of George Bannatyne*. Edinburgh: A. Murray and J. Cochran for John Blafour, 1770. Pp. 134–35.

Laing, David, ed. "The Ressoning betwixt Deth and Man." In *The Poems and Fables of Robert Henryson: Now First Collected with Notes, and a Memoir of his Life*. Edinburgh: William Paterson, 1865. Pp. 27–29.

Murdoch, James Barclay, ed. "The Ressoning betuix Deth and Man." In *The Bannatyne Manuscript*. 4 vols. in 11 parts, paged continuously. Glasgow: Anderson, 1873–96: 2.153–55.

Smith, G. Gregory, ed. "The Ressoning betwixt Deth and Man." In *The Poems of Robert Henryson*. 3 vols. STS 1st series 55, 58, 64. Edinburgh: William Blackwood and Sons, 1906–14. Rpt. New York, 1968: 3.134–38.

Ritchie, W. Tod, ed. "The Ressoning betuix Deth and Man." In *The Bannatyne Manuscript Written in Tyme of Pest, 1568, by George Bannatyne*. 4 vols. STS 3rd series 5; 2nd series 22, 23, 26. Edinburgh and London: William Blackwood and Sons, 1928–34. 1:71–73; 2:139–41.

Wood, Henry Harvey, ed. "The Ressoning betuix Deth and Man." In *The Poems and Fables of Robert Henryson*. 2nd Edition. Edinburgh, London: Oliver and Boyd, 1933; Rpt., 1958: 211–12.

Fox, Denton, and William A. Ringler, eds. "The Ressoning betuix Deth and Man." *The Bannatyne Manuscript: National Library of Scotland Advocates' MS. 1.1.6*. London: Scolar Press, in Association with The National Library of Scotland, 1980. Pp. 43–44. Fols. 56r–57r.

Parkinson, David J., ed. "The Ressoning betwix Deth and Man." In *Robert Henryson, The Complete Works*. Kalamazoo, MI: Medieval Institute Publications, 2010. Pp. 155–56.

Title	*The Ressoning betuix Deth and Man.* So BM. Omitted in BD.
Before 1	*Deth.* So BM. BD: *Mors.* (Death.) *Mors* appears as a speaker for the remainder of the text.
2	*sowld.* So BM. BD: *sall.*
5	*stait.* So BM. BD: *estait.*
6	*not.* So BM. BD: *nocht.*
	the. So BM. BD: *this.*
7	*castelis and towris.* So BM. BD: *castells towiris.*
	wicht. So BM. BD: *hicht wicht.*
Before 9	*The man.* So BM. BD: *Homo.* (Man.) *Homo* appears as a speaker for the remainder of the text.
12	*that thuw sall sone.* So BM. BD: *that that thow sall.*
14	*outhir.* So BM. BD: *owyr.*
15	*wicht or stark.* So BM. BD: *wicht so stark.*
16	*But.* So BM. BD: *Nor.*
17	*forsuith.* So BD. BM: *forswth.*
	speiris. So BM. BD: *speirs.*
18	*Thay.* So BM. BD: *Tha.*
19	*thair.* So BM. BD: *ther.*
	beiris. So BM. BD: *beirs.*
23	*owthir.* So BM. BD: *ouyr be it.*
26	*awld with riche.* So BM. BD: *auld riche.*
29	*deids.* So BM. BD: *deidis.*
30	*ay yowtheid wold with me.* So BM. BD: *youtheid wald with me ay.*
34	*wordis.* So BM. BD: *wirds.*
35	*full.* So BM. BD: *wofull.*
36	*sall richt deir.* So BM. BD: *sall deir.*
37	*thy self.* So BM. BD: *for the.*
	in hye. So BM. BD: *and fre.*
43	*thee Deid to lurk.* So BM. BD: *to deid to luke.*
44	*humly.* So BM. BD: *humily.*
45	*Beseiking.* So BM. BD: *Beseikand.*
Explicit	*Finis quod Hendersone.* So BM. BD: *Finis.*

"The Dawnce of Makabre" (DIMEV 4104)

Manuscript:

London, British Library Additional 37049 fols. 31v–32r

Editions:

Brunner, Karl, ed. "Dance of Makabre." In "Mittelenglische Todesgedichte." *Archiv für das Studium der neueren Sprachen und Literaturen* 167 (1935), 27–28, 30.

Doty, Brant Lee, ed. "Dawnce of Makabre." In "An Edition of British Museum Manuscript Additional 37049: a Religious Miscellany." Ph.D. Dissertation: Michigan State University, 1969. Pp. 206–11.

Hogg, James, ed. "A Morbid Preoccupation with Mortality? The Carthusian London British Library MS. Add. 37049." *Zeit, Tod und Ewigkeit in der Renaissance Literatur* 2 (1986): 52–54.

1	*that.* Inserted above line in A1.
48	*As.* So Doty, A1. Brunner emends to *as that.*
51	*nover.* So Brunner. A1, Doty: *neir.*

"CAN YE DANCE THE SHAKING OF THE SHEETS" (DIMEV 956)

MANUSCRIPT:
London, British Library Additional MS 15225, fols. 15r–16r

EARLY PRINT EDITIONS:
The dolefull dance and song of death; intituled, dance after my pipe. [London]: F. Coles, J. Wright, T. Vere, and W. Gilbertson, [1655–58]. (Wing H2013A)

The dolefull dance and song of death; intituled; Dance after my pipe. London: F. Coles, T. Vere, and W. Gilbertson, [1658–64]. (Wing H2013B)

The doleful Dance and Song of Death; Intituled, Dance after my Pipe. [London]: F. Coles, T. Vere, and J. Wright, [1663–74?]. (Rawl. 566)

The doleful Dance, and Song of Death; Intituled, Dance after my pipe. [London]: T. Vere, I. Wright, J. Clarke, W. Thackeray, and T. Passenger, [1678–81]. (Pepys Ballads 2.62)

EDITIONS:
Chappell, W., ed. "The Dance and Song of Death." In *Roxburghe Ballads*, vol. 3. Hertford: Stephen Austin & Sons, 1880; Rpt. New York: AMS Press, 1966, pp. 183–86.

Gray, Douglas, ed. "A Dolfull Daunce & Song of Death Intituled: the Shakeing of the Sheetes." In "Two Songs of Death." *Neuphilologische Mitteilungen* 64 (1963), 64–67.

2	*man.* So A2. P, R, W1, W2: *one.*
4	*that.* So A2. P, R, W2: *as.*
10	*Bring away both.* So A2. P, R, W1, W2: *Bring the.*
14	*And.* So A2. P, R, W1, W2: omitted.
	beating hookes. So A2. P, R, W1, W2: *baiting hooks.*
15	*that make your.* So A2. P, R, W1, W2: *have you made your.*
18	*With both our heeles.* So A2. P, R, W1, W2: *Both our heeles.*
22	*Thinke on.* So A2. P, R, W1, W2: *Thinke you on.*
24	*agast.* So A2. P, R, W1, W2: *all agast.*
29	*Thinke you.* So A2. P, R, W2: *you that I.*
	in scooles. So A2. P, R, W1, W2: *to scholes.*
31	*Take not I away.* So A2. P, W2: *Take I not always.*
36	*busie-headed.* So A2. R: *bustheaded.* This stanza appears after line 56 in the printed versions.
37	*To brawle for everie.* So A2. P: *to bubble of a*; R: *to babble of a*; W1: *to brabble for a*; W2: *to brabble of a.*

39	*To cut away.* So A2. R: *To cut you from.*
40	*foolishly.* So A2. W1: *falsely*; P, R, W2: *safely.*
45	*Doe yea acount.* So A2. P, R, W1, W2: *do you make account.*
46	*To have all the world.* So A2. P, R, W2: *to have the world.*
48	*This night thy soule must sure goe hence.* So A2. P, R, W1, W2: *Full soon thy soul must needs go hence.*
51	*her knee.* So A2. P, R, W1, W2: *their knee.*
52	*Doe you thinke to play.* So A2. P, R, W1, W2: *Think you for to play.*
54	*Noe faith.* So A2. P, R, W1, W2: *Noe.*
	laddes. So A2. P, R, W1, W2: *lords.*
58	*he learnes.* So A2. P, R, W1, W2: *she loves.*
60	*doth.* So A2. P, W2: *can.*
61	*swash and flash.* So A2. P, R, W1, W2: *flash and swash.*
68	*ladie.* So A2. P, R, W1, W2: *ladies.*
	beldam. So A2. P, R, W1, W2: *beldams.*
72	*Prepare yourselves.* So A2. P, R, W1, W2: *with me your selves.*
76	*pypes his play.* So A2. P, R, W1, W2: *pipe doth play.*
77	*daunce readie way.* So A2. P, R, W1, W2: *dance the way.*
Explicit	*finis Thomas Hill.* So A2. No attribution is given in the printed broadsides.

LA DANSE MACABRE, TRANSLATION BY ELIZAVETA STRAKHOV

Our edition of the *Danse macabre* intentionally uses an early manuscript, Paris, BNF fonds francaise MS 14989, containing the name "Machabre Docteur," as its base-text (see Headnote to Explanatory Notes for the *Danse macabre* on p. 142), whereas other modern editions of the *Danse* all take Guyot Marchant's 1485 and 1486 editions as their base-text. Warren also opts for a manuscript as her base-text: British Library, Additional MS 38858. Emendations of our base-text have been made simply for grammatical clarity, but we adduce the other modern editions as parallels to our editorial choices; in a few cases obviously corrupt readings have been emended in accordance with the other editions.

MANUSCRIPTS:
1. Chantilly, Bibliothèque et Archives du Château, MS 502 (olim 1920), fols. 1r–20v.
2. Lille, Bibliothèque municipale, MS 139 (*olim* 364), fols. 233v–39v.
3. London, British Library, Additional, MS 38858, fols. 2r–12r.
4. Paris, Bibliothèque Mazarine, 3896, fols. 237r–64v.
5. Paris, Bibliothèque nationale de France, fonds latin MS 14904, fols. 64r–72r.
6. Paris, Bibliothèque nationale de France, fonds français MS 995, fols. 1r–17r.
7. Paris, Bibliothèque nationale de France, fonds français MS 1055, fols. 68r–75r.
8. Paris, Bibliothèque nationale de France, fonds français MS 1181, fols. 137v–40v (fragment).
9. Paris, Bibliothèque nationale de France, fonds français MS 1186, fols. 89r–98v.
10. Paris, Bibliothèque nationale de France, fonds français MS 14989, fols. 1r–12v (base text for this edition).
11. Paris, Bibliothèque nationale de France, fonds français MS 25434, fols. 18r–35v.

12. Paris, Bibliothèque nationale de France, fonds français MS 25550, fols. 235r–49v.
13. Paris, Bibliothèque nationale de France, nouvelles acquisitions françaises MS 10032, fols. 209r–23v.
14. Saint-Omer, Bibliothèque municipale, MS 127, fols. 201r–06r.
15. Tours, Bibliothèque municipale, MS 907, fols. 99v–114v.

INCUNABULA: For a comprehensive list of incunabula printing the *Danse macabre*, see the *Universal Short Title Catalogue* (https://ustc.ac.uk/index.php/search), using the keyword "Danse macabre" to search.

EDITIONS:

La grande danse macabre des hommes et des femmes precédée du dict des trois mors et des trois vifz, du debat du corps et de l'âme, et la complaincte de l'âme dampnée. Paris: Bailleu, 1862.

de Lincy, Le Roux, and L. M. Tisserand, eds. "La danse macabre reproduite textuellement d'apres l'unique exemplaire connu de l'édition princeps de Guyot Marchant (Paris, 1485) et completée avec l'édition de 1486." In *Paris et ses historiens aux XIVe et XVe Siècles.* Paris: Imprimerie Impériale, 1867. Pp. 291–317.

Dufour, Valentin, ed. *La dance macabre peinte sous les charniers des Saints Innocents de Paris (1425): reproduction de l'édition princeps donnée par Guyot Marchant, texte et gravures sur bois (1485).* Paris: Féchoz, 1874. Rpt. 1875. Rpt. 1891.

Champion, Pierre, ed. *La danse macabre, reproduction en fac-similé de l'édition de Guy Marchant, Paris, 1486.* Paris: Éditions des Quatre Chemins, 1925.

Warren, Florence, and Beatrice White, eds. "The French Text." In *The Dance of Death, Edited from MSS. Ellesmere 26/A.13 and B.M. Lansdowne 699, Collated with the Other Extant MSS.* EETS o.s. 181. London: Oxford University Press, 1931; Rpt. New York: Klaus Reprint Co., 1971. Pp. 79–96.

Chaney, Edward F., ed. *La danse macabré des charniers des Saints Innocents à Paris.* Manchester: Manchester University Press, 1945.

Saugnieux, Joël, ed. "*La danse macabre* française de Guyot Marchant (1486)." In *Les danses macabres de France et d'Espagne et leurs prolongements littéraires.* Lyon: Emmanuel Vitte, 1972. Pp. 143–64.

Kaiser, Gert, ed. and trans. "La danse macabre" in *Der tanzende Tod: Mittelalterliche Totentänze.* Frankfurt am Main: Insel-Verlag, 1982. Pp. 72–107.

Fein, David A., ed. and trans. *The* Danse Macabre *Printed by Guyot Marchant, 1485.* Tempe: Arizona Center for Medieval and Renaissance Studies, 2013.

14	*Mort n'espargne.* F: *Mort* ~~le~~ *nespargne.*
42	*timbre.* So Lincy, Dufour, Saugnieux, Fein. F: *timble.* Warren: *tymbre.*
55	*ce.* So Warren, Lincy, Dufour, Saugnieux, Fein. F: *se.*
83	*tout.* So Warren, Lincy, Dufour, Saugnieux, Fein. F: *teut.*
102	*le.* So Warren, Lincy, Dufour, Saugnieux, Fein. F: *les.*
134	*contrainte.* So Warren, Lincy, Dufour, Saugnieux, Fein. F: *centrainte.*
149	*cop suis.* F: ~~cop~~ *cop suis.*
178	*rire.* So Warren, Lincy, Dufour, Saugnieux, Fein. F: *vivre.*
184	*chiere.* So Lincy, Dufour, Saugnieux, Fein. F: *cheere.* Warren: *chere.*
185	*que.* So Warren, Lincy, Dufour, Saugnieux, Fein. F: *qui.*
198	*On s'advise tart en mourant.* Added in space between stanzas by the scribe.

Before 199	¶ *Le mort* added in the margin by the scribe.
317	*Homme n'est fors que vent et cendre.* Added in the outer margin by the scribe with a *signe de renvoi* (an insertion mark) in the form of a circle and cross.
318	*est peu.* F: *est ~~moult~~ peu.*
332	*se.* So Warren, Lincy, Dufour, Saugnieux, Fein. F: *ce.*
347	*ma main.* So Warren, Lincy, Dufour, Saugnieux, Fein. F: *main.*
380	*Souviegnez.* F: *souviegne.* Warren, Lincy, Dufour, Saugnieux, Fein all have forms of *souvienne*, but the verb form should be in the second person plural, as we have emended it.
403	*Monstrer.* So Warren, Lincy, Dufour, Saugnieux, Fein. F: *monstres.*
Before 423	¶ *Le cure.* F: omitted.
440	*la.* So Lincy, Dufour, Saugnieux. F, Warren: *le.* Omitted in Fein.
456	*n'y demeure.* F: *ny demeure ~~demeure~~.* The first *demeure* has been written over a word that has been scraped away. The second, crossed out *demeure* occurs in the right-hand margin next to the line, with traces of a third *demeure* written above it.
470	*a a souffrir.* So Warren, Lincy, Dufour, Saugnieux, Fein. F: *a assouffrir.*
472	*la.* So Warren, Lincy, Dufour, Saugnieux, Fein. F: *le.*
483	*Qu'on.* So Warren, Lincy, Dufour, Saugnieux, Fein. F: *Quen.*
511	A copy of lines 519–24 with the speaker marker are written out here but crossed out.
526	*aux vers donnez.* So Warren, Lincy, Dufour, Saugnieux, Fein. F: *donnez aux vers.*
553	*amens.* F: illegible, supplied by Fein.

BIBLIOGRAPHY

EDITIONS (IN CHRONOLOGICAL ORDER)

The dolefull dance and song of death; intituled, dance after my pipe. [London]: F. Coles, J. Wright, T. Vere, and W. Gilbertson, [1655–58]. [Shaking of the Sheets]

The dolefull dance and song of death; intituled; Dance after my pipe. London: F. Coles, T. Vere, and W. Gilbertson, [1658–64]. [Shaking of the Sheets]

The doleful Dance and Song of Death; Intituled, Dance after my Pipe. [London]: F. Coles, T. Vere, and J. Wright, [1663–74?]. [Shaking of the Sheets]

The doleful Dance, and Song of Death; Intituled, Dance after my pipe. [London]: T. Vere, I. Wright, J. Clarke, W. Thackeray, and T. Passenger, [1678–81]. [Shaking of the Sheets]

Dalrymple, Sir David, ed. "The Ressoning betwixt Deth and Man." *Ancient Scottish Poems. Published from the MS. of George Bannatyne.* Edinburgh: A. Murray and J. Cochran for John Balfour, 1770. Pp. 134–35.

La grande danse macabre des hommes et des femmes, precédée du dict des trois mors et des trois vifz, du debat du corps et de l'âme et la complaincte de l'âme dampnée. Paris: Bailleu, 1862. [French *Danse Macabre*]

Laing, David, ed. "The Ressoning betwixt Deth and Man." In *The Poems and Fables of Robert Henryson: Now First Collected with Notes, and a Memoir of his Life.* Edinburgh: William Paterson, 1865. Pp. 27–29.

de Lincy, Le Roux, and L. M. Tisserand, eds. "La danse macabre reproduite textuellement d'apres l'unique exemplaire connu de l'édition princeps de Guyot Marchant (Paris, 1485) et completée avec l'édition de 1486." In *Paris et ses historiens aux XIVe et XVe Siècles.* Paris: Imprimerie Impériale, 1867. Pp. 291–317. [French *Danse macabre*]

Murdoch, James Barclay, ed. "The Ressoning betuix Deth and Man." In *The Bannatyne Manuscript.* 4 vols. in 11 parts, paged continuously. Glasgow: Anderson, 1873–96. 2.153–55.

Dufour, Valentin, ed. *La dance macabre peinte sous les charniers des Saints Innocents de Paris (1425): reproduction de l'édition princeps donnée par Guyot Marchant, texte et gravures sur bois (1485).* Paris: Féchoz, 1874. Rpt. 1875, 1891. [French *Danse macabre*]

Horstmann, Carl, ed. "The Messengers of Death." In "Naträge zu den Legenden." *Archiv für das Studium der neueren Sprachen und Literaturen* 79 (1887), 432–34.

Chappell, W., ed. "The Dance and Song of Death." In *Roxburghe Ballads* vol. III. Hertford: Stephen Austin & Sons, 1880; Rpt. New York: AMS Press, 1966, pp. 183–86. [Shaking of the Sheets]

Furnivall, Frederick James, ed. "Of Þre Messagers of Deeth." In *The Minor Poems of the Vernon MS., Part II (with a few from the Digby MSS. 2 and 86).* 2 Vols. EETS o.s. 177. London: Kegan Paul, Trench, Trübner & Co., 1901. 2:443–48.

Söderhjelm, Werner, ed. "Le miroir des dames et demoiselles," *Neuphilologische Mitteilungen* 6.2 (1904), 29–35.

Glixelli, Stefan, ed. *Les cinq poèmes des trois morts et des trois vifs.* Paris: Honoré Champion, 1914.

Champion, Pierre, ed. *La danse macabre, reproduction en fac-similé de l'édition de Guy Marchant, Paris, 1486.* Paris: Éditions des Quatre Chemins, 1925. [French *Danse macabre*]

Hammond, Eleanor Prescott, ed. "The Dance Macabre." *English Verse between Chaucer and Surrey: Being Examples of Conventional Secular Poetry, Exclusive of Romance, Ballad, Lyric, and Drama, in the Period from Henry the Fourth to Henry the Eighth.* Durham, NC: Duke University Press, 1927. Pp. 131–42. [Lydgate's *Dance of Death*, A version]

Ritchie, W. Tod, ed. "The Ressoning betuix Deth and Man." In *The Bannatyne Manuscript Written in Tyme of Pest, 1568, by George Bannatyne*. 4 vols. STS 3rd series 5; 2nd series 22, 23, 26. Edinburgh and London: William Blackwood and Sons, 1928–34. 1:71–73; 2:139–41.

Warren, Florence, and Beatrice White, eds. "The Daunce of Death." In *The Dance of Death, Edited from MSS. Ellesmere 26/A.13 and B.M. Lansdowne 699, Collated with the Other Extant MSS*. EETS o.s. 181. London: Oxford University Press, 1931; Rpt. New York: Klaus Reprint Co., 1971. Pp. 1–77. [Lydgate's *Dance of Death*, A and B versions]

———. "The French Text." In *The Dance of Death, Edited from MSS. Ellesmere 26/A.13 and B.M. Lansdowne 699, Collated with the Other Extant MSS*. EETS o.s. 181. London: Oxford University Press, 1931; Rpt. New York: Klaus Reprint Co., 1971. Pp. 79–96. [French *Danse macabre*]

Brunner, Karl, ed. "Dance of Makabre." In "Mittelenglische Todesgedichte." *Archiv für das Studium der neueren Sprachen und Literaturen* 167 (1935), 27–28, 30. [Dawnce of Makabre]

Brown, Carleton Fairchild, ed. "A Mirror for Young Ladies at their Toilet." In *Religious Lyrics of the XVth Century*. Oxford: Clarendon, 1939. P. 241.

Chaney, Edward F., ed. *La danse macabré des charniers des Saints Innocents à Paris*. Manchester: Manchester University Press, 1945. [French *Danse macabre*]

Cutler, John L., ed. "No. 2136, A Mirror for Young Ladies at their Toilet." In "A Middle English Acrostic." *Modern Language Notes* 70.2 (1955), 88.

Wood, Henry Harvey, ed. "The Ressoning betuix Deth and Man." In *The Poems and Fables of Robert Henryson*. Second Edition. Edinburgh and London: Oliver and Boyd, 1933; Rpt. 1958. Pp. 211–12.

MacCracken, Henry Noble, ed. "Death's Warning." In *The Minor Poems of John Lydgate, Edited from all Available MSS., with an Attempt to Establish the Lydgate Canon. Part II: Secular Poems*. EETS o.s. 192. London: Oxford University Press, 1934. Rpt. 1961. Pp. 655–57.

Gray, Douglas, ed. "A Dolfull Daunce & Song of Death Intituled: the Shakeing of the Sheetes." In "Two Songs of Death." *Neuphilologische Mitteilungen* 64 (1963), 64–67.

Rosenfeld, Hellmut, ed. "Die Vado-Mori-Elegie." In *Der mittelalterliche Totentanz: Entstehung—Entwicklung—Bedeutung*. Cologne: Böhlau Verlag, 1968. Pp. 323–26.

Smith, G. Gregory, ed. "The Ressoning betwixt Deth and Man." In *The Poems of Robert Henryson*. 3 vols. STS 1st series 55, 58, 64. Edinburgh: William Blackwood and Sons, 1906–14. Rpt. New York, 1968. 3.134–38.

Woolf, Rosemary, ed. "Mi Leeve Liif." In *The English Religious Lyric in the Middle Ages*. Oxford: Clarendon Press, 1968. Pp. 317–18. [Warning Spoken by the Soul of a Dead Person]

Doty, Brant Lee, ed. "Dawnce of Makabre." In "An Edition of British Museum Manuscript Additional 37049: a Religious Miscellany." Ph.D. Dissertation: Michigan State University, 1969. Pp. 206–11. [Dawnce of Makabre]

Silverstein, Theodore, ed. "Cest le Myrroure pur les Iofenes Dames." In *Medieval English Lyrics*. London: Edwin Arnold Ltd., 1971. Pp. 121–22. [A Mirror for Young Ladies]

Saugnieux, Joël, ed. "*La danse macabre* française de Guyot Marchant (1486)." In *Les danses macabres de France et d'Espagne et leurs prolongements littéraires*. Lyon: Emmanuel Vitte, 1972. Pp. 143–64. [French *Danse macabre*]

———. "*Danza general*." In *Les danses macabres de France et d'Espagne et leurs prolongements littéraires*. Lyon: Emmanuel Vitte, 1972. Pp. 165–82.

Hirsh, John C., ed. "*Index of Middle English Verse* No. 2255." In "Prayer and Meditation in Late Mediaeval England: MS Bodley 789." *Medium Ævum* 48 (1979), 61–62. [Warning Spoken by the Soul of a Dead Person]

Fox, Denton, and William A. Ringler, eds. "The Ressoning betuix Deth and Man." *The Bannatyne Manuscript: National Library of Scotland Advocates' MS. 1.1.6*. London: Scolar Press, in Association with The National Library of Scotland, 1980. Pp. 43–44. Fols. 56r–57r.

Kaiser, Gert, ed. and trans. "La danse macabre" in *Der tanzende Tod: Mittelalterliche Totentänze*. Frankfurt am Main: Insel-Verlag, 1982. Pp. 72–107. [French *Danse macabre*]

Hogg, James, ed. "A Morbid Preoccupation with Mortality? The Carthusian London British Library MS. Add. 37049." *Zeit, Tod und Ewigkeit in der Renaissance Literatur* 2 (1986), 52–54. [Dawnce of Makabre]

Doyle, I. A., ed. *The Manuscript. A Facsimile of Bodleian Library, Oxford, MS. Eng. Poet.a.1, with an introduction by A.I. Doyle*. Cambridge: D. S. Brewer, 1987. Fols. 297vc–98rb. [Three Messengers of Death]

Parkinson, David J., ed. "The Ressoning betwix Deth and Man." In *Robert Henryson: The Complete Works*. Kalamazoo, MI: Medieval Institute Publications, 2010. Pp. 155–56.

Scase, Wendy, and Nick Kennedy, eds. (software). *A Facsimile Edition of the Vernon Manuscript: Oxford, Bodleian Library, MS. Eng. Poet. A. 1*. Oxford: The Bodleian Library, 2011. Fols. 297vc–98rb. [Three Messengers of Death]

Fein, David A., ed. and trans. *The* Danse Macabre *Printed by Guyot Marchant, 1485*. Tempe: Arizona Center for Medieval and Renaissance Studies, 2013. [French *Danse macabre*]

OTHER WORKS

Ackerman, Robert W. "*The Debate of the Body and the Soul* and Parochial Christianity." *Speculum* 37.4 (1962), 541–65.

Appleford, Amy. "The Dance of Death in London: John Carpenter, John Lydgate, and the *Daunce of Poulys*." *Journal of Medieval and Early Modern Studies* 38.2 (2008), 285–314.

———. *Learning to Die in London, 1380–1540*. Philadelphia: University of Pennsylvania Press, 2015.

Ariès, Philippe. *The Hour of Our Death*. Trans. Helen Weaver. New York: Knopf, 1981.

Ashley, Kathleen, and Robert L. A. Clark, eds. *Medieval Conduct*. Minneapolis: University of Minnesota Press, 2001.

Audelay, John. "Three Dead Kings." In *John the Blind Audelay, Poems and Carols* (Oxford, Bodleian Library MS Douce 302). Ed. Susanna Fein. Kalamazoo, MI: Medieval Institute Publications. Pp. 218–22.

Backer, George de, ed. *Dictionnaire des proverbes françois avec l'explication de leurs significations, & une partie de leur origine. Le tout tiré & recueilli des meilleurs autheurs de ce dernier siecle. Par G. D. B.* Brusselles: Coerge de Backer, 1710.

Batiouchkof, Theodore. "Le débat de l'âme et du corps (Part 1)." *Romania* 20.77 (1891), 1–55.

———. "Le débat de l'âme et du corps (Part 2)." *Romania* 20.80 (1891), 513–78.

Beaune, Colette, ed. *Journal d'un bourgeois de Paris de 1405 à 1449*. Paris: Librairie générale française, 1990.

Becker, Karin. "La danse macabre au féminin: *La danse des femmes* de Martial d'Auvergne." In *La mort dans la littérature française du Moyen Âge*. Ed. Jean-François Kosta-Théfaine. Villers-Cotterêts: Ressouvenances, 2013. Pp. 282–302.

Bellis, Joanna. *The Hundred Years War in Literature: 1337–1600*. Woodbridge: D. S. Brewer, 2016.

Binski, Paul. *Medieval Death: Ritual and Representation*. London: British Museum Press, 1996.

Blatt, Heather. *Participatory Reading in Late-Medieval England*. Manchester: Manchester University Press, 2018.

Boccaccio, Giovanni. *Famous Women*. Ed. and trans. Virginia Brown. Cambridge, MA: Harvard University Press, 2001.

Boffey, Julia. *Manuscripts of English Courtly Love Lyrics in the Later Middle Ages*. Woodbridge: D. S. Brewer, 1985.

The Book of Hours of Charles V. Madrid, Biblioteca Nacional de Espana, Cod. Vitr, 24–3, 2008–18. Online at http://bdh-rd.bne.es/viewer.vm?id=0000051953.

The booke of the common prayer and administraction of the Sacramentes, and other rites and ceremonies of the Churche. London: Edward Whitchurch, 1549.

Brunner, Karl. "Mittelenglische Todesgedichte." *Archiv für das Studium der neueren Sprachen und Literaturen* 167 (1935), 20–35.

Burger, Glenn D. *Conduct Becoming: Good Wives and Husbands in the Later Middle Ages*. Philadelphia: University of Pennsylvania Press, 2018.

Butterfield, Ardis. *The Familiar Enemy: Chaucer, Language, and Nation in the Hundred Years War*. Oxford: Oxford University Press, 2009.

Caciola, Nancy. "Wraiths, Revenants and Ritual in Medieval Culture." *Past & Present* 152 (1996), 3–45.

Carruthers, Mary J. *The Book of Memory: A Study of Memory in Medieval Culture*. Second edition. Cambridge: Cambridge University Press, 2008.

The Catholic Encyclopedia. Vol. 1–15. New York: Robert Appleton Company, 1907–12. Online at https://www.catholic.org/encyclopedia/.

Chaganti, Seeta. "*Danse Macabre* and the Virtual Churchyard." *Postmedieval* 3.1 (2012), 7–26.

———. *Strange Footing: Poetic Form and Dance in the Late Middle Ages*. Chicago: University of Chicago Press, 2018.

Chappell, William, ed. *Popular Music of the Olden Time*. 2 vols. London: Cramer, Beale, & Chappell, 1885–86.

Chaucer, Geoffrey. *The Riverside Chaucer*. Third edition. Gen. ed. Larry D. Benson. Boston: Houghton Mifflin, 1987.

Clark, James M. *The Dance of Death in the Middle Ages and the Renaissance*. Glasgow: Jackson, Son and Company, 1950.

Cohen, Kathleen. *Metamorphosis of a Death Symbol: The* Transi *Tomb in the Late Middle Ages and the Renaissance*. Berkeley: University of California Press, 1973.

Cooper, Lisa, and Andrea Denny-Brown, eds. *Lydgate Matters: Poetry and Material Culture in the Fifteenth Century*. New York: Palgrave MacMillan, 2008.

Copeland, Rita. *Rhetoric, Hermeneutics, and Translation in the Middle Ages: Academic Traditions and Vernacular Texts*. Cambridge: Cambridge University Press, 1991.

Cutler, John L. "A Middle English Acrostic." *Modern Language Notes* 70.2 (1955), 87–89.

Daniell, Christopher. *Death and Burial in Medieval England, 1066–1550*. London: Routledge, 1997.

Davis, Matthew Evan. "Lydgate at Long Melford: Reassessing the *Testament* and 'Quis Dabit Meo Capiti Fontem Lacrimarum' in Their Local Context." *Journal of Medieval Religious Cultures* 43.1 (2017), 77–114.

"Detailed Record for Harley 116." *Catalogue of Illuminated Manuscripts*. British Library. Online at http://www.bl.uk/catalogues/illuminatedmanuscripts/record.asp?MSID=3466&CollID=8&Nstart=116.

Dictionnaire du Moyen Français (1330–1500). Analyse et traitement informatique de la langue française, Université de Lorraine, 2015. Online at http://www.atilf.fr/dmf.

DIMEV: An Open-Access, Digital Edition of the Index of Middle English Verse. Ed. Linne R. Mooney, Daniel W. Mosser, Elizabeth Solopova, Deborah Thorpe, and David Hill Radcliffe. Virginia Polytechnic Institute and State University, 1995. Online at www.dimev.net.

Dictionary of the Scots Language. Ed. William A. Craigie. Online at http://www.dsl.ac.uk.

DuBruck, Edelgard. "Another Look at 'Macabre.' Nouveau c. r. de Robert Eisler (*Danse macabre dans traditio*, VI, 1948) suivi de remarques de M. Félix Lecoy (auteur du premier c. r. dans *Romania*, LXXI, 1950)." *Romania* 79.316 (1958), 536–44.

DuBruck, Edelgard E., and Barbara I. Gusick, eds. *Death and Dying in the Middle Ages*. New York: Peter Lang, 1999.

Dujakovic, Maja. "The Dance of Death, the Dance of Life: Cemetery of the Innocents and the *Danse Macabre*." In *Out of the Stream: Studies in Medieval and Renaissance Mural Painting*. Ed. Luís Urbano Alfonso and Vítor Serrão. Newcastle upon Tyne: Cambridge Scholars Publishing, 2007. Pp. 206–32.

Dymond, David, and Clive Paine. *The Spoil of Melford Church: the Reformation in a Suffolk Parish*. Ipswich: Salient Press, 1989.

Erler, Mary C. *Women, Reading, and Piety in Late Medieval England*. Cambridge: Cambridge University Press, 2002.

Euripedes. *Children of Heracles: Hippolytus; Andromache; Hecuba*. Ed. and trans. David Kovacs. Cambridge, MA: Harvard University Press, 1995.

Eustace, Frances, with Pamela M. King. "Dances of the Living and the Dead: A Study of *Danse Macabre* Imagery within the Context of Late-Medieval Dance Culture." In Oosterwijk and Knöll, *Mixed Metaphors*, pp. 43–71.

Floyd, Jennifer Eileen. "St. George and the 'Steyned Halle': Lydgate's Verse for the London Armourers." In Cooper and Denny-Brown, *Lydgate Matters*, pp. 139–64.

———. "Writing on the Wall: John Lydgate's Architectural Verse." Ph.D. Dissertation: Stanford University, 2008.

Furnivall, Frederick James, ed. *The Minor Poems of the Vernon MS., Part II (with a few from the Digby MSS. 2 and 86)*. EETS o.s. 177. London: Kegan Paul, Trench, Trübner & Co., 1901.

———. *Political, Religious, and Love Poems from the Archbishop of Canterbury's Lambeth MS. No. 306, and Other Sources*. EETS o.s. 15. London: N. Trübner & Co., 1866.

Gayk, Shannon. *Image, Text, and Religious Reform in Fifteenth-Century England*. Cambridge: Cambridge University Press, 2010.

Geanakoplos, Deno John. *Constantinople and the West: Essays on the Late Byzantine (Paleologan) and Italian Renaissances and the Byzantine and Roman Churches*. Madison: The University of Wisconsin Press, 1989.

Gérold, Théodore. *Le Manuscrit de Bayeux: texte et musique d'un recueil de chansons du XVe siècle*. Strasbourg: Librairie Istra, 1921.

Gertsman, Elina. *The Dance of Death in the Middle Ages: Image, Text, Performance*. Turnhout: Brepols, 2010.

———. "Pleyinge and Peyntinge: Performing the Dance of Death." *Studies in Iconography* 27 (2006), 1–43.

Gower, John. *Traitié selonc les auctours pour essampler les amantz marietz*. In *The French Balades*. Ed. and trans. R. F. Yeager. Kalamazoo, MI: Medieval Institute Publications, 2011. Pp. 12–33.

Gray, Douglas. "Two Songs of Death." *Neuphilologische Mitteilungen* 64.1 (1963), 52–74.

———, ed. *The Oxford Book of Late Medieval Verse and Prose*. Oxford: Clarendon Press, 1985.

Griffith, David. "A Newly Identified Verse Item by John Lydgate at Holy Trinity Church, Long Melford, Suffolk." *Notes and Queries* 58.3 (2011), 364–67.

Guillebert de Mets. *Description de la ville de Paris 1434*. Ed. and trans. Evelyn Mullally. Turnhout: Brepols, 2015.

Harris, Jonathan. *The End of Byzantium*. New Haven: Yale University Press, 2010.

Harrison, Ann Tukey. "The Danse Macabre de Femmes." In *The Danse Macabre of Women: MS. Fr. 995 of the Bibliothèque Nationale*. Kent, OH: Kent State University Press, 1994. Pp. 46–133.

———. "La Grant Dance Macabre des Femmes." *Fifteenth-Century Studies* 3 (1980), 81–91.

Hassell, James Woodrow, Jr. *Middle French Proverbs, Sentences, and Proverbial Phrases*. Toronto: Pontifical Institute of Mediaeval Studies, 1982.

Hélinant, Cistercian monk at Froidmont. *Les vers de la mort par Hélinant, moine de Froidmont*. Ed. Fredrik Wulff and Emmanuel Walberg. Paris: Firmin Didot, 1905.

Holinshed, Raphael. *The First and Second Volumes of Chronicles*. London: [Henry Denham] for John Harrison, George Bishop, Rafe Newberie, Henrie Denham, and Thomas Woodcocke, 1587.

The Holy Bible: Douay-Rheims Version. Rockford, IL: Tan Books and Publishers, 1899.

Infantes, Víctor. *Las danzas de la muerte: Génesis y desarrollo de un género medieval (siglos XIII–XVII)*. Salamanca: Ediciones Universidad de Salamanca, 1997.

Keene, Derek, Arthur Burns, and Andrew W. Saint, eds. *St. Paul's: The Cathedral Church of London, 604–2004*. New Haven: Yale University Press, 2004.

Kinch, Ashby. *Imago Mortis: Mediating Images of Death in Late Medieval Culture*. Leiden: Brill, 2013.

Kralik, Christine. "Dialogue and Violence in Medieval Illuminations of the Three Living and the Three Dead." In Oosterwijk and Knöll, *Mixed Metaphors*, pp. 133–54.

Kurtz, Leonard Paul. *The Dance of Death and the Macabre Spirit in European Literature*. New York: Columbia University Press, 1934.

Laidlaw, James C. "The *Cent Balades*: The Marriage of Content and Form." In *Christine de Pizan and Medieval French Lyric*. Ed. Earl Jeffrey Richards. Gainesville: University Press of Florida, 1998. Pp. 53–82.

Laing, Margaret. "Confusion 'Wrs' Confounded: Litteral Substitution Sets in Early Middle English Writing Systems." *Neuphilologische Mitteilungen* 100.3 (1999), 251–70.

Le Fèvre, Jean. *Le respit de la mort par Jean le Fèvre*. Ed. Geneviève Hasenohr-Esnos. Paris: A. & J. Picard, 1969.

Le Goff, Jacques. *Your Money or Your Life: Economy and Religion in the Middle Ages*. Trans. Patricia Ranum. New York: Zone Books, 1988.

Lydgate, John. *The Dance of Death, Edited from MSS. Ellesmere 26/A.13 and B.M. Lansdowne 699, Collated with the Other Extant MSS*. Ed. Florence Warren and Beatrice White. EETS o.s. 181. London: Oxford University Press, 1931; Rpt. New York: Klaus Reprint Co., 1971.

———. *The Fall of Princes*. Ed. Henry Bergen. EETS e.s. 121–24. Oxford: Oxford University Press, 1924–27.

———. *The Pilgrimage of the Life of Man, English by John Lydgate, A.D. 1426, from the French of Guillaume de Deguileville, A.D. 1330, 1355*. Ed. Frederick James Furnivall and Katharine B. Locock. 3 vols. EETS e.s. 77, 83, 92. London: K. Paul, Trench, Trübner & Co., 1899–1904.

———. *The Minor Poems of John Lydgate, Edited from all Available MSS., with an Attempt to Establish the Lydgate Canon*. Ed. Henry Noble MacCracken. 2 vols. EETS o.s. 192. London: Oxford University Press, 1934. Rpt. 1961.

MacDonald, Alasdair A. "The Bannatyne Manuscript — A Marian Anthology." *The Innes Review* 37.1 (1986), 36–47.

Mann, Jill. *Chaucer and Medieval Estates Satire: The Literature of Social Classes and the* General Prologue *to the* Canterbury Tales. Cambridge: Cambridge University Press, 1973.

Middle English Dictionary. Ed. Frances McSparran, et al. Ann Arbor: University of Michigan Library, 2000–18. Online at http://quod.lib.umich.edu/m/middle-english-dictionary/.

Mitchell, W. J. T. *Iconology: Image, Text, Ideology*. Chicago: University of Chicago Press, 1986.

———. *Picture Theory: Essays on Verbal and Visual Representation*. Chicago: University of Chicago Press, 1994.

Nash, W. L. "Ancient Egyptian Draughts-Boards and Draughts-Men." *Proceedings of the Society of Biblical Archæology* 24 (1902), 341–48.

Oosterwijk, Sophie. "Of Corpses, Constables and Kings: the *Danse Macabre* in Late Medieval and Renaissance Culture." *Journal of the British Archaeological Association* 157.1 (2004), 61–90.

———. "Money, Morality, Mortality: The Migration of the *Danse Macabre* from Murals to Misericords." In *Freedom of Movement in the Middle Ages: Proceedings of the 2003 Harlaxton Symposium*. Ed. Peregrine Horden. Donington: Shaun Tyas, 2007. Pp. 37–56.

———. "Of Dead Kings, Dukes and Constables: The Historical Context of the *Danse Macabre* in Late Medieval Paris." *Journal of the British Archaeological Association* 161.1 (2008), 131–62.

———. "Dance, Dialogue and Duality: Fatal Encounters in the Medieval *Danse Macabre*." In Oosterwijk and Knöll, *Mixed Metaphors*, pp. 9–42.

Oosterwijk, Sophie, and Stefanie Knöll, eds. *Mixed Metaphors: The* Danse Macabre *in Medieval and Early Modern Europe*. Newcastle upon Tyne: Cambridge Scholars Publishing, 2011.

Ouy, Gilbert. *Les manuscrits de l'Abbaye de Saint-Victor: Catalogue établi sur la base du répertoire de Claude de Grandrue (1514)*. 2 vols. Turnhout: Brepols, 1999.

Ovid. *Tristia; Ex Ponto*. Trans. Arthur Leslie Wheeler. Rev. G. P. Goold. Cambridge, MA: Harvard University Press, 1988.

Oxford Dictionary of National Biography. Oxford University Press, 2004–18. http://www.oxforddnb.com.

Oxford English Dictionary. Oxford University Press. Online at http://www.oed.com/.

Oxford Music Online. Oxford University Press, 2007–18. Online at http://www.oxfordmusiconline.com.

Paris, Gaston. "Le Danse Macabré de Jean Le Fèvre." *Romania* 24.93 (1895), 129–32.

Perry, R. D. "Lydgate's *Danse Macabre* and the Trauma of the Hundred Years War." *Literature and Medicine* 33.2 (2015), 326–47.

Pollen, John Hungerford, ed. *Unpublished Documents Relating to the English Martyrs*. Vol 1. Leeds: J. Whitehead and Son for the Catholic Record Society, 1908.

Raskolnikov, Masha. *Body Against Soul: Gender and* Sowlehele *in Middle English Allegory*. Columbus: Ohio State University Press, 2009.

Reynolds, Catherine. "'Les angloys, de leur droicte nature, veullent touzjours guerreer': Evidence for Painting in Paris and Normandy, c. 1420–1450." In *Power, Culture, and Religion in France, c. 1350–c. 1550*. Ed. Christopher Allmand. Woodbridge: The Boydell Press, 1989. Pp. 37–55.

Rollins, Hyder Edward. *Old English Ballads, 1553–1625*. Cambridge: Cambridge University Press, 1920.

Saugnieux, Joël. *Les danses macabres de France et d'Espagne et leurs prolongements littéraires*. Lyon: Emmanuel Vitte, 1972.

Scase, Wendy. *The Making of the Vernon Manuscript: The Production and Contexts of Oxford, Bodleian Library, MS Eng. poet.a.1*. Turnhout: Brepols, 2013.

Schwab, Winfried. "Letters without Words? The *Danse Macabre* Initials by Hans Holbein and His Followers." In Oosterwijk and Knöll, *Mixed Metaphors*, pp. 361–84.

Shailor, Barbara A. *Catalogue of Medieval and Renaissance Manuscripts in the Beinecke Rare Book and Manuscript Library Yale University*. Vol. 2. Binghamton, NY: Medieval and Renaissance Texts and Studies, 1984.

A Short-Title Catalogue of Books Printed in England, Scotland and Ireland and English Books Printed Abroad 1473–1640. Ed. A. W. Pollard and G. R. Redgrave. Second edition. Rev. W. A. Jackson, F. S. Ferguson and K. F. Pantzer. 3 vols. London: Bibliographical Society, 1976–91. Online at http://estc.bl.uk.

Söderhjelm, Werner. "Le miroir des dames et des demoiselles." *Neuphilologische Mitteilungen* 6.2 (1904), 29–35.

Sperber, Hans. "The Etymology of Macabre." In *Studia Philologica et Litteraria in Honorem L. Spitzer*. Ed. A. G. Hatcher and K. L. Selig. Bern: Francke Verlag, 1958. Pp. 391–401.

Sponsler, Claire. "Text and Textile: Lydgate's Tapestry Poems." In *Medieval Fabrications: Dress, Textiles, Clothwork, and Other Cultural Imaginings*. Ed. E. Jane Burns. New York: Palgrave Macmillan, 2004. Pp. 19–34.

———. "Lydgate and London's Public Culture." In Cooper and Denny-Brown, *Lydgate Matters*, pp. 13–33.

———. *The Queen's Dumbshows: John Lydgate and the Making of Early Theater*. Philadelphia: University of Pennsylvania Press, 2014.

Stow, John. *A Survey of London, Written in the Year 1598*. Ed. William J. Thoms. London: Whittaker and Co., 1842.

Strakhov, Alexander. "Russkie slova so znacheniiami 'obmanut'sia' i 'obmanut,'" 'obmanshchik' i 'prostak' v krugu narodnoetimologicheskikh i uchenykh sblizheniiakh." *Palaeoslavica* 21.2 (2013), 260–87.

Stratford, Jenny. "The Manuscripts of John, Duke of Bedford: Library and Chapel." In *England in the Fifteenth Century: Proceedings of the 1986 Harlaxton Symposium*. Ed. Daniel Williams. Suffolk: The Boydell Press, 1987. Pp. 329–50.

Taylor, Jane H. M. "*Danse Macabré* and Bande Dessinée: A Question of Reading." *Forum for Modern Language Studies* 25.4 (1989), 356–69.

———. "Que signifiait 'danse' au quinzième siècle?: Danser la danse macabré." *Fifteenth-Century Studies* 18 (1991), 259–77.

Trapp, J. B. "Verses by Lydgate at Long Melford." *Review of English Studies* 6.21 (1955), 1–11.

Universal Short Title Catalogue. University of St Andrews. Online at https://www.ustc.ac.uk/index.php.

Utley, Francis Lee. *The Crooked Rib: An Analytical Index to the Argument about Women in English and Scots Literature to the End of the Year 1568*. Columbus: Ohio State University, 1944.

Vasari, Giorgio. *Le vite de' più eccellenti pittori scultori e architettori nelle redazioni del 1550 e 1568*. Ed. Rosanna Betarini and Paola Barocchi. 9 vols. Florence: Sansoni, 1966–87.

Veenstra, Jan R. *Magic and Divination at the Courts of Burgundy and France: Text and Context of Laurens Pignon's* Contre les devineurs *(1411)*. Leiden: Brill, 1998.

Vogel, Sister Mary Ursula. "Some Aspects of the Horse and Rider Analogy in 'The Debate Between the Body and the Soul.'" Ph.D. Dissertation: The Catholic University of America, 1948.

Whiting, Bartlett Jere, and Helen Wescott Whiting. *Proverbs, Sentences, and Proverbial Phrases from English Writings mainly before 1500*. Cambridge, MA: Belknap Press of Harvard University Press, 1968.

Wijsman, Hanno. "*La danse macabre* du cimetière des Saints-Innocents et un manuscrit de Philippe Le Bon." In *12ème Congrès International d'études sur les danses macabres et l'art macabre en général, Gand du 21 au 24 septembre, 2005*. Volume 1. Meslay-le-Grenet: Association Danses macabres d'Europe, 2006. Pp. 135–44.

❧ GLOSSARY

The following definitions and etymologies have been established by consulting the *Middle English Dictionary* and the *Oxford English Dictionary*. The meanings given here correspond with the marginal glosses found in the edition; for full definitions, the reader is encouraged to consult the dictionaries noted above.

ABBREVIATIONS: **1**: first person; **2**: second person; **3**: third person; **adj.**: adjective; **adv.**: adverb; **AF**: Anglo-French; **art.**: article; **conj.**: conjunction; **impers.**: impersonal construction; **indef.**: indefinite; **Lat.**: Latin; **ME**: Middle English; **n.**: noun; **neg.**: negative; **num.**: number; **OE**: Old English; **OF**: Old French; **ON**: Old Norse; **pl.**: plural; **past part.**: past participle; **poss.**: possessive; **prep.**: preposition; **pron.**: pronoun; **sing.**: singular; **v.**: verb.

abaisshid, abaissht, abassht (adj. & v., past part.) *upset* [OF]

afore, afforn, aforn (prep.) *before, in advance* [OE]

agayne, agein, agens, ageyn, ageyns, ayenst (prep.) *against* [OE]

amys (n.) *Eucharistic vestment, amice (garment worn over the head and shoulders)* [OF]

apelen, appelen (v.) *to appeal* [OF, Lat.]

aray (n.) *adornment, attire, clothing* [AF]

arestid *arrested* (v., past part.) *detained* [OF]

availe, availle (n.) *aid, help* [prob. AF]

ay (adv.) *always* [ON]

beldam (n.) *grandmother* [OF]

bellewedir (n.) *bellweather* [OE]

ben (v.) *to be* (1 pl. **ben**) [OE]

bihoven (v.) *to be appropriate* (3 sing. **bihoveth**) [OE]

busie-headed (adj.) *"busy-headed," i.e. distracted* [OE]

chaipen (v.) *to escape* [AF]

cheer, chere (n.) *attitude, expression* [OF]

constreinen, constreynen (v.) *to detain, compel* [OF]

contre, cuntre (n.) *country, region* [OF]

devise (n.) *scheme, intrigue* [OF]

deynous (adj.) *scornful, arrogant* [from ME **disdeinous**, OF]

disheriten (v.) *to disinherit* [OF]

disseveren (v.) *to fall away* [OF]

domofyeng (v.) *calculating and locating the position of the stars and planets* [OF, Lat.]

drad, drede (n.) *fear* [OE]

dressen (v.) *to prepare, direct* [OF]

eiyen (n.) *eyes* [OE]

eke (adv. and conj.) *also* [OE]

emprice, emprise, empryse (n.) *undertaking, enterprise* [OF]

entencion, entencioun (n.) *desire, intent* [OF, Lat.]

etik (n.) *consuming passion, desire* [OF]
everech (n. & adj.) *every, all* [OE]

fine, fine, fyne (n.) *end, outcome* [OF, Lat.]
fitt (n.) *tune* [OE]
fotyng (n.) *steps, footing (of a dance)* [OE]
fra, fro (prep.) *from* [OE]
fressh, fresshe (adj.) *youthful, cheerful* [OE]
ful, full (adv.) *very, entirely* [OE]

ganestainden (v.) *to put up a fight* [OE]
genolagie (n.) *descendants, lineage* [OF, Lat.]
gentil, gentyl (adj.) *noble* [OF, Lat.]
geynchar (n.) *escape* [OE]
gostli, gostly (adj.) *spiritual* [OE]
greithen (v.) *to prepare, make ready* [ON]
grotchen, grucchen, grutchen (v.) *to complain* [OF]
gynne (n.) *aid, expedient* [OF]

hafen, haifen (v.) *to have* [OE]
helewowe (n.) *end wall of a building* [OE]
hem (pron. pl.) *them, themselves* [OE]
her, heore (pron. poss. pl.) *their* [OE]
hih (adj.) *high, elevated* [OE]

ilk, ilke (pron.) *each, every* [OE]
in (n.) *home, dwelling* [OE]

kempe (n.) *wrestler, warrior* [OE]
kevere (v., past part.) *delivered* [OE, OF]
kind, kynde (n.) *nature* [OE]

lad (v., past part.) *led (conducted)* [OE]
legerdemeyn (n.) *sleight of hand, leger-de-main* [AF]
liff (n.) *life* [OE]
listen (v., impers.) **him** (**hire**, etc.) **list, lust, lyst, lyste, he** (**she**, etc.) *chooses, desires* [OE]
lucre (n.) *profit* [OF, Lat.]

maistresse (n.) *mistress* [OF]
manacen, mannissen (v.) *to threaten* [OF]
mathe (n.) *worm, maggot* [OE]
mede, meede (n.) *reward, compensation* [OE]
mete (n.) *food, nourishment* [OE]
moten (v) *to be allowed to, to be permitted to, may, must* (3 sing. **moot, most, mot, mote, must**) [OE]

nighene (num.) *nine* [OE]
nis (v., 3 sing., neg. of **ben**) *is not* [OE]
non, none, noon (pron.) *no one* [OE]
not (v., 3 sing., neg. of **witen**) *know not* [OE]
nouther (conj.) *neither* [OE]

o, oo (indef. art.) *a, an, one* [OE]
or (prep.) *before* [OE, ON]

passing, passinge (adj.) *exceeding, great* [OF]
peur, peure (adj.) *poor* [OF]
phidil (n.) *fiddle* [OE]
phisik (n.) *medicine* [Lat.]
picois (n.) *pickaxe* [OF]
platis (n.) *plate-armor* [OF]
plesance, plesaunce (n.) *delight, pleasure, charm* [OE]

reden, reeden (v.) *to instruct, advise* [OE]
respite (n.) *reprieve* [OF]
riggeboon (n.) *vertebral column, spine* [OE]
rympled (adj & v., past part.) *wrinkled* [OE]

sal, sall (v., 3 sing of **shulen**) *shall, will* [OE]
sautry (n.) *psaltery* [OF, Lat.]
schaft (n.) *appearance, likeness;* **monnes schaft,** *human shape* [OE]
see (n.) *position of authority, status* [OF]

sen (v.) *to see* (3 sing. **se**) [OE]

sentence (n.) *wisdom, judgment* [OF]

shalmuse (n.) *reed flute* [OF]

shortly (adv.) *concisely, quickly* [OE]

sich, syche (adj.) *such* [OE]

sikir (adj.) *safe, protected, secure*; **sikir of heaven**, *bound to obtain heaven* [OE]

sith, syth (conj.) *because* [OE]

sithol (n.) *stringed instrument* [OF]

socour (n.) *assistance, help* [AF]

sodein, soden (adj.) *sudden* [OF, AF]

sone (adv.) *soon* [OE]

sore (adv.) *powerfully, fervently* [OE]

sowpouailen (v.) *to encourage* [AF]

speiren (v.) *to ask* (2 sing. **speiris**) [OE]

strange, straunge (adv.) *haughty, aloof* [OF, AF]

strangenesse, straungenesse (n.) *haughtiness* [OF]

surquidous (adj.) *haughty* [AF]

taken tent (v.) *pay heed, pay attention to* [OF]

tarie, tarye (n.) *delay* [origin debated]

thorwsouht (v., past part.) *dug through, penetrated through* [OE]

tofore, toforn (prep. & conj.) *before* [OE]

tracen (v.) *follow* [OF]

uche (pron.) *each* [OE]

unknyt (v., past part.) *loosened* [OE]

unset (adj & v., past part.) *unspecified*; **unset our, unsett howr**, *unspecified hour* [OE]

ur, ure (pron.) *our* [OE]

wacche (n.) *wakefulness (e.g., for a vigil)* [OE]

watris (n. pl.) *urine* [OE]

wich, wiche (pron.) *who* [OE]

wight, wiht (n.) *person* [OE]

wol, wole, woll (v., 3 sing. of **willen**) *will* [OE]

woot, wot (v., 3 sing of **witen**) *knows* [OE]

yeven, yiven (v.) *to give* [OE, ON]

ygrounde (v., past part.) *honed, whetted* [OE]

yit (adv. & conj.) *yet* [OE]

youwtheid (n.) *youth* [OE]

Typeset in 10/13 New Baskerville
and Golden Cockerel Ornaments display

Medieval Institute Publications
College of Arts and Sciences
Western Michigan University
1903 W. Michigan Avenue
Kalamazoo, MI 49008-5432
http://www.wmich.edu/medievalpublications

 WESTERN MICHIGAN UNIVERSITY

William Dunbar, *The Complete Works*, edited by John Conlee (2004)

Chaucerian Dream Visions and Complaints, edited by Dana M. Symons (2004)

Stanzaic Guy of Warwick, edited by Alison Wiggins (2004)

Saints' Lives in Middle English Collections, edited by E. Gordon Whatley, with Anne B. Thompson and Robert K. Upchurch (2004)

Siege of Jerusalem, edited by Michael Livingston (2004)

The Kingis Quair and Other Prison Poems, edited by Linne R. Mooney and Mary-Jo Arn (2005)

The Chaucerian Apocrypha: A Selection, edited by Kathleen Forni (2005)

John Gower, *The Minor Latin Works*, edited and translated by R. F. Yeager, with *In Praise of Peace*, edited by Michael Livingston (2005)

Sentimental and Humorous Romances: Floris and Blancheflour, Sir Degrevant, The Squire of Low Degree, The Tournament of Tottenham, and The Feast of Tottenham, edited by Erik Kooper (2006)

The Dicts and Sayings of the Philosophers, edited by John William Sutton (2006)

"Everyman" and Its Dutch Original, "Elckerlijc," edited by Clifford Davidson, Martin W. Walsh, and Ton J. Broos (2007)

The N-Town Plays, edited by Douglas Sugano, with assistance by Victor I. Scherb (2007)

The Book of John Mandeville, edited by Tamarah Kohanski and C. David Benson (2007)

John Lydgate, *The Temple of Glas*, edited by J. Allan Mitchell (2007)

The Northern Homily Cycle, edited by Anne B. Thompson (2008)

Codex Ashmole 61: A Compilation of Popular Middle English Verse, edited by George Shuffelton (2008)

Chaucer and the Poems of "Ch," edited by James I. Wimsatt (revised edition 2009)

William Caxton, *The Game and Playe of the Chesse*, edited by Jenny Adams (2009)

John the Blind Audelay, *Poems and Carols*, edited by Susanna Fein (2009)

Two Moral Interludes: The Pride of Life and Wisdom, edited by David Klausner (2009)

John Lydgate, *Mummings and Entertainments*, edited by Claire Sponsler (2010)

Mankind, edited by Kathleen M. Ashley and Gerard NeCastro (2010)

The Castle of Perseverance, edited by David N. Klausner (2010)

Robert Henryson, *The Complete Works*, edited by David J. Parkinson (2010)

John Gower, *The French Balades*, edited and translated by R. F. Yeager (2011)

The Middle English Metrical Paraphrase of the Old Testament, edited by Michael Livingston (2011) *The York Corpus Christi Plays*, edited by Clifford Davidson (2011)

Prik of Conscience, edited by James H. Morey (2012)

The Dialogue of Solomon and Marcolf: A Dual-Language Edition from Latin and Middle English Printed Editions, edited by Nancy Mason Bradbury and Scott Bradbury (2012)

Croxton Play of the Sacrament, edited by John T. Sebastian (2012)

Ten Bourdes, edited by Melissa M. Furrow (2013)

Lybeaus Desconus, edited by Eve Salisbury and James Weldon (2013)

The Complete Harley 2253 Manuscript, Vol. 2, edited and translated by Susanna Fein with David Raybin and Jan Ziolkowski (2014); Vol. 3 (2015); Vol. 1 (2015)

Oton de Granson, Poems, edited and translated by Peter Nicholson and Joan Grenier-Winther (2015)

The King of Tars, edited by John H. Chandler (2015)

John Hardyng Chronicle, edited by James Simpson and Sarah Peverley (2015)

Richard Coer de Lyon, edited by Peter Larkin (2015)

Guillaume de Machaut, The Complete Poetry and Music, Volume 1: The Debate Poems, edited and translated by R. Barton Palmer (2016)

Lydgate's Fabula Duorum Mercatorum and Guy of Warwyk, edited by Pamela Farvolden (2016)

The Katherine Group (MS Bodley 34), edited by Emily Rebekah Huber and Elizabeth Robertson (2016)

Sir Torrent of Portingale, edited by James Wade (2017)

The Towneley Plays, edited by Garrett P. J. Epp (2018)

The Digby Mary Magdalene Play, edited by Theresa Coletti (2018)

Guillaume de Machaut, The Complete Poetry and Music, Volume 9: The Motets, edited by Jacques Boogart (2018)

Six Scottish Courtly and Chivalric Poems, Including Lyndsay's Squyer Meldrum, edited by Rhiannon Purdie and Emily Wingfield (2018)

Gavin Douglas, *The Palyce of Honour*, edited by David John Parkinson (2018)

Guillaume de Machaut, The Complete Poetry and Music, Volume 2: The Boethian Poems, Le Remede de Fortune and Le Confort d'Ami, edited by R. Barton Palmer (2019)

✒ COMMENTARY SERIES

Haimo of Auxerre, *Commentary on the Book of Jonah*, translated with an introduction and notes by Deborah Everhart (1993)

Medieval Exegesis in Translation: Commentaries on the Book of Ruth, translated with an introduction and notes by Lesley Smith (1996)

Nicholas of Lyra's Apocalypse Commentary, translated with an introduction and notes by Philip D. W. Krey (1997)

Rabbi Ezra Ben Solomon of Gerona, *Commentary on the Song of Songs and Other Kabbalistic Commentaries*, selected, translated, and annotated by Seth Brody (1999)

John Wyclif, *On the Truth of Holy Scripture*, translated with an introduction and notes by Ian Christopher Levy (2001)

Second Thessalonians: Two Early Medieval Apocalyptic Commentaries, introduced and translated by Steven R. Cartwright and Kevin L. Hughes (2001)

The "Glossa Ordinaria" on the Song of Songs, translated with an introduction and notes by Mary Dove (2004)

The Seven Seals of the Apocalypse: Medieval Texts in Translation, translated with an introduction and notes by Francis X. Gumerlock (2009)

The "Glossa Ordinaria" on Romans, translated with an introduction and notes by Michael Scott Woodward (2011)

Nicholas of Lyra, *Literal Commentary on Galatians*, translated with an introduction and notes by Edward Arthur Naumann (2015)

Early Latin Commentaries on the Apocalypse, edited by Francis X. Gumerlock (2016)

Rabbi Eliezer of Beaugency: Commentaries on Amos and Jonah (with selections from Isaiah and Ezekiel), by Robert A. Harris (2018)

Carolingian Commentaries on the Apocalypse by Theodulf and Smaragdus, edited and translated by Francis X. Gumerlock (2019)

✒ SECULAR COMMENTARY SERIES

Accessus ad auctores: Medieval Introduction to the Authors, edited and translated by Stephen M. Wheeler (2015)

The Vulgate Commentary on Ovid's Metamorphoses, Book 1, edited and translated by Frank Coulson (2015)

Brunetto Latini, *La rettorica*, edited and translated by Stefania D'Agata D'Ottavi (2016)

✒ DOCUMENTS OF PRACTICE SERIES

Love and Marriage in Late Medieval London, selected, translated, and introduced by Shannon McSheffrey (1995)

Sources for the History of Medicine in Late Medieval England, selected, introduced, and translated by Carole Rawcliffe (1995)

A Slice of Life: Selected Documents of Medieval English Peasant Experience, edited, translated, and with an introduction by Edwin Brezette DeWindt (1996)

Regular Life: Monastic, Canonical, and Mendicant "Rules," selected and introduced by Douglas J. McMillan and Kathryn Smith Fladenmuller (1997); second edition, selected and introduced by Daniel Marcel La Corte and Douglas J. McMillan (2004)

Women and Monasticism in Medieval Europe: Sisters and Patrons of the Cistercian Reform, selected, translated, and with an introduction by Constance H. Berman (2002)

Medieval Notaries and Their Acts: The 1327–1328 Register of Jean Holanie, introduced, edited, and translated by Kathryn L. Reyerson and Debra A. Salata (2004)

John Stone's Chronicle: Christ Church Priory, Canterbury, 1417–1472, selected, translated, and introduced by Meriel Connor (2010)

Medieval Latin Liturgy in English Translation, edited by by Matthew Cheung Salisbury (2017)

Henry VII's London in the Great Chronicle, edited by Julia Boffey (2019)

✒ MEDIEVAL GERMAN TEXTS IN BILINGUAL EDITIONS SERIES

Sovereignty and Salvation in the Vernacular, 1050–1150, introduction, translations, and notes by James A. Schultz (2000)

Ava's New Testament Narratives: "When the Old Law Passed Away," introduction, translation, and notes by James A. Rushing, Jr. (2003)

History as Literature: German World Chronicles of the Thirteenth Century in Verse, introduction, translation, and notes by R. Graeme Dunphy (2003)

Thomasin von Zirclaria, *Der Welsche Gast (The Italian Guest)*, translated by Marion Gibbs and Winder McConnell (2009)

Ladies, Whores, and Holy Women: A Sourcebook in Courtly, Religious, and Urban Cultures of Late Medieval Germany, introductions, translations, and notes by Ann Marie Rasmussen and Sarah Westphal-Wihl (2010)

Neidhart: Selected Songs from the Riedegg Manuscript, introduction, translation, and commentary by Kathryn Starkey and Edith Wenzel (2016)

✒ VARIA

The Study of Chivalry: Resources and Approaches, edited by Howell Chickering and Thomas H. Seiler (1988)

Studies in the Harley Manuscript: The Scribes, Contents, and Social Contexts of British Library MS Harley 2253, edited by Susanna Fein (2000)

The Liturgy of the Medieval Church, edited by Thomas J. Heffernan and E. Ann Matter (2001; second edition 2005)

Johannes de Grocheio, *Ars musice*, edited and translated by Constant J. Mews, John N. Crossley, Catherine Jeffreys, Leigh McKinnon, and Carol J. Williams (2011)

Aribo, "De musica" and "Sententiae," edited and translated by T. J. H. McCarthy (2015)

Guy of Saint-Denis, *Tractatus de tonis*, edited and translated by Constant J. Mews, Carol J. Williams, John N. Crossley, and Catherine Jeffreys (2017)